Studies in Church History

Subsidia

13

MISSIONS AND MISSIONARIES

MISSIONS AND MISSIONARIES

EDITED BY

PIETER N. HOLTROP

and

HUGH McLEOD

PUBLISHED FOR

THE ECCLESIASTICAL HISTORY SOCIETY

BY

THE BOYDELL PRESS

2000

First published 2000

A publication of the Ecclesiastical History Society
in association with The Boydell Press
an imprint of Boydell & Brewer Ltd
PO Box 9, Woodbridge, Suffolk IP12 3DF, UK
and of Boydell & Brewer Inc.
PO Box 41026, Rochester, NY 14604-4126, USA

ISBN 0 9529733 6 7

A catalogue record for this book is available
from the British Library

Library of Congress Cataloging-in-Publication Data
Missions and missionaries/edited by Pieter N. Holtrop and Hugh McLeod.
p cm. – (Studies in church history. Subsidia; 13)
Includes bibliographical references and index.
ISBN 0-9529733-6-7 (hardback: alk. paper)
1. Missions, British – History – Congresses. 2. Missions, Dutch – History – Congresses. I. Holtrop, Pieter. II. McLeod, Hugh. III. Series.
BV2121.G7 M57 2001
266'.009–dc21 00-042998

Details of previous volumes available from Boydell & Brewer Ltd

This book is printed on acid-free paper

Typeset by Joshua Associates Ltd, Oxford
Printed in Great Britain by
St Edmundsbury Press Ltd, Bury St Edmunds, Suffolk

CONTENTS

CONTRIBUTORS

GUUS BOONE
Historisch Documentatiecentrum, Free University of Amsterdam

JOHN CASSON
Civil servant, British Foreign Office, formerly Research Assistant, Faculty of Divinity, University of Cambridge

ANNA MARIA LUISELLI FADDA
Professor of Anglo-Saxon and Germanic Philology, University of Rome 3

MYRTLE HILL
Director, Centre for Women's Studies, Queen's University, Belfast

PIETER N. HOLTROP
Professor, Theological University of Kampen

EUGÈNE HONÉE
Emeritus Professor of Church History, Catholic Theological University of Utrecht

LIESBETH LABBEKE
Doctoral student, Catholic Theological University of Utrecht

KATE LOWE
Senior Lecturer, Department of Historical and Cultural Studies, Goldsmiths' College, University of London

H. L. MURRE-VAN DEN BERG
Docent in Missiology and Ecumenics, Research Group on Church History and History of Dogma, Faculty of Theology, University of Leiden

HENDRIK E. NIEMEIJER
Research Fellow, Institute for the History of European Expansion and its Aftermath, University of Leiden

ANDREW PORTER
Rhodes Professor of Imperial History, King's College, University of London

RACHEL A. RAKOTONIRINA
Recently completed PhD, Department of Theology, University of Birmingham

BRIAN STANLEY
Director, Currents in World Christianity Project, and Fellow of St Edmund's College, University of Cambridge

JORIS VAN EIJNATTEN
Research worker, Institute for European History, Mainz, and Free University, Amsterdam

EDITORS' PREFACE

The sixth British–Dutch Colloquium on Ecclesiastical History took place at Newnham College, Cambridge, from 2 to 5 April 1998, organized by the British and Dutch Sub-Commissions of the Commission Internationale d'Histoire Ecclésiastique Comparée. The theme was 'Missions and Missionaries', and this volume provides a selection from the twenty-five papers presented on that occasion. The papers of the fifth Colloquium, held in Groningen in 1992, were published in the Subsidia series of *Studies in Church History*. We are delighted to be following in our predecessors' footsteps.

Pieter N. Holtrop
Hugh McLeod

ABBREVIATIONS

AHR	*American Historical Review* (New York, 1895–)
BJRL	*Bulletin of the John Rylands Library* (Manchester, 1903–)
CathHR	*Catholic Historical Review* (Washington, D.C., 1915–)
CChr.SL	*Corpus Christianorum, series Latina* (Turnhout, 1953–)
EETS	*Early English Text Society* (London, 1864–)
EHR	*English Historical Review* (London, 1886–)
GBM	*Geschichtsquellen des Bisthums Münster*
IBMR	*International Bulletin of Missionary Research*
JMH	*Journal of Modren History* (Chicago, 1929–)
MGH	*Monumenta Germaniae historica inde ad a. 500 usque ad a. 1500*, ed G. H. Pertz *et al.* (Hanover, Berlin, etc., 1826–)
Ep. Sel.	*Epistolae Selectae*
SRM	*Scriptores rerum merovingicarum*
nd	no date
np	no place of publication
os	old series
PBA	*Proceedings of the British Academy* (London, 1904–)
PL	*Patrologia Latina*, ed. J. P. Migne, 217 vols + 4 index vols (Paris, 1841–61)
RS	*Rerum Britannicarum medii aevi scriptores*, 99 vols (London, 1858–1911) = *Rolls Series*
SCH	*Studies in Church History* (London/Cambridge/Oxford/Woodbridge, 1964–)
Speculum	*Speculum: a Journal of Medieval Studies* (Cambridge, MA, 1925–)

THE VERNACULAR AND THE PROPAGATION OF THE FAITH IN ANGLO-SAXON MISSIONARY ACTIVITY

by ANNA MARIA LUISELLI FADDA

THE fundamental problem that every religious conversion process grapples with – at all times and in all areas – is that of finding a linguistic medium, as a suitable means of facilitating an easy communication with pagans. Undoubtedly, to overcome this otherwise almost insuperable language barrier, the use of native tongues seems to be crucial.

Turning our attention to the Carolingian period, although several contemporary writers made it clear that the use of political force and coercion was justifiable and even praiseworthy to initiate the conversion process, evidence gleaned from missionaries' biographies and correspondence suggests that the question of linguistic intelligibility and communication was ever-present in missionary discussions.[1] Nor should we be surprised at this. There can be no doubt that the early phase of Carolingian missionary work was strongly dominated by the Anglo-Saxon missions. There is enough evidence to suggest that those most astonishing results achieved by Willibrord, Boniface, and the Anglo-Saxon monks on the Continent can be traced back to the conversion of England, to the policy of the first Roman missionaries, and ultimately that of Gregory the Great. This evidence of Anglo-Saxon influence is a most significant element. Closer investigation of the sources reveals that missionary work in England was carried out by language interaction and never by forcing and coercing pagan audiences to accept Christianity. Without awareness of this fact, it would be difficult to understand the whole process of the religious and doctrinal formation of the Anglo-Saxons, who were pagans and spoke

[1] See Richard E. Sullivan, 'Carolingian missionary theories', *CathHR*, 42/3 (1956), pp. 273–95; idem, 'The Carolingian missionary and the pagan', *Speculum*, 28 (1953), pp. 705–40; idem, 'The papacy and missionary activity in the early Middle Ages', *Mittelalterliche Studien*, 17 (Stuttgart, 1955), pp. 46–106; Frederick Prinz, *Klerus und Krieg im früheren Mittelalter* (Stuttgart, 1971); Rosamond McKitterick, *The Frankish Kingdoms under the Carolingians. 751–987* (London and New York, 1983); Janet L. Nelson, 'Kingship and empire in the Carolingian world', in Rosamond McKitterick, ed., *Carolingian Culture: Emulation and Innovation* (Cambridge, 1994), pp. 52–87.

Germanic dialects rather than Latin, the language of the Roman Church.

Nonetheless, considering the importance of the problems the missionaries had to face, it is surprising that there is little evidence of their method of contacting the pagans: we are given very few details of what linguistic techniques and procedures were thought suitable to pagan audiences. As a result, then, the vital role of the vernacular in the history of Roman missions to England has largely been neglected and underestimated, and needs to be investigated. What methods of evangelization were used by the missionaries? How did the pagan tribes in England become acquainted with Christian doctrine and the difficult theological concepts of the new religion? How could the vernacular communicate the Christian message to pagan audiences? In search of an answer to these crucial questions, I will begin by examining the principal records for Anglo-Saxon missionary activity.

I

The surviving documentary and historical records dealing with the spread of Christianity to England supply clear evidence that the first and fundamental problem which Gregory the Great had sought to solve as far back as the inauguration of the English mission was the whole question of language. Language differences in that far-off land, forgotten and neglected by *sacerdotes qui in uicino sunt*, according to the bitter words of the Pope,[2] represented a real threat to the successful outcome of the mission, since the crucial step for an efficient missionary policy was the ability to communicate with pagans.

In a famous letter dated September 595 to the priest Candidus, rector of the papal patrimony in Gaul,[3] Gregory ordered that young Angles, aged about seventeen or eighteen, were to be ransomed from the continental slave-markets and, once baptized and educated in monasteries, were then to be used as missionaries. This clearly indicates that the Pope, fully aware of the difficult linguistic situation which the Church was about to face in the conversion of England, intended to entrust a group of local missionaries with the main task of communication. The valuable aid provided to Christianity by this

[2] Gregory the Great, *Registrum Epistularum*, vi, 60, ed. Dag Norberg, *CChr.SL*, 140 (Turnhout, 1982), p. 433 (*Sacerdotes e uicino*: vi, 51, p. 424). The date is 23 July 596.

[3] Ibid., vi, 10, p. 378.

policy seems to be proved by its renewal during the conversion of the Frisians.[4]

The second piece of evidence, referred to by Bede,[5] is even more significant. In 596 Gregory dispatched Augustine, together with a group of other monks *timentes Dominum*, to preach the gospel to the pagan Angles. The missionaries had already completed part of their journey when, overcome by paralysing fear, they considered returning home rather than facing 'a cruel, barbarous and pagan people, whose language they did not understand'. This last piece of evidence indicates that the problem of communication was a cause of serious concern at this time. In the following year, 597, Gregory instructed Augustine and his companions, nearly forty in number, to go to the Isle of Thanet accompanied, this time, by *interpretes* from the Frankish race.[6] The Pope thus offered his first official solution to the question of the communication barrier. Subsequent history tells us that this was effective, because these *interpretes*, whatever their real role,[7] clearly served as co-workers in spreading the Christian message. They forged contacts between the missionaries and the royal Kentish court of King Æthelbert and his queen, Bertha, the Christian daughter of Charibert, King of Paris. Although no explicit statement can be produced to prove in what language, and with the aid of whom, these contacts and discussions took place – Bede is silent on this point – undoubtedly we should assume that there was language communication between speakers. West Frankish may not have been so different from Kentish: the situation was probably one of mutual intelligibility of varying degrees within the West Germanic language

[4] Anon., *Vita Amandi episcopi*, ch. 9, ed. Bruno Krusch, *MGH, SRM*, 5 (Hannover and Leipzig, 1910), p. 435 : 'Si quos etiam captivos vel pueros transmarinus invenisset, dato pretio redimebat, spiritalique eos regenerans lavacro, litteris affatim imbui praecipiebat, praemissaque libertate, per diversis relinquebat ecclesias, pluresque ex his postea episcopos vel presbiteros seu honorificos abbates fuisse audivimus.'

[5] Bede, *Historia ecclesiastica gentis Anglorum*, i, 23, ed. Bertram Colgrave and Roger Aubrey Baskerville Mynors (Oxford, 1972), p. 68 [hereafter Bede, *HE*].

[6] Bede, *HE*, i, 25, p. 72.

[7] On the Frankish interpreters, their role and language, see James Campbell, 'The first century of Christianity in England', in idem, ed., *Essays in Anglo-Saxon History* (London and Ronceverte, 1986), p. 54; André Crépin, 'Bede and the vernacular', in Gerald Bonner, ed., *Famulus Christi: Essays in Commemoration of the Thirteenth Centenary of the Birth of the Venerable Bede* (London, 1976), pp. 176–7; René Derolez, 'Language problems in Anglo-Saxon England: *barbara loquella* and *barbarismus*', in Michael Korhammer *et al.*, eds, Words, Texts and Manuscripts (Cambridge, 1992), pp. 288–9; Helmut Gneuss, '*Anglicae linguae interpretatio*: language contact, lexical borrowing and glossing in Anglo-Saxon England', *PBA*, 82 (London, 1992), pp. 131–2.

group rather than of mutually incomprehensible and fully distinct different languages.[8]

In recounting subsequent events, and throughout his discussion of the conversion of Kent, Bede allows us to see that the methods of Augustinian evangelization were based on personal contacts, on dialogue, and on persuasion. Only through discussion could pagans be convinced to abandon their old religion. The nature of the impact of the new faith on Anglo-Saxon pagan society is clearly indicated by Bede. Being in a good position to know, he records that King Æthelbert 'compelled no one to accept Christianity. . . . He had learned from his teachers and guides in the way of salvation that the service of Christ was voluntary and ought not to be compulsory.'[9] The granting of a religious seat at Canterbury, the capital of the Kentish kingdom, the permission to build or restore churches, and above all the freedom to preach the word of God everywhere,[10] unmistakably show that the missionaries could communicate with the King, the court, and the whole pagan population without great difficulty. Most important of all, it reveals that the native tongues were the most efficient medium for the transmission of the new doctrine and that obstacles between the different languages were overcome in quite a short time. Thus Pope Gregory, fully aware of the progress of the new religion and of the magnitude of the successes achieved by Augustine and his monks, described the new Anglo-Saxon situation in words of great admiration: 'Lo, the mouth of Britain, which once only knew how to gnash its barbarous teeth, has long since learned to sing the praises of God with the alleluia of the Hebrews.'[11]

That preaching – the principal means of spreading Christianity amongst the pagans – should have taken place in the native language is not surprising. The use of the vernacular as a worthy medium of expression in situations which the clergy usually dealt with in Latin, seemed to be the most appropriate method Roman missionaries had to employ in making Anglo-Saxon pagans receptive to Christian ideas. One possible reading of canon three of the Council of Clofesho in 747,

[8] Roger Lass, *Old English* (Cambridge, 1994), pp. 13–15.

[9] Bede, *HE*, i, 26, pp. 76–8.

[10] Ibid., i, 25, p. 74.

[11] Gregory the Great, *Moralia in Iob*, xxvii, 11, 21, ed. Marci Adriaen, *CChr.SL*, 143 B (Turnhout, 1985), p. 1346: 'Ecce lingua Britanniae, quae nihil aliud nouerat, quam barbarum frendere, iam dudum in diuinis laudibus Hebraeum coepit Alleluia resonare.' See also Bede, *HE*, ii, 1, p. 130.

according to which bishops were commanded to call the people together to hear the Scriptures, is that doctrinal instruction of pagans was to be performed in the vernacular.[12] Canon ten of the same Council openly prescribed that priests should not only understand but also explain in the native tongue the liturgical services, the Creed, and *Pater noster*.[13] There is therefore a good case for assuming that even sermons to the masses, though not recorded in Old English prior to the tenth century,[14] had yet to be spoken in the vernacular. Indeed, no great flight of imagination is needed to assume that the missionaries were forced to adapt themselves to the ways and expressions of the people they came to instruct.

But it is perhaps worth remembering that native tongues were also used in contexts other than preaching. At the Council of Nidd in 703, Archbishop Berhtwald was asked to provide a translation of the papal letters, which he did by summarizing their contents.[15] At the famous Council of Whitby in 663/4, not only was the debate conducted in the languages of the Anglo-Saxons and Irish,[16] but in order to overcome the language barrier, 'the venerable bishop Cedd, who had been consecrated long before by the Irish, . . . acted as a most careful interpreter for both parties at the council.'[17]

Missionary work could not succeed, however, without the support of the kings. Anglo-Saxon royal personages were very careful to implement the new religion in line with the strategy of the missionaries. Most of them felt the need to contribute to the acceptance of Christianity by requesting monks or bishops who could eliminate any possible source of religious tension and uneasiness among the pagans. The case of King Oswald of Northumbria sheds light on the kind of

[12] Canon three, *HS*, III, p. 363. There is a thorough discussion of this Council in Catherine Cubitt, *Anglo-Saxon Church Councils c.650–c.850* (London and New York, 1995), pp. 99–152.

[13] Canon ten, *HS*, III, p. 366.

[14] The first two sermon-collections compiled in Old English are eighteen homilies for Sundays and Saints' Days, known as 'Blickling homilies' (Titusville, USA, collection of William H. Scheide, s.X/XI), ed. Richard Morris, *The Blickling Homilies of the Tenth Century*, *EETS* (os), 29, 34 (London, 1880, repr. 1953), and twenty-three homilies, preserved in the 'Vercelli Book' (Vercelli, Biblioteca capitolare CXVII, s.X^{2}), ed. Donald Scragg, *The Vercelli Homilies*, *EETS* (os), 300 (Oxford, New York and Toronto, 1992).

[15] Eddius Stephanus, *Vita Wilfridi I episcopi Eboracensis*, ch. 60, ed. Wilhelm Levison, *MGH*, *SRM*, 6 (Hannover and Lipsia, 1913), p. 255. See also Catherine Cubitt, *Councils*, pp. 88–9.

[16] Bede, *HE*, iii, 25, pp. 294–308.

[17] Ibid., p. 298.

personal involvement of monarchs in the Christianization process. On becoming king in 635, Oswald requested the Irish to send a bishop 'by whose teaching and ministry the English race over whom he ruled might learn the privileges of faith in our Lord and receive the sacraments. His request was granted without delay.'[18] The Irish first of all sent Cormán, who preached unsuccessfully to the English for some time; later, seeing that the people were unwilling to listen to him, he returned to Iona.[19] The story goes that Aidan, 'a man of outstanding gentleness, devotion, and moderation', was sent instead.[20] On the bishop's arrival, the king gave him a place for his episcopal see on the island of Lindisfarne. Oswald himself acted as *interpres* of the heavenly word for his ealdormen and thegns when Aidan was preaching the gospel, 'for the bishop was not completely at home in the English tongue, while the king had gained a perfect knowledge of Irish during the long period of his exile'.[21] Bede also relates[22] that King Cenwealh, who knew only the Saxon language, grew tired of the *barbara loquella* of Bishop Agilbert, a Gaul by birth, who had spent a long time in Ireland studying the Scriptures. He then imposed upon the kingdom a bishop named Wine, who had been consecrated in Gaul but who spoke the king's own tongue.

About sixty years after the death of Gregory the Great, the information we have about Pope Vitalianus suggests that the papacy adopted the same missionary policy. When the Pope, urged in 663 by Egbert of Kent and Oswiu of Northumbria, showed himself willing to restore the authority of the Roman Church in England, he made the most of the missionary experience by sending to England in 669 Theodore, a sixty-seven-year-old monk from Tarsus in Cilicia. He was appointed as Archbishop of Canterbury so that '*uiua uoce* [that is, "by preaching"] and with the help of the word of God' he might 'entirely root out with His blessing the tares sown by the enemy throughout the island'.[23] The high-sounding expression used by the Pope, *uiua uoce*, points once again to the importance of oral communication, of human and personal bonds, and of peaceful persuasion in converting pagans, and explains the deep concern and preoccupation of the missionaries

[18] Bede, *HE*, iii, 3, p. 218.
[19] Bede, *HE*, iii, 5, p. 228.
[20] Bede, *HE*, iii, 3, p. 218.
[21] Ibid., p. 220.
[22] Bede, *HE*, iii, 7, p. 234.
[23] Bede, *HE*, iii, 29, p. 320.

with such matters as the need for trust and confidence in convincing pagans to accept the new faith.

It is therefore not surprising to find further proof of the same kind of missionary policy in surviving sources dealing with the work of the Anglo-Saxon missionaries in bringing Christianity to the Continent. One revealing account concerns St Boniface, during his mission to the continental Saxons in the early eighth century, and Gregory, one of his earliest Frankish disciples. Boniface, before consenting to Gregory's missionary activity, wanted to make sure that he could understand what he read in Latin and could develop it fully in his own language and in the natural speech of his parents.[24] Another source[25] reveals that sometime after 785 the eastern Frisians 'surrendered themselves to the Frankish kingdom and promised that they would accept Christianity if someone, whose native speech they could understand, would have been sent and taught them letters'. Liudger, a native Frisian, was chosen to head the mission. In the account of the evangelization of the region of Ghent,[26] St Amand's tactic of buying English slaves and training them as missionaries was a policy aimed at bridging the linguistic gap between a missionary from Aquitaine and the Flemings. It thus appears beyond dispute that the first and most pressing task that faced missionaries was the mastery of native tongues.

These reflections on the language problem in Anglo-Saxon missionary method lead me to another crucial point of discussion. Deep concern for the salvation of souls necessarily implied that great attention had to be paid by the missionaries to the needs of the society in which they worked and, consequently, to the native tongues in order to respond to the social demands of the conversion process. Inevitably, the practice of giving doctrinal instruction and of discussing

[24] Liudger, *Vita Gregorii abbatis Traiectensis*, ch. 2, ed. Oswald Holder-Egger, *MGH, SS*, 15 (Hannover, 1887/8), p. 68: 'Sanctus autem doctor prosecutus eum secundum ordinem rationis, ait: <<Dic mihi, quomodo intelligis quae legis>>. Ipse vero repetebat ab exordio lectionem suam et coepit iterum legere velle sicut prius. Egregius ergo praeceptor paululum eum distulit et dixit: <<Non ita, fili, quaero, ut mihi dicas modo lectionem tuam, sed secundum proprietatem linguae tuae et naturalem parentum tuorum locutionem edissere mihi lectionem tuam>>.'

[25] Anon., *Vita secunda sancti Liudgeri*, i, 16, ed. Wilhelm Diekamp, *Geschichtsquellen des Bisthums Muenster*, 4 (Münster, 1881), pp. 61–2: 'His quoque temporibus orientalis Frisiae quinque pagi cum una insula, que dicitur Band, Francorum regno se subdiderunt promittentes fidem Christianam se suscepturos, si erudiendis eis aliquis daretur, cuius loquelam intelligere possent. Porro imperator hoc gratanter accipiens Liudgero opus istud commendavit.'

[26] See above, n. 6.

any other matters by *uiua uoce* procedures called attention to the fact that the use and role of the vernacular in clerical education should now be part of a new Christian missionary *paideia*. In line with the teaching of Gregory the Great,[27] the speech of the teachers should adapt itself to the nature of the audience, to the characteristic of any individual person, and to all the qualities, abilities, and experiences which make one race of people different from another. The sources available to us are few and often vague on this point, but however meagre they may be, they point towards a full understanding of the character of the pagan audience as the real missionary goal.

First, let me direct attention to the Anglo-Saxon glosses which accompanied biblical commentaries in Latin from the so-called 'Canterbury school' of Theodore of Tarsus and Hadrian.[28] It seems clear that the vernacular served to draw close to the world of Christian culture and education the day-to-day world of the Anglo-Saxons. Vernacular glosses never explained doctrinal or theological concepts but involved, instead, the realities of daily life. They offered many translations for terminology relating to money or animals, and even in one case, an accessory for clothing.[29] This evidence suggests that far from exclusively involving the rich inheritance of classical and Christian tradition, Anglo-Saxon missionary education stressed the need for a basic knowledge of local institutions, ideas, realities, and modes and forms of expression. This new range of culture made it imperative that ability in speaking native languages and competence in a variety of social situations and usages became a significant and essential aspect of Anglo-Saxon missionary training.

[27] Gregory the Great, *Regula pastoralis*, iii, prologue, *PL* 77, p. 49: 'Quia igitur qualis esse debeat pastor ostendimus, nunc qualiter doceat demonstremus. . . . Non una eademque cunctis exhortatio congruit, quia nec cunctos par morum qualitas astringit. . . . Pro qualitate igitur audientium formari debet sermo doctorum, ut et ad sua singulis congruat, et tamen a communis aedificationis arte numquam recedat. . . . Unde et doctor quisque, ut in una cunctos virtute charitatis aedificet, ex una doctrina, non una eademque exhortatione tangere corda audientium debet.'

[28] The first mention of the 'school' is in Bede, *HE*, iv, 2. For discussion of the whole matter, see Bernard Bischoff and Michael Lapidge, eds, *Biblical Commentaries from the Canterbury School of Theodore and Hadrian* (Cambridge, 1994). See also J. D. Pheifer, 'The Canterbury Bible glosses: facts and problems', in Michael Lapidge, ed., *Archbishop Theodore* (Cambridge, 1995), pp. 281–333.

[29] For example, Old English *cesaring, pending* for Latin *solidus*; Old English *lopustrae* for Latin *locustae*; Old English *hupupa* for Latin *opupa*; Old English *uuf* for Latin *bubo*; Old English *greshoppae* for Latin *locusta*; Old English *hod* for Latin *capellus*. See B. Bischoff and M. Lapidge, *Biblical Commentaries*, p. 588.

Bede says[30] that Bishop Cormán, whom the monastery of Iona had sent to further the Christian faith in Oswald's kingdom, could make no headway with the English, because he had probably been 'unreasonably harsh' with his *indoctis auditoribus.* He did not first offer them 'the milk of simpler teaching until, little by little, as they grew strong on the food of God's word, they were capable of receiving more elaborate instruction and of carrying out the more transcendent commandments of God'. Pope Gregory II, in a letter of 15 May 719, entrusted Boniface with a mission to the heathens in Thuringia,[31] and ordered him 'to teach them the service of the kingdom of God by persuading them to accept the truth . . . , doing this in a spirit of love and moderation, and with arguments suited to their understanding'. In a long letter written to him by Daniel, Bishop of Winchester, in 723/4,[32] Boniface, then a missionary in Thuringia, was advised to communicate with pagan people 'not in an offensive and irritating way but calmly and with great moderation', and by using persuasion and dialogue. Still more significant is the account of how Aldhelm, then Abbot of Malmesbury, in agreement with his people's interest in old heroic tales, used to please the crowds on a bridge over the river by singing the sacred texts in his native tongue and in the manner of the secular poets.[33]

II

We should now be asking about the linguistic techniques and procedures and the principles guiding choice of vocabulary which were devised to make the Christian message fully understandable.

[30] Bede, *HE*, iii, 5, p. 228.

[31] *Bonifatius-Briefe*, n.12, ed. Michael Tangl, *MGH, Ep.sel. in usum schol. separ. ed.* (Berlin, 1916), pp. 17–18: 'Praecipimus, ut in verbo gratiae Dei, quo igne salutifero, quem mittere Dominus venit in terram, enitere videris, ad gentes quascumque infidelitatis errore detentas properare Deo comitante potueris, ministerium regni Dei per insinuationem nomini Christi domini dei nostri veritatis suasione designes et per spiritum virtutis et dilectionis ac sobrietatis praedicationem utriusque testamenti mentibus indoctis consona ratione transfundas.'

[32] Ibid., p. 40, n. 23.

[33] William of Malmesbury, *Gesta pontificum Anglorum*, v, ed. N. E. S. A. Hamilton, *RS*, 52 (London, 1870), p. 336: 'Litteris itaque ad plenum instructus, nativae quoque linguae non negligebat carmina. . . . Populum eo tempore semibarbarum, parum divinis sermonibus intentum, statim, cantatis missis, domos cursitare solitum. Ideo sanctum virum, super pontem qui rura et urbem continuat, abeuntibus se opposuisse obicem, quasi artem cantitandi professum. Eo plusquam facto, plebis favorem et concursum emeritum. Hoc commento sensim ludicra verbis Scripturarum inseritis, cives ad sanitatem reduxisse.'

Indeed, the deep concern of the missionaries over language differences, to which I have already drawn attention, suggests that they were perfectly conscious of the obstacles inherent in what Michel Banniard has called 'vertical communication'. By 'vertical communication'[34] we mean any factual situation in which speakers are needed to transmit foreign concepts and words to hearers who belong to a completely different cultural and linguistic milieu. No doubt problems of this order constituted very major difficulties in the missionaries' rendering of Christian written doctrine into the native language of the Anglo-Saxons, whose linguistic models and training were based exclusively on oral tradition. It is not my intention to discuss here such key problems as the channels of transmission of Latin loans, the various forms of contact, or the different periods of their interference, about which there is a great variety and wealth of studies.[35] Rather, what I shall now attempt briefly to investigate is the missionaries' mastering both of the native language and of a foreign language such as Latin in order to explain the new religion.

The first point to be made is that to assist the full integration of new converts into the newly established Church system at all levels, a basic technical vocabulary was developed, primarily made up of loanwords. As far as the chronological distribution of Latin loans is concerned, Professor Gneuss has recently pointed out that the traditional periodization into three groups (words from the Continental period, up to

[34] Michel Banniard, *Viva Voce: communication orale et communication écrite en occident latin (IVe–IXe siècle)* (Paris, 1992), pp. 38–9.

[35] See, for example, Alois Pogatscher, *Zur Lautlehre der griechischen, lateinischen und romanischen Lehnwörter im altenglischen, Quellen und Forschungen zur Sprach- und Kulkturgeschichte der Germanischen Voelker*, 64 (Strasburg, 1888); Otto Funke, *Die gelehrten lateinischen Lehn- und Fremdwörter in der altenglischen Literatur von der Mitte des X. Jahrhunderts bis zum Jahr 1066* (Halle, 1914); Mary Serjantson, *A History of Foreign Words in English* (London, 1935); Alistair Campbell, *Old English Grammar* (Oxford, 1954), pp. 199–219; Helmut Gneuss, *Lehnbildungen und Lehnbedeutungen im altenglischen* (Berlin, 1955); idem, 'Some problems and principles of the lexicography of Old English', in E. S. Dick and K. R. Jankowsky, eds, *Festschrift für Karl Schneider* (Amsterdam, 1982), pp. 153–68; idem, '*Anglicae linguae interpretatio*', pp. 107–48; idem, 'Latin loans in Old English: a note on their inflexional morphology', in Helmut Gneuss, ed., *Language and History in Early England* (Variorum, 1996), ch. 6, pp. 1–12; Alfred Wollmann, *Untersuchungen zu den frühen Lehnwörtern im altenglischen. Phonologie und Datierung, Texte und Untersuchungen zur Englischen Philologie*, 15 (München, 1990); idem, 'Lateinisch-altenglische Lehnbeziehungen im 5. und 6. Jahrhundert', in Alfred Bammesberger and Alfred Wollmann, eds, *Britain 400–600: Language and History* (Heidelberg, 1990), pp. 373–96; idem, 'Early Latin loan-words in Old English', in *Anglo-Saxon England*, 22 (Cambridge, 1993), pp. 1–26; idem, 'Early Christian loan-words in Old English', in Tette Hofstra, Luuk A. J. R. Houwen and Alasdair A. MacDonald, eds, *Pagans and Christians, Germania latina*, II (Groningen, 1995), pp. 175–210.

about 400; words borrowed in Britain, 450–650; words borrowed after 650) is now no longer generally accepted, since there seem to be no safe criteria for drawing a fixed borderline between them.[36] Only by means of phonological criteria can we roughly date the introduction of loanwords into Old English, but no significant change in their inflexional distribution during the three periods can be ascertained.[37] Moreover, if we consider that very few borrowings are believed to have belonged to a pre-597 stratum, going back to an earlier period of the Germanic languages,[38] the lack of persuasive evidence in support of the setting of a minimum amount of Christian literature into the new language before Augustine's first mission to England provides an extra-linguistic chronological criterion, pointing to the end of the sixth century as the *terminus post quem* for the greater part of Christian borrowings.[39]

There can hardly be any doubt that Latin Christian loans which entered the Anglo-Saxon language quite quickly became basic components of a newly established vocabulary. A considerable number of them retained typically Anglo-Saxon phonological changes, thus providing valuable evidence for a wide adoption of such words from the very beginning and involving a clear on-going interaction between the native sound-system and the newcomers.[40] What is significant, though, is the record of varying phonological forms for the very same ecclesiastical and liturgical loans.[41] This would indicate that an outstanding role in social life ought to be ascribed to these occurrences, the majority of which entered the Anglo-Saxon language in different periods and changed in conformity with the multifarious needs of users and the inherent tendencies of the language system itself.

[36] Helmut Gneuss, 'Latin loans in Old English', p. 6.

[37] Ibid., p. 8.

[38] A few examples are Old English *cirice* < Latin *kyricón* < Greek *kuriakón*; Old English *deofol* < Latin *diabolus* < Greek *diábolos*; Old English *engel* < Latin *angelus* < Greek *ággelos*; Old English *mæsse* < Latin *missa*. For a list, see Wollmann, 'Early Christian loan-words in Old English', pp. 178–9.

[39] Wollmann, 'Early Christian loan-words in Old English', pp. 177–8.

[40] For a detailed list of Christian loanwords borrowed in the early stages of Christianization, see ibid., pp. 177–8, 186–90.

[41] Ibid., pp. 186–210; Helmut Gneuss, 'Liturgical books in Anglo-Saxon England and their Old English terminology', in Michael Lapidge and Helmut Gneuss, eds, *Learning and Literature in Anglo-Saxon England. Studies presented to Peter Clemoes on the occasion of his sixty-fifth birthday* (Cambridge, 1985), pp. 91–141; idem, 'Linguistic borrowing and Old English lexicography: Old English terms for the books of the liturgy', in Alfred Bammesberger, ed., *Problems of Old English Lexicography. Studies in Memory of Angus Cameron* (Regensburg, 1985), pp. 107–29.

The second significant point to be made concerns the creative dimension of the vernacular in enlarging its Christian technical vocabulary and, above all, the essential role played by the study of etymology, grammar, and meaning in Anglo-Saxon missionaries' education.[42] Not only were new words formed on a native basis from Latin models (loan-formations), but native words were given new additional meanings adopted from Latin (semantic loans), and even newly formed words were produced to deal with new institutions, values, and concepts (loan-creations).[43]

Loan-formations were formed from native elements in complete or partial correspondence to the structural elements of their Latin (or Greek, via Latin) models, in order to explain or paraphrase the originals. There can be no doubt that such operations were the results of the missionaries' exegetical methods and of the wide interpenetration of their teaching. The case of such loan-formations as Old English *ælmihtig* for Latin *omnipotens*, Old English *inflæscnes, inlichomung, onflæscnes* for Latin *incarnatio*, Old English *anboren, ancenned* for Latin *unigenitus*, Old English *godspell* for Greek (via Latin) *evangelium*, and so on, is most instructive.

The same linguistic sensibility and missionary aims may be recognized in native words with additional Christian meanings. That many terms assume new significance under the influence of social and cultural developments is in no way problematic. But it is difficult to escape the conclusion that the joining of new Christian ideas with native words specifically connected with secular situations was the response of missionaries to the need to render intelligible to the masses conditions and concepts of an entirely new world. One of the most significant examples is Anglo-Saxon terminology for the Latin word *Dominus*. The regular Old English development from Latin *Dominus* was *domne*, which was only used as determiner of a person's rank or status (*Domne Augustinus*; *Domne bisceop*), and never as a noun as it is in Latin. Instead, a range of synonyms for God as *Dominus* was taken from secular Anglo-Saxon society: *hlaford, frea, dryhten, theoden*. It is well known that those terms were not strict semantic equivalents, their employment being dependent on the particular meaning to be embedded in texts. Thus, in reference to God, Old English *hlaford*

[42] A comprehensive survey of the question appears in Helmut Gneuss, 'The study of language in Anglo-Saxon England', *BJRL* (1990), pp. 3–32.
[43] See Gneuss, '*Anglicae linguae interpretatio*', p. 143.

pointed not only to the notion of God as Father, as the custodian of men and provider of their needs (Psalm 120.5–7), but also to the notion of God as the superior Authority, to whom belongs the right (*ius in re*) to supreme power over people and to their submission (Psalm 71.8). The term *frea* (*heahfrea*) underlined the role of God as king, as the leader of believers (Psalm 43.5). *Dryhten* (*freadrihten*) preserved the meaning of 'lord of the *dryht*, chief of the armies', in close correspondence to 1 Kings 15.2, *Dominus exercituum.* Finally, *theoden*, which means 'lord of the *theod*, chief of the same descent or tribal communities' (Latin *gens*), pointed to the link between the Christian God, who chose to make a man of himself, and mankind (Psalm 88.28–9).

Other examples are native terms for God as Creator and for creation *ex nihilo*. The Anglo-Saxon words *scippend* ('He who shapes') and *scippan* ('to shape', 'to form'), which translated the Latin *creator/creare*, went back to textual exegetical variants of the *Vetus latina* in Genesis 1.27, where the readings *fecit, finxit, figuravit, plasmavit*, and *formavit* were alternative to the Vulgate's *creavit* in Genesis 1.1. There can be no doubt that the Old English lexical choice ('to shape') aimed not only at thorough intelligibility of the Christian meaning but also at preserving a full interpretative orthodoxy. The same conformity to the Christian concept of *creator* may be found in Old English *frumscepend*, where the emphasis was placed on God *auctor ab initio* (Old English *frum* = 'first'). Two other native terms, *metod* and *metend*, used for the secular concepts of 'destiny', 'fate', 'death', and consequently the 'distributor/measurer of destiny', were also used with a clear Christian meaning to indicate the Creator who holds the power of life and death (Ecclesiasticus 11.14; 39.30; Wisdom 16.13).

Another illuminating example of the adaptation of the vernacular for doctrinal teaching is to be found in the frequent use of the native word *thegn* for Latin *discipulus, apostolus.* Even if the Latin term was rendered either with the loanword *discipul* or with the loan-translation *leorningcniht*, the choice of the native word *thegn* – a term of very great social and political importance in Anglo-Saxon times[44] – as a semantic correspondent to its Latin model gives further support to the idea that

[44] Hector Munro Chadwick, *Studies on Anglo-Saxon Institutions* (Cambridge, 1905), pp. 333–54; Rachel R. Reid, 'Barony and Thanage', *EHR*, 35 (1920), pp. 161–99; Eric John, *Orbis Britanniae* (Bristol, 1966), pp. 128–53; Henry Loyn, 'Gesiths and thegns in Anglo-Saxon England from the seventh to the tenth century', *HER*, 70 (1955), pp. 529–49; idem, 'Kings, gesiths and thegns', in Martin Carver, ed., *The Age of Sutton Hoo* (Woodbridge, 1992), pp. 75–9.

this was an attempt to achieve the consent of pagans through intercomprehension. It is well known that *thegn* (over and above its general meaning of 'servant') could signify a noble in charge of the personal service of the king, a man who could belong to the household of the king in peace and war, and could follow him everywhere in battle and even into exile, a *miles* or *minister regis* who could be part of a king's *comitatus*. Thus, pagan people could be made more aware of the special link of protection and of loyalty which had bound Christ and His twelve apostles together, if local customs were employed as examples by which to understand the meaning of such an important dimension of Christianity.

Even more illustrative support is given by the Anglo-Saxon rendering of Church Latin *baptizare/baptidiare* (from Greek *baptízo*). Just as in Latin, in all Old Germanic languages the corresponding semantic loans strictly alluded to the act of immersion in water, a rite in which even Jesus submitted himself to receive baptism from John (Gothic *daupjan*; *Old English dyppan/dippan/diepan*; Old Saxon *dopian*; Old High German *toufen*; Old Islandic *deypa*). But in Old English the common term was a newly formed word, the impressive loan-creation *fulwian, fullian, fulligan*, which evoked for the converts not the material act but the spiritual, transcendental significance of immersion in water. Indeed, the Old English verb – sometimes glossed with Latin *albare* or *candidum facere* and probably related to Gothic *weihan* ('to purify', 'to make sacred') – transmitted with extraordinary intensity the theological meaning of the Christian rite, which exalts the recovery of purity of the soul stained by original sin, and displays the new condition of life of new Christian believers. (See Old English *fulluht/fulwiht/fulwuht* 'Baptism' = *full/ful* 'complete', 'entire', and *wiht* 'creature', 'wight'.)

In conclusion, I hope that I have been able to show that in Roman missionaries' policy of overcoming the language barrier with pragmatic solutions is to be found the secret of their spectacular successes. Gregory the Great, the first Pope who made the conversion of the Anglo-Saxon pagans the central focus of his pastoral activity, died without seeing his project of the Catholic unity of all the insular Churches fulfilled. What he nevertheless left as his extraordinary inheritance was the fertile idea that in order to transmit the Christian message it was necessary to establish solid human contacts and a solid intercomprehension between missionaries and their audience. This suggestion, which is strongly reflected and illustrated in the history of

Anglo-Saxon Christianization and that of Anglo-Saxon missions to the Continent, cannot be confined to that period. In response to the pressures of the contemporary Church, which still today grows up out of diversity, Gregory's pleading for the *qualitas* of the Christian shepherd, the *qualitas* of his teaching, and the *qualitas* of the audience is expected to govern the conduct of missionaries themselves and of those who support missionary efforts.

University of Rome

ST WILLIBRORD IN RECENT HISTORIOGRAPHY

by EUGÈNE HONÉE

INTRODUCTION

IN contrast to his fellow-countryman Boniface, Willibrord did not leave any correspondence or other writings. As a matter of fact, the only thing known to us is a small private note, consisting of a few lines. This note was written when he was seventy years old and is part of the liturgical calendar which he carried with him on his missionary travels. Here Willibrord, speaking about himself in the third person, mentions two events from his eventful life: first, that he came across the sea to the Frankish Kingdom in 690, secondly, that he was consecrated bishop by Pope Sergius in Rome five years later. These are the only things he says about himself.[1]

We may assume that Willibrord looked upon these two facts as the most important events in his life. It is remarkable that they both belong to the second half of that life, which he spent on the continent. About the thirty-two years which had preceded his coming to Francia nothing at all is mentioned.

In contrast to Willibrord himself, subsequent historiographers could not of course leave the first half of the saint's life undiscussed. As a matter of fact not only his biographer Alcuin, but also many twentieth-century historians, have paid explicit attention to the period prior to Willibrord's missionary work. This period, in its turn, is also to be divided into two halves. The first phase of his life is connected with his native country, Northumbria, and the monastery of Ripon situated there. It is followed by a second phase, related to Ireland and the Irish monastery of Rath Melsighi. For at the age of twenty, Willibrord made the journey to Rath Melsighi in south Ireland, where he stayed for more than twelve years before undertaking the crossing to the continent. After having arrived in Francia, he was granted a period of fifty years of mission among the Frisians and

[1] H. A. Wilson, ed., *The Calendar of St. Willibrord, from Ms. Paris Lat. 10837. A Facsimile with Transcription, Introduction and Notes*, Henry Bradshaw Society 55 (London, 1918), Pl. XI (facsimile) and p. 13 (transcription).

other Germanic tribes. The life of the saint is therefore to be divided into three periods. We may speak of an English, an Irish, and a continental period.[2]

The first and second periods not only constitute the prelude to the third, but also contain the key to understanding it. All modern, that is to say twentieth-century, authors agree on this. Opinions are only divided as to the importance to be attached to the first two periods. The past fifty years have shown a remarkable development in historiography about Willibrord. It can be summarized as follows. Around the middle of the present century most specialists described Willibrord's missionary activities against an Anglo-Roman background. From the seventies onwards more and more attention has been paid to the Irish elements in the Anglo-Saxon mission. In the following sections we shall briefly describe the outlines of this change.

I. THE OLDER VIEW

The chief representative of the older view, which was generally prevalent around the middle of the present century, was no doubt Wilhelm Levison. In 1939, this German medievalist who had fled to England from the Nazis gave a brilliant lecture at Durham to commemorate the twelve-hundredth anniversary of Willibrord's death.[3] A few years later he repeated his views in the Ford Lectures, held at Oxford, which were published in one volume entitled *England and the Continent in the Eighth Century*.[4] Other representatives of the older view are the Dutch expert Reinier Post and the Luxemburger Camille Wampach, who became especially known through his edition of the charters concerning Echternach.[5]

[2] Willibrord's life can be summarized as follows: 658 birth in Northumbria, *c.* 665 admission as *puer oblatus* to the monastery of Ripon, 678 departure to Ireland (Rath Melsighi), 690 departure to the continent, 739 death in Echternach. For Rath Melsighi as the monastery where Willibrord spent his Irish years, see D. Ó'Croinin, 'Rath Melsighi, Willibrord and the Earliest Echternach Manuscripts', *Peritia*, 3 (1984), pp. 17–49, here pp. 22–3 and n. 1.

[3] W. Levison, 'St. Willibrord and his place in history', in ibid., *Aus rheinischer und fränkischer Frühzeit. Ausgewählte Aufsätze* (Düsseldorf, 1948), pp. 314–29.

[4] Oxford, 1946.

[5] R. R. Post, 'Sint Willibrord in Noord en Zuid. Eenige kantteekeningen bij de jubileumliteratuur', *Nederlandse Historiebladen*, 3 (1940/41), pp. 1–14; idem, *De overgang van de Friezen tot het christendom*, Frisia Catholica 1948 (brochure); idem, 'Nieuwe

The tone for the older research was unmistakably set by Levison. In his 1939 address he emphasized the epoch-making character of Willibrord's work, by comparing him with, and contrasting him to, Columbanus, the monk and missionary who one hundred years before had gone to the continent *from Ireland*. 'Willibrord', as Levison expresses it, 'was to England what Columbanus had been to Ireland. He inaugurated a century of English spiritual influence on the Continent.'[6] In Levison's view, the remarkable thing about Willibrord was that he put his missionary work under the authority of the pope.

We do indeed read in Bede that Willibrord, after having arrived in the regions of the lower Rhine basin, first paid his respects to the Frankish ruler Pepin and then 'hurried to Rome' (*acceleravit venire ad Romam*), for the purpose of obtaining the licence and the blessing from Pope Sergius to undertake the conversion of the Frisians.[7] Willibrord was probably the first missionary of the early Middle Ages who for this reason paid his respects to the bishop of Rome. Many missionaries before him had undertaken the conversion of the Gentiles inhabiting the border regions of the Frankish Kingdom. Indigenous, that is to say Frankish, followers of Columbanus had already engaged in the Christianization of these border regions. However, in this so-called Iro-Frankish missionary movement it had by no means been customary to go to Rome in order to get the pope's approval and blessing for missionary work.

In the older literature, Willibrord's performance is invariably explained against the background of his first monastic period. It is assumed that Wilfrid, the famous abbot of Ripon, who was also bishop of York, left his mark on Willibrord's spirituality and view of the Church.

It is an established fact that the Northumbrian Wilfrid zealously promoted Roman customs as well as the Benedictine rule. At the synod of Whitby in 664 he arranged for the Irish influence to be reduced and

argumenten voor Sint Willibrords missiearbeid in Antwerpen en Noord-Brabant?', *Studia Catholica*, 29 (1954), pp. 165–77; idem, *Kerkgeschiedenis van Nederland*, 2 vols (Utrecht, 1957), I, pp. 14–29; C. Wampach, *Geschichte der Grundherrschaft Echternach im Frühmitteltelater*, 1,1 (Textband), 1, 2 (Quellenband) (Luxemburg, 1929–30); idem, *Sankt Willibrord. Sein Leben und Lebenswerk* (Luxemburg, 1953). For a more complete survey see my 'Sint Willibrord in wisselend historisch perspectief. Recente discussies over zijn geestelijke herkomst en missiewerk', *Tijdschrift voor Theologie* 31 (1991), pp. 357–80, here pp. 362–5.

[6] Levison, 'St. Willibrord', 320.

[7] Bede, *Historia Ecclesiastica Gentis Anglorum*, v, 11 (ed. C. Plummer, *Venerabilis Baedae opera historica*, vol. 1 [Oxford, 1896], p. 301) [hereafter *HE*].

for the king of Northumbria to decide in favour of the Roman observance. As a result, the bishops' seats throughout England came to have a lead over the monasteries, and in Northumbria, too, monastic organization was replaced by an episcopal church structure.[8]

According to the older historiography, Willibrord is said to have come to the continent full of the same Roman spirit which had inspired Wilfrid. Willibrord is described as a Benedictine monk who had devoted his heart and soul to the pope and who transplanted the diocesan structure of the Church as well as the Benedictine rule from England to the continent.

One more special characteristic of the older view must be emphasised here. Willibrord was not only looked upon as a pupil of Wilfrid, but also as predecessor of Boniface. It is generally known that this younger contemporary not only worked as a missionary but also as a reformer of the Frankish church. In this capacity he made every effort, at a great many synods, to bring about the introduction of the Roman liturgy, the Benedictine rule, and the strict observance of the old canonical rules as they had been preserved in Rome. The truth is that the Willibrord experts were inclined to attribute to Willibrord the same qualities which were demonstrably present in Boniface. They assumed as a matter of course that the old canonical regulations were as directive for Willibrord as they had been for Boniface.

2. NEW INSIGHTS

During the seventies and eighties there was a change in the insights concerning Willibrord's spiritual profile. This was the result of a renewed attention to the first two periods of his life, the years of his youth at Ripon and the years he spent in Ireland. Two authors deserve special mention in this connection: the Dutch Benedictine Augustinus van Berkum and the German medievalist Michael Richter. Both researchers arrived, independently of each other, at the conclusion that Willibrord must have been influenced by Irish-Columban traditions much more profoundly that had been assumed so far.[9]

[8] R. Fletcher, *The Conversion of Europe. From Paganism to Christianity 371–1386 AD* (London, 1997), ch. 6.

[9] A. van Berkum, 'Willibrord en Wilfried. Een onderzoek naar hun wederzijdse betrekkingen', *Sacris erudiri*, 23 (1978/79), pp. 347–415; idem, 'Iers-Columbaanse achtergronden in het leven en beleid van Willibrord en de zijnen' (Louvain, 1980) (dissertation in

We should not form an over-simple idea of that influence. For example, it would certainly be wrong to suppose that Willibrord only came into contact with the Irish way of thinking in Rath Melsighi and that this way of thinking remained outside his field of vision during the first, English, period. Richter and van Berkum established the likelihood that Willibrord did not find a strictly Benedictine monastic environment at Ripon, as used to be the prevailing opinion, but an environment in which a great deal of the Irish spirituality was still to be found. During the reign of King Oswald (634–42), Irish monks had swarmed out all over Northumbria and they had been able to hold their ground for three decades, more or less until the time when Willibrord was born. Even after the synod of Whitby, the way of living and thinking of the Irish monks continued to exert a great influence. During the last three decades of the seventh century many Englishmen even decided to leave Northumbria to settle in Ireland. Willibrord became one of these immigrants.

It can be indicated fairly accurately what inspired him and his fellow-immigrants. Bede mentions for the year 664 that there were many then who left 'their native island' (*insula patriae*), either for the sake of religious studies or to live a more ascetic life. 'In course of time', Bede continues, 'some of these devoted themselves faithfully to the monastic life, while others preferred to travel round to the cells of various teachers and apply themselves to study.'[10] Obviously Ireland was very popular because of its high level of culture and because of the special monastic ascesis which could be practised there. Just as a great many Irish ascetics had swarmed out both to the continent and to Britain for the past one hundred years, likewise now English Christians went the same route in the opposite direction. Those who moved away

typescript); idem, 'Réflexions sur la physionomie spirituelle de Saint Willibrord et de ses compagnons', *Echternacher Studien/Études Epternaciennes*, 2 (1982), pp. 7–18. M. Richter, 'Der irische Hintergrund der angelsächsischen Mission', in H. Löwe, ed., *Die Iren und Europa im frühen Mittelalter*, 2 vols (Stuttgart, 1982), I, pp. 120–37; idem, 'The young Willibrord', in G. Kiesel and J. Schroeder, eds, *Willibrord. Apostel der Niederlande – Gründer der Abtei Echternach. Gedenkgabe zum 1250. Todestag des angelsächsischen Missionars* (2nd edn, Luxembourg 1990 [1st edn 1989]), pp. 25–30; idem, 'England and Ireland in the time of Willibrord', in P. Bange and A. G. Weiler, eds, *Willibrord, zijn wereld en zijn werk. Voordrachten gehouden tijdens het Willibrordcongres Nijmegen, 28–30 september 1989*, Middeleeuwse Studies, VI (Nijmegen, 1990), pp. 35–50.

[10] 'Erant ibidem eo tempore multi . . . qui . . . relicta insula patriae, vel divinae lectionis vel continentioris vitae gratia illo secesserant. Et quidam quidem mox se monasticae conversationi fideliter mancipaverunt: alii magis circumeundo per cellas magistrorum lectioni operam dare gaudebant, Bede, *HE*, iii, 27 (ed. Plummer, p. 192).

from the 'insula patriae' practised a well-defined ascesis which had sprung up in Ireland, namely that of the *peregrinatio pro Christo*, a voluntary form of exile, chosen for the sake of Christ.

The ideal of the *peregrinatio* had traditionally assumed different forms.[11] The first, and perhaps even most important, variant was monastic life. 'Peregrination' and monastic life do not exclude each other, but essentially belong together. Most peregrinations took a monastery as their point of departure and in the end resulted in the permanent residence in another monastery, with the distinction that the latter monastery was situated *extra patriam.*

The monastic way of life, however, was not the only destination of itinerant ascetics. In many cases staying abroad was used 'to bring blessing to many' (*pluribus prodesse*), to use Bede's expression.[12] In that way preaching and ministry, in short, mission, became a second important goal of the 'peregrination'. This second purpose mostly followed naturally from the first: it was only chosen at a later stage and in close connection with monastic life abroad. It is this sequence and this connection that we also find with Willibrord.[13]

We should indeed understand the beginning of the third phase of Willibrord's life in terms of the ideal of the *peregrinatio pro Christo.* Sadly enough, Bede does not mention anything about Willibrord's personal motives for exchanging Ireland for the continent. However, he does tell extensively about the ideals which had come to inspire Egbert, Willibrord's abbot in Rath Melsighi, in the course of his development. Everything that we learn about this can also be applied to Willibrord.

Like Willibrord, Egbert was of English descent. A long time before Willibrord, he had set out for Ireland. At first he had only intended to stay for a short period and especially for study. Once he had arrived at his new destination, he, together with a great many others, fell victim to an epidemic. In these distressing circumstances he made a vow to stay away from England once and for all if he recovered, or, as Bede phrases it, 'that he would live as an exile [*peregrinus*] to such a degree that he would never return into the island of Britain where he was born'.[14] His prayer for recovery was granted and therefore he remained

[11] A. Angenendt, 'Die irische Perigrinatio und ihre Auswirkungen auf dem Kontinent vor dem Jahre 800', in Löwe, *Iren*, pp. 124–75.

[12] Bede, *HE*, v, 9 (ed. Plummer, p. 296).

[13] See Richter, 'Hintergrund', pp. 123–7.

[14] 'Vovit etiam votum, quia adeo peregrinus vivere vellet, ut nunquam in insulam, in qua natus est, id est Brittanniam, rediret', Bede, *HE*, iii, 27 (ed. Plummer, p. 193).

in Ireland, where he rose to be abbot of Rath Melsighi. Again some time afterwards, however, Egbert also decided to leave Ireland. He turned his eyes to the continent and 'proposed to himself', as Bede says, 'to carry the word of God . . . to some of those nations that had not yet heard it.[15]

It may be concluded from Bede's account that Egbert looked upon the conversion of the Gentiles as a continuation and completion of his destiny as a *peregrinus*. In fact, all his missionary plans came to nothing. On account of bad weather conditions, Egbert had to give up his crossing. Afterwards, others went instead of him to the continent, starting from Rath Melsighi to be sure: first Wigbert, then Willibrord with eleven companions, and finally also two other Englishmen, the priests White Hewald and Black Hewald who were to die martyrs' deaths in Saxony.[16] The successive missionary initiatives, briefly mentioned by Bede, belong together. This means that Willibrord was a missionary from the school of Egbert and that the latter's ideal of *peregrinatio* must also have inspired him.

3. NEW LIGHT ON THE MISSIONARY WORK

After the English and the Irish periods of life, the third, continental period, should be discussed. We have to deal with the obvious question of how the research into Willibrord's origins has been productive for the interpretation of his work as a founder of monasteries and as a missionary.

Some authors have managed to demonstrate that Willibrord continued to maintain relations with Ireland from the continent. David Ó'Croinin, for example, proved that the earliest Echternach manuscripts show Irish features. He is right in concluding that the scriptorium of Willibrord's monastery was at first inhabited by monks who had been trained at Rath Melsighi.[17]

The same author also made a new study of Willibrord's liturgical calendar (see p. 16 above). He was able to show that this famous manuscript was built up in several layers which were prepared at separate moments and in places that were far apart. The oldest

[15] 'Proposuit animo . . . verbum Dei aliquibus earum, quae nondum audierant, gentibus evangelisando committere', Bede, *HE*, v, 9 (ed. Plummer, p. 296).

[16] Bede, *HE*, v, 9 (ed. Plummer, pp. 296–303).

[17] D. Ó'Croinin, 'Rath Melsighi', pp. 17–49.

fragment consists of calendar leaves which were probably not written at Echternach, but at Rath Melsighi. They must have been handed to Willibrord there when he was making preparations for the crossing to the Low Countries.[18]

Nowadays the inhabitants of the monasteries founded by Willibrord are no longer looked upon as Benedictines. In the charters of foundation of Echternach and Susteren we find the designation *monachi peregrini* and in the rule of Benedict one will look in vain for a description of monastic life as a *peregrinatio*.[19] Obviously, in Willibrord's time the monastic customs of Rome and Monte Cassino had not yet found acceptance in Frisia. Also it is now generally supposed that Willibrord's followers were not yet, or only to a limited extent, familiar with Roman liturgy. The latter was only fully introduced at the instigation of his successor Boniface.[20]

Previously it was assumed that the ideal of the *peregrinatio* was experienced differently among the Anglo-Saxon missionaries than among the followers of Columba and Columbanus. Willibrord and his followers were supposed to have been 'professional missionaries' in contrast to the Irish and Iro-Frankish *peregrini*. The Dutch medievalist Reinier Post was the first scholar to use this definition. He wished to express by it that Willibrord and his companions came to the Low Countries 'for no other purpose than to preach the gospel'.[21] It is far more likely, however, that Willibrord continued to attach an independent importance to a monastic life abroad, which means that the monastic way of life remained as important for him as mission and preaching.

In this connection, it is important to ask with what purpose Echternach was founded. Post and others assumed that this monastery, which was situated close to Trier, was only of derivative importance. It was supposed to have been intended as an operating base and a safe haven for the missionaries who were active in Frisia.[22] A simple argument, to begin with, against this supposition is the great distance (about 400 kilometres, or 250 miles) between Echternach and Utrecht.

18 Ibid., pp. 28–36.

19 Wampach, *Geschichte*, I, 2, No. 3 and No. 15 (p. 19 and p. 42).

20 H. Wegman, 'De praktijk van de eredienst in het leven van Willibrord', in Bange and Weiler, *Willibrord*, pp. 221–36.

21 Post, *Kerkgeschiedenis*, p. 17.

22 Ibid., p. 21. See also Weiler, *Willibrords missie. Christendom en cultuur in de zevende en achtste eeuw* (Hilversum, 1989), pp. 112–13 and 115.

Nor can we rely on the idea that Willibrord set up his monastery as a missionary centre for the immediate surroundings. The Christianization of the Moselle and the Eifel regions had already made too much progress to make such a centre necessary. Another solution forces itself upon us: Willibrord may have wished to have a monastery which resembled the centres of prayer and study which he had got to know in Ireland. It is quite conceivable that Echternach was for him another Rath Melsighi: a place where ascetics could retire as 'exiles', for praying and studying, and also for preparing themselves for the proclamation of the faith in the broadest sense of the word, not only to the Frisians, but to all the Germanic peoples who were still unconverted.[23]

We must point to another misunderstanding in connection with Echternach. Until recently it was generally assumed that Willibrord's patron Pepin played an essential role in the foundation of Echternach. Just as Pepin had assigned Frisia to Willibrord as a missionary region,[24] likewise he was supposed afterwards to have wished to give the Frisian mission a solid backing in the Frankish hinterland.[25] This view is no longer tenable. It is based on the misconception that the actual foundress, Lady Irmina, was closely related to Pepin, namely that she was his mother-in-law. In 1982, however, Matthias Werner showed that Pepin has no place whatsoever in the genealogy of the foundress of Echternach.[26]

It is quite certain that the Frankish ruler, just like the foundress Irmina, favoured Echternach with liberal gifts. However, he did so only at a later stage and certainly not in close consultation with Irmina, but only after he had driven her away from the scene. Nor, according to Werner, was Pepin's patronage of the monastery prompted by the idea that he wanted to give the mission in the North a solid backing. The *major domus* was driven by a far more

[23] See for this my *Willibrord, asceet en geloofsverkondiger. De lijn van zijn leven en de structuur van zijn levenswerk* (Zoetermeer, 1995), pp. 49–58.

[24] Bede, *HE*, *V*, 10 (ed. Plummer, p. 299).

[25] H. Büttner, 'Mission und Kirchenorganistation des Frankenreiches bis zum Tode Karls des Grossen', in H. Braunfels, ed., *Karl der Grosse. Lebenswerk und Nachleben, I: Persönlichkeit und Geschichte* (Düsseldorf, 1965), pp. 462–3.

[26] M. Werner, *Adelsfamilien im Umkreis der frühen Karolinger. Die Verwandtschaft Irminas von Oeren und Adelas von Pfalzel*, Vorträge und Forschungen hrsg. vom Konstanzer Arbeitskreis für mittelalterliche Geschichte, Sonderband 28 (Sigmaringen, 1982), pp. 98–121. Werner's argumentation did not convince E. Hlawitschka, as may be clear from the latter's contribution: 'Zu den Grundlagen des Aufstiegs der Karolinger', *Rheinische Vierteljahrsblätter*, 49 (1985), pp. 1–48.

direct self-interest. Willibrord's monastery was situated in the centre of Austrasia, the ancestral region of the Pepinides. The family had numerous possessions here. The monastery could serve as an important base for the consolidation of Pepin's power in the region. It was upon this consideration that he strengthened the position of the monastery.[27]

Apart from clarifying Pepin's objectives, Werner also shed new light on the goals of the foundress, Irmina.[28] This woman had entered the religious life after her husband's death. At the moment when she presented Willibrord with the monastery and the church at Echternach, she herself was also head of a monastic community. She was abbess of Oeren and the convent with the same name was just outside the walls of Trier. In the famous Echternach foundation charter there is the hint of a possible motive for Irmina's generosity towards Willibrord. The latter was given the monastery and the church at Echternach because of his unceasing attention to and care for Irmina and her fellow-nuns in Trier.[29] Unfortunately, we are not given any further information about the nature of Willibrord's attention and care. It is certain, however, that there must already have been a connection between Willibrord and Irmina at the time when he received gifts from her in 697. Apparently Willibrord more than once found himself in Trier and its surroundings during the years prior to the foundation of Echternach.

Possibly the contacts with Irmina had already been established at the time of his first journey to Rome, around 690. The most common route from the Low Countries to Italy was by way of Trier. If Willibrord used this route on his first journey to Rome, he may have taken a break in Trier and have found accommodation in Irmina's convent. Once the contact had been established, he must have returned to her convent more than once. During his visits he may have taught Irmina and her fellow-nuns in some way, giving them spiritual counselling, and this may be the attention and care which Irmina mentions in her foundation charter.

27 Werner, *Adelsfamilien*, pp. 84–5 and 96–8.

28 Ibid., pp. 44–8 and 60–83.

29 'Dum sanctitas et dilectio vestra erga me vel monasterium meum assidue agitur', Wampach, *Echternach*, I, 2, No. 3 (p. 19).

4. ECHTERNACH AND UTRECHT

Although Willibrord's missionary work shows Irish characteristics, this does not mean that we should have any doubts about his bond with the Holy See. Most authors are not concerned about replacing the older view by its counterpart, so as to highlight Willibrord's missionary work exclusively in an Irish perspective. Rather they try to replace the mono-causal explanation of their predecessors by a multi-causal scheme, in which some data are drawn from Irish-Celtic, others from Anglo-Roman, influences. This is by no means an easy task. It is even more difficult to bring the various research findings together into one meaningful whole.

With respect to some aspects of Willibrord's lifework, diverging views are held to this day. This applies especially to Willibrord's position as a bishop. To conclude this survey, we shall give a brief exposition of the various opinions on this point and comment on them.

To begin with, we have to stick to the fact that Willibrord's two journeys to Rome are clear evidence of an Anglo-Roman bias in his activities. The first journey, to be sure, was much more than a pilgrimage to the graves of the Apostles, for example. Pilgrimages to Rome had always been popular, including with Willibrord's Irish and Irish-Frankish predecessors. Willibrord's first journey, on the other hand, was a direct 'visit to the pope' especially undertaken to obtain the latter's permission for the vast missionary project that had been agreed on with Pepin.[30]

The second visit only strengthened the bond with the Holy See. This time the initiative was on Pepin's side. At the latter's request Willibrord was consecrated 'archbishop of the Frisians' in Rome.[31] According to Alcuin, Willibrord was handed the pallium by the pope as a sign of this high authority.[32] A comparison with Augustine of Canterbury forcefully suggests itself. One hundred years earlier this Roman missionary had been sent the same decoration in England. As we know, Augustine had received instructions through the same post

[30] J. Schroeder, 'Willibrord und Rom. Zu den beiden Papstbesuchen des Apostels der Friesen', *Hémecht. Zeitschrift für Luxemburgische Geschichte*, 37 (1985), pp. 5–13, here pp. 10–11.

[31] 'misit Pippin . . . Uilbrordum Romam . . . postulans ut eidem Fresonum genti archiepiscopus ordinaretur', Bede, *HE*, v, 11 (ed. Plummer, p. 302).

[32] *Vita s. Willibrordi archiepiscopi Traiectensis auctore Alcuino*, cap. 7, ed. W. Levison, *MGH, SRM*, 7 (Hanover, 1919), pp. 113–41, 122.

for founding two archdioceses and twice twelve dioceses.[33] If the comparison with Augustine holds good, it must have been the intention of Pope Sergius in 695 to plant the diocesan structure, which meanwhile had fully developed in England, into Willibrord's missionary region.

There is no evidence, however, of the fact that an episcopal church structure was actually achieved at the time of Willibrord's missionary activity. According to Bede, Willibrord appointed 'bishops' *(antistites)*.[34] Probably these were auxiliary bishops without their own jurisdiction.[35] At the time of Willibrord's death the Utrecht see itself was in an extremely vulnerable position and even remained unoccupied for three years at a stretch. Only at the end of the eighth century is it possible to speak of a regular succession. Then, however, Utrecht is not the centre of an archdiocese, but the seat of a bishop, subordinate to the archbishop of Cologne.

In order to explain this development, Father van Berkum pointed to Willibrord's Irish-Columban background. According to him, with this missionary 'the monastic element prevailed over the function of bishop' and therefore he was not the right man for helping to carry out the Roman project of a Utrecht archdiocese.[36] In van Berkum's opinion, Willibrord can only have looked upon Utrecht as a mission post which was completely subordinate to his monastery in Echternach. In short, in this author's view the 'failure of the Frisian archdiocese' is related to the 'Irish spirituality' of the archbishop consecrated in Rome.[37]

In the eyes of other Dutch authors, the fiasco which Father van Berkum tries to explain never took place. The medievalist Anton Weiler argues as follows. In the year in which Willibrord was consecrated, nothing like a Frisian archdiocese was designed in Rome. Utrecht did not even become the seat of a bishop during Willibrord's lifetime. None of the charters preserved contains any mention of Willibrord calling himself 'bishop of Utrecht'. Such a title is lacking because he did not have that title. Willibrord, so Weiler argues, had been consecrated archbishop in Rome without any canonically

[33] Gregory the Great, *Registrum Epistularum*, XI, 39 (22.6.601), ed. Norberg, *CChr.SL*, CXLA (Turnhout, 1996), pp. 934–5.

[34] Bede, *HE*, v, 11 (ed. Plummer, p. 303).

[35] Levison,'St. Willibrord', pp. 326–8.

[36] Van Berkum, 'De constituering en mislukking van de Friese kerkprovincie', in Bange and Weiler, *Willibrord*, pp. 159–71, here 169.

[37] Van Berkum, 'Reflexions', p. 17.

founded see being joined to the title. According to Bede, Utrecht was assigned to him by Pepin, and this initiative on the part of a worldly ruler is not sufficient to allow one to speak of an ecclesiastical see.[38] Therefore, we have to imagine Willibrord as a missionary bishop without an ecclesiastically recognized see or residence. He was even a missionary archbishop, in which capacity he was authorized to appoint suffragan bishops to assist him, but not the head of an archdiocese.

This view cannot be quite convincing. Apart from Bede, Boniface, in a famous letter dating from the year 753, also asserts that Willibrord had a bishop's see in Utrecht. Boniface even speaks of an 'episcopalis sedes Romano pontifici subjecta', a see which was directly subordinate to the pope in Rome.[39] Partly on the basis of this statement, the German church historian Arnold Angenendt again expressed himself positively with respect to Willibrord's episcopal office. In Angenendt's view, it is almost a matter of course that Willibrord was bishop of Utrecht. He even goes one step further and regards Willibrord as a 'Roman archbishop', that is to say, a bishop who came back from Rome with the pallium and who, therefore, was authorized to establish an archdiocese in Frisia.[40]

It really seems as if history has retraced its own footsteps. All things considered, Angenendt holds the same view as Levison: for him, too, Willibrord's consecration in Rome implies that the Holy See had the intention of transplanting to the continent an ecclesiastical structure which had developed in England. This does not mean, however, that an answer has been found to the old question of why the intended Frisian archdiocese in fact never came about.

In trying to resolve this question Angenendt broke new ground. Just as Father van Berkum, he holds the view that Willibrord assigned a priviliged position to Echternach in relation to Utrecht. He derives the evidence for this from the famous gift that Willibrord made to the remote monastery some ten years before he died.[41]

[38] A. Weiler, *Willibrords missie*, pp. 103–9, 144 and 153. See also P. Leupen, 'Sint Salvator en Sint Maarten: Willibrord en Bonifatius', in Bange and Weiler, *Willibrord*, pp. 317–27. Bede's brief account runs as follows: 'Donavit autem ei Pippin locum cathedrae episcopalis in castello suo inlustri, quod . . . lingua . . . Gallica Traiectum vocatur', *HE*, v, 11 (ed. Plummer, p. 303).

[39] Boniface, *Epistulae*, ed. M. Tangl, *MGH, Epp. Sel.* (²1955), No 109.

[40] 'Willibrord als römischer Erzbischof', in Kiesel and Schroeder, *Willibrord. Apostel der Niederlande*, pp. 31–41.

[41] 'Willibrord im Dienste der Karolinger', *Annalen des historischen Vereins für den Niederrhein*, 175 (1973), pp. 63–113, here 91–4.

In a charter dating from the year 726 Willibrord gave up a great many possessions in land and farms which he had acquired through the years. All the property made over by him belonged to the Frankish hinterland of the Frisian mission, namely the county of Toxandria which borders the Meuse and Rhine delta in the North.[42] What surprises the reader of the charter is the fact that Willibrord bequeathed his vast possessions to Echternach, instead of to his own nearby bishop's see.

Willibrord must have had a special reason for endowing Echternach so lavishly with property. In the opening line of the charter he expresses the wish that he may be buried in Echternach after his death. Apparently he made the endowment in 726 to guarantee the continued existence of a monastic community in Echternach which would maintain his *memoria* and would never cease praying for the salvation of his soul.

According to Angenendt, however, there may also have been another reason for the fact that Echternach was favoured in preference to Utrecht. Perhaps, according to his hypothesis, Willibrord also assigned to Echternach the position of a head monastery and this may have been the reason why he wished to strengthen its economic basis.[43] Angenendt does not look upon Echternach as another Rath Melsighi. He prefers to compare Willibrord's first and most important monastery with Iona. Perhaps, he argues, the missionary wanted to join the various monasteries in his vast missionary region into a similar organizational framework to that which had existed in the British Isles in the days of his youth. The monasteries which the Irish monks, taking Iona as their base, had founded in Northumbria were part of a network, a so-called *paruchia*. The abbot of Iona kept control over the other foundations, and the monks who had swarmed out in every direction came under his authority.[44] Perhaps, Angenendt suggests, we may look upon Echternach as the centre of a new *paruchia* in the making. Several monasteries were founded or planned by Willibrord. Apart from Echternach, we have to mention Susteren on the river

[42] Wampach, *Echternach*, I, 2, No 39.

[43] 'Willibrord tussen bischopszetel en klooster', *Millennium. Tijdschrift voor middeleeuwse studies*, 10 (1996), pp. 100–10.

[44] H. Moisl, 'Das Kloster Iona und seine Verbindungen mit dem Kontinent im siebenten und achten Jahrhundert', in H. Dopsch and R. Juffinger, eds, *Virgil von Salzburg. Missionar und Gelehrter. Beiträge des internationalen Symposiums vom 21.–24. Sept. 1984* (Salzburg, 1985), pp. 27–37.

Meuse, as well as Utrecht where at the time there was also a monastic settlement, fourthly Rindern on the lower Rhine and finally Hammelburg on the river Saale.[45] Angenendt thinks it is quite conceivable that Willibrord on the one hand let himself be consecrated a Roman archbishop and on the other wished to build up and supervise a network of monasteries which was conceived after the Irish model. In support of his view he refers to a charter of Charles Martel relating to Utrecht (723). Here a gift is made to a *monasterium* in Utrecht which is supervised by *pater noster Vuillibrordus archiepiscopus*.[46]

From the phrases used in the charter it may indeed be inferred that Willibrord carried out his activities as archbishop from the monastery situated in Utrecht. I doubt, however, whether Angenendt is right when he goes much further in supposing that the Utrecht monastery was *subordinate* to Echternach. The idea that Willibrord was engaged in creating a kind of *paruchia* for his monasteries, with Echternach as centre, cannot be made to fit the available information. It is true that he was at the same time abbot in Echternach, Susteren, and Utrecht, but there is no evidence at all for the fact that he wished to supervise Susteren and Utrecht from Echternach or intended to put them into a position in which they were dependent on Echternach.

CONCLUSION

All things considered, another, more limited, conclusion forces itself upon us, namely that Willibrord's missionary work cannot be understood from the perspective of one particular model which was the diocesan ecclesiastical framework. Apparently, the monasteries occupied an important place next to the bishop's see. The authority of bishop and archbishop which he received in Rome was not the only

[45] See for the geographical situation of these places Wampach's map of 'Echternachs entfernter Klosterbesitz in Friesland, am Niederrhein und in Franken-Thüringen' in Wampach, I, 1. With regard to Susteren see Werner, *Adelsfamilien*, pp. 157, 289; and idem, *Der Lütticher Raum in frühkarolingischer Zeit*, Veröffentlichungen des Max-Planck-Instituts für Geschichte, 62 (Göttingen, 1980), p. 170. In Hammelburg a monastery was only planned, not realized; see Werner, *Adelsfamilien*, pp. 156–9. For the presumptive evidence of a monastery in Rindern see Angenendt, 'Willibrord . . . bisschopszetel', p. 106.

[46] M. Gijsseling and A. C. F. Koch, eds, *Diplomata Belgica ante annum millesimum centesimum scripta*, 2 vols (Brussels, 1950), I, 305, No 173: 'monasterium, quod est infra muros Traiecto castro situm constructum, ubi apostolicus vir et in Christo pater noster Vuillibrordus archiepiscopus sub sancte conversationis cenobitali ordine custos preesse videtur.'

thing which determined the structure of Willibrord's missionary work. His authority as abbot of a monastery had an influence which was at least as powerful.

It is not possible for us to get an idea of the way in which Willibrord experienced the tension between his two authorities. The vulnerable position in which the Utrecht diocese was left by his death demonstrates that he did not succeed in fully integrating these authorities. He may not have done enough to strengthen his see, and perhaps this negligence is related to a clear preference for the other centre of his missionary work: Echternach.

Catholic Theological University of Utrecht

POLITICAL RIVALRY AND EARLY DUTCH REFORMED MISSIONS IN SEVENTEENTH-CENTURY NORTH-SULAWESI (CELEBES)

by HENDRIK E. NIEMEIJER

THE northernmost region of North Sulawesi, Minahasa, is one of the most Christian provinces of Eastern Indonesia. About ninety per cent of its total population of approximately one million is Protestant. The upland province capital of Tomohon and the city of Manado – the capital of North Sulawesi – are important centres for Christian education. On Sundays, the sound of bells of the white cathedral-style churches can be heard in almost every Minahasan town. Travellers who venture out to the beach villages on the Sangihe-Talaud islands north of Manado experience the same Protestant features of this part of the eastern archipelago.

When asking the ordinary Minahasan village people when their community became Christian, they usually recall two famous nineteenth-century missionaries of the Dutch Missionary Society (NZG): J. F. Riedel and J. G. Schwarz. The former worked in the upland town of Tondano (1831–53), and the latter in Langowan (1832–59). Their mission work made a great impact on the indigenous people and their traditional religions. During his twenty-two years' residence, Riedel baptized 9,341 people and admitted another 3,851 to the Communion celebrations. In two of his most successful years, 1850–2, Schwarz baptized 2,473 adults and 1,942 children. When he died, he left twenty-seven churches and fifteen mission schools. The other eight Minahasan missionary districts were successfully evangelized by other NZG missionaries. As a result, eighty per cent (80,000 people) of the Minahasans formally belonged to the Protestant Church by the end of the nineteenth century.[1]

Interestingly, collective memory does not recall the first Protestant missions in North Sulawesi, which date back to the time of the Dutch East India Company (VOC, 1602–1795). In this article I attempt to

[1] S. Coolsma, *De Zendingseeuw voor Nederlandsch Oost-Indië* (Utrecht, 1901), pp. 562–92. J. W. Gunning, 'Uit en over de Minahasa II; De protestantsche zending in de Minahasa', *Bijdragen tot de Taal-, Land- en Volkenkunde* (1924), 80, pp. 451–520.

place the early conversions to Protestantism in its political and religious contexts. In the first sections attention is paid to North Sulawesi as a subordinate part of a political rivalry between European and indigenous powers over the Malukan spice islands. As rivalry ended during the 1660s, peripheral North Sulawesi found itself in a power vacuum, which was filled by the VOC. As a result of a new political equilibrium, Dutch Reformed missions were unexpectedly welcomed in remote places where the Calvinist ministers would not normally have expected to make converts.

CONTESTING THE SPICE ISLANDS

During the period 1450–1680 Southeast Asia went through the so-called 'Age of Commerce'.[2] First, trade relations between much of the region, including the Indonesian archipelago and Chinese, Arab, and Indian merchants were considerably strengthened, while the Europeans opened the world market further. Increasing trade activity also gave a boost to the spice trade of the four ancient Malukan kingdoms of Ternate, Tidore, Jailolo, and Bacan. In 1511, the Portuguese took the great trade entrepot of Melaka, with a view to establishing their headquarters on the odorous spice island of Ternate, which they accomplished eleven years later in 1522. Sadly enough for the Europeans, the spice islands were already influenced by Islam and had become sultanates in the late fifteenth century. But the constant rivalry between Ternate and the neighbouring sultanate of Tidore helped the Portuguese to conclude exclusive spice contracts with Ternate despite the religious differences. For nearly half a century, the royal clove ships from Ternate set sail for the bay of Ambon, joined the nutmeg ships from the southern Banda islands, and returned with the favourable monsoon winds to Goa to deliver the costly cargo.

This favourable situation changed drastically after a series of conflicts with the Ternaten elite, and the assassination of Sultan Hairun by the Portuguese in 1570. To avenge his father, the newly elected sultan, Babullah, laid siege to the Portuguese fortress of Gammalama, which was not rigidly enforced anymore. After five years of war, the Portuguese were forced to withdraw to Amboina,

[2] Reid, 'Islamization and Christianization in Southeast Asia: The Critical Phase, 1550–1650', in A. Reid (ed.), *Southeast Asia in the Early Modern Era. Trade, Power, and Belief* (Ithaca and London, 1993), pp. 151–80.

where they settled permanently, and built the city of Ambon. From now on, they supported Ternate's arch-rival Tidore. The Spaniards, after the incorporation of the Portuguese crown into the Spanish kingdom (1580), succeeded in reconquering the old Portuguese fortress of Gammalama in 1606.[3] They also maintained three strong fortresses on Tidore, well defended with three to five hundred troops. North Sulawesi and the Sangihe-Talaud islands (especially Siau), lying half-way to the Manila headquarters, supplied the Spanish garrisons with rice, slaves, coconut oil, and a variety of marine products.

Despite growing animosities with the Iberians, the Ternatens still traded with other Europeans. When Sir Francis Drake visited Ternate in 1579, he was warmly welcomed by Babullah in the reception hall of the former Portuguese fortress of Gammalama. The visit of the English trader Henry Middleton in 1605, however, was not a success. The Ternaten sultan was more impressed by the naval firepower of the Dutch East India Company (1602). Their anti-Iberian sentiments, fed by the Eighty Years War between Spain and the Low Countries, made them an attractive counterpart, while the English had done little to fight the Spaniards since Drake's visit.

Under the Spanish attack of 1606, Ternate desperately tried to contact a Dutch fleet under commander Cornelis Matelief. But when Matelief arrived, the Spaniards had already captured the sultan and some of his nobles and sent them to Manila. The remaining Ternaten nobility, who had fled to Jailolo on Halmahera, anxiously concluded a treaty with Matelief. The VOC promised full protection of the Ternaten sultanate in return for an exclusive monopoly in the clove trade. Matelief now quickly built and occupied a new fortress close to the sultan's kraton (Fort Oranje, 1607–8).[4]

The Twelve Years' Truce between Spain and the Dutch Republic (1609–21) did not ease rivalry over the spice islands. The VOC's first main concern was the conquest of Banda and Jayakarta (Batavia). It temporarily occupied Siau in 1614, but showed no intention of expanding in North Sulawesi. This part of the archipelago was not of vital strategic value. It also was a highly unstable region frequently raided by several local maritime warlords and regional competitors, including the sultans of Ternate, Tidore, Mindanao, and the Bugis-

[3] During the years 1521–34, Spaniards from Manila had also settled on Tidore, but were forced to give up their claims under papal restrictions.

[4] F. W. Stapel, *Pieter van Dam, Beschryvinge van de Oostindische Compagnie*, II, 1 (The Hague, 1931), pp. 31–2.

Makassarese kings. As Ternate's allies, the Dutch from time to time supported the sultan in his territorial claims over a number of small kingdoms and islands. Even after a joint Dutch-Ternaten attack on the Spanish stronghold Timon in 1644, which caused the Spaniards to leave Minahasa for seven years, the Dutch showed no interest in a costly occupation which required permanent manned strongholds and provisioning.

The proclamation of the end of the Eighty Years War in 1648 (the Peace of Westphalia) was received with much scepticism by the Spanish side. It forbade any Iberian presence in North Sulawesi, yet as soon as the treaty was publicly announced in the fortress of Gammalama, the Spaniards sent soldiers to Minahasa to secure their territorial claims and rice supplies.[5] Reports of Minahasan resistance and refusals to serve the Spaniards now tempted the Dutch to build a wooden barricade in the town of Manado, which sympathized with the sultan. The Dutch rightly feared that the Spaniards would take possession of all Minahasan lands to back up their presence on the spice islands.

When the Spanish-Tidorese alliance finally broke down, the roles were reversed. In 1657 the Dutch agreed with the Tidorese sultan to extirpate all clove trees on his island (including those around the three Spanish fortresses) in return for a yearly payment of 3,000 rixdollars.[6] This severely damaged Spanish involvement in the spice trade and made the continuation of the fortresses on Tidore far too expensive. Meanwhile a Dutch expedition convinced the Minahasan village heads that local tribal conflicts and their troubles with the Spaniards could best be solved by contracts with the alleged legitimate overlord (the sultan of Ternate) and the Company. From 1662 onwards, the Spaniards gradually withdrew. A Chinese attack on Manila accelerated the depature of 'Speck Jan' or 'De Sinjoor', as the Dutch still nicknamed the Spaniards.

THE FALL OF MAKASSAR

The Spanish withdrawal from the eastern archipelago practically coincided with the fall of the great kingdom of Gowa in South Sulawesi in 1667. The king of Gowa, residing in a fortress near the port

[5] Algemeen Rijksarchief Den Haag (ARA), VOC 1225, fos 374–84, Letter of the Political Council of Ternate to Batavia, 1 Nov. 1657.

[6] Ibid.

town of Makassar, had gained much strength after converting to Islam in 1603. During the first half of the seventeenth century, he was able to conquer almost every part of Sulawesi. The busy port of Makassar became an Islamic centre with strong Malay, Indian, and Arab mercantile connections, and also a *rendezvous* for European nations at conflict with the Dutch, especially the British and Portuguese.

The fact that all these maritime powers were gathered in such a vital trading entrepot as Makassar was a continuous irritation to the Company and a constant threat to the Dutch spice monopoly. With the help of Arung Palakka, the king of a nearby kingdom subjugated by Gowa, the Dutch finally succeeded in taking Makassar after a three years war. The British and the Portuguese – the latter two thousand persons strong – had to leave Makassar, while the peace treaty (the Treaty of Bungaya, 18 November 1667) completely forbade Makassarese precense in Maluku. The ruler of Makassar was also forced not to claim any authority anymore over northeastern Sulawesi, the island of Sula, and some places in the Sangihe-Talaud archipelago. The Makassar trading state being destroyed, Gowa's political expansion in the peripheries was stopped and Islamization severely diminished, especially in Maluku and North Sulawesi. All this was crucial in encouraging the VOC policy of forging new alliances with local kings, containing the further spread of Islam, and promoting Protestant missions.

ACCEPTING 'BAPAK KUMPENI'

After the Spanish withdrawal and the fall of Makassar, the VOC Governor and the sultan agreed to leave a number of small North Sulawesian kingdoms to Ternate's overlordship. Supporting the sultan's claims on several coastal settlements and Minahasan lands seemed the cheapest and easiest way to secure Minahasa as 'the rice-barn of Maluku' for the Company. A decade later, however, the sultan's claims had utterly failed, while the VOC revealed itself once again as an expanding state. A direct expansion was considered necessary to control the rich clove islands Tagulandang, Siau, and Sangihe north of Manado, and secure the spice monopoly in a difficult periphery full of 'illegal' Makassar/Bugis and Mindanao vessels.

A few examples may serve to demonstrate that accepting 'Father Company' (*Bapak Kumpeni*) appeared to be the most attractive way for a number of kings to secure their rule and stabilize their territories. The Malukan kingdoms no longer provided the best security or represented the highest regional authority from which the local kings derived their prestige. The impressive guns of Company ships, the sealed contracts drawn up in Fort Oranje, and the European cultural attraction set the new norms. The kings of Tabukan and Manganitu on Sangihe still acknowledged Ternaten suzerainty in 1662. But seven years later, the rulers of the other Sangihe kingdoms, Candahar, Taruna, and Saban, decided to request Company protection, repudiating everyone else.[7] Others followed. In 1675, the new Ternaten sultan Kaicili Sibori was still received with great ceremony during a royal visit to Manado, the island of Tagulandang, and Tabukan, but two years later the rulers of these places denied their vassalage to Ternate.[8]

Similar political reversals can be observed in the coastal kingdoms of North Sulawesi. When a VOC delegation visited the kingdom of Kaidipan in 1671, it was warmly welcomed. In former wars, Kaidipan had been divided into Dauw, belonging to Manado, and Bolaang-Itam, under the king of Siau. In an attempt to re-unite his kingdom, the king of Kaidipan first allied with the rulers of Gowa, but when Makassar was defeated and Manado became a vassal of Ternate, the anti-Siau faction of Kaidipan had only one option to escape increasing pressure from Siau: request Company protection.[9] The governors of Ternate repeatedly received messages from Kaidipan for help, and in 1677, Governor Padtbrugge restored the old king, Binangkal, to his possessions. Padtbrugge convinced the Queen of Bolaang-Itam to conclude a treaty with the VOC. The Catholic mission undertaken from Siau was immediately stopped, and the priest who served the local village church was forced to leave his parishioners and sell his house, utterly disturbed by this violation of a Spanish possession.[10]

After this success, Padtbrugge set sail for Siau to remove an old obstacle on that island: the Jesuit priests. Siau could not be taken openly, as the Dutch Republic was no longer at war with Spain, and had even allied with Spain against the aggression of the French king

[7] ARA, VOC 1271, fol. 593r; *Memorie van Overgave* Governor Maximilian de Jongh, 14 May 1669.

[8] D. Henley, 'A Superabundance of Centers: Ternate and the Contest for North Sulawesi, *Cakalele*, 4 (1993), pp. 39–60. P. A. Leupe, 'Het journaal van Padtbrugge's reis naar Noord-Celebes en de Noordereilanden', *Bijdragen tot de Taal-, Land- en Volkenkunde*, 2 (1867), pp. 105–340.

[9] ARA, VOC 1286, fos 705r-722r; letter from the Ternaten PC to Batavia, 20 May 1671; ARA, VOC 1301, fos 378r-382r; letter from Jochum Sipman in Manado to the Ternaten PC, 10 Aug. 1673.

[10] Leupe, 'Het journaal van Padtbrugge's reis', pp. 126–7.

Louis XIV. After waiting long for a favourable opportunity, Padtbrugge used a quarrel between the sultan of Ternate and the king of Siau to take possession of the island. He engineered a maritime expedition with Ternate as the actual aggressor, and only watched the sultan's troops landing on Siau's beaches from his ship. After this 'Ternaten' victory, the Spaniards requested that the Siauese Christians be placed under Company protection, fearing that Padtbrugge would 'turn them over to the Moors'. However, as soon as the Spanish garrison fell, the sultan handed over the island to the VOC. The Catholic priests were immediately removed from the island, kept in Ternate, and sent as far away as possible to prevent them from coming back.[11]

Only two years later, Manado also decided for direct Company rule.

Interestingly, the upland Minahasan people had their own internal political motives to try an alliance with the VOC. Their leaders wished to avoid the violent raids of the Manadonese ruler, who had earlier become a Muslim under Ternaten influence. The Reverend Montanus wrote in 1673 that the king was attracted to several wives and daughters of the nineteen or twenty village heads in the Manado hinterlands. In raids he frequently captured the women, only to sell them back later to their fathers. Montanus expected the political allegiance of Manado to be followed by religious conversions in the hinterlands, if only because the Minahasan uplanders seemed to have acquired an 'eternal hatred' for their Muslim kings.[12]

In fact, however, this did not happen, and the Minahasans remained culturally and religiously independent. In his *Memorie van Overgave* (1682), Governor Robertus Padtbrugge describes the 'mountain people' (*bergboeren*) around Lake Tondano (*ton-danau*, people of the lake), and Tonseca (*ton-sea*, people of the waterfalls) as resentful and difficult to control.[13] Many Minahasans were also inclined to recognize the suzerainty of the nearby kingdom of Bolaang. The problematic relationship with the VOC after the 1679 treaty with Manado often led the Minahasans to seek refuge there.[14] As the VOC governors'

[11] R. van der Aa, 'De vermeestering van Siauw door de Oost-Indische Compagnie', *Bijdragen tot de Taal-, Land- en Volkenkunde*, 2 (1867), pp. 95–104.

[12] ARA, VOC 1294, fos 169r–181r, visitation report from the Revd Jacobus Montanus, 9 June to 30 September 1673.

[13] Arsip National Republik Indonesia (The National Archives of Indonesia; ANRI), Ternate 67, *Memorie van Overgave* Governor Robertus Padtbrugge, 31 Aug. 1682.

[14] D. Henley, *Nationalism and Regionalism in a Colonial Context. Minahasa in the Dutch East Indies* (Leiden, 1996), p. 33.

main interest was in the compulsory rice supplies, they avoided direct rule over much of the interior of Minahasa. 'As far as I can understand the old papers', Governor Jacob Claasz wrote in 1710, 'the Minahasans are no subjects of the Company, but only have a permanent treaty with us.'[15] J. S. Wigboldus writes that the contracts between the Company and the greater number of Minahasan *walak* were not followed by Dutch Protestant missions in the interior until the 1820s.[16]

These short impressions of incorporating local kingdoms and rulers within the VOC realm as a result of the new political vacuum, provide a backdrop against which to understand the political nature of conversion to Protestantism. During the 1670s the VOC profited from its growing image of being *Bapak Kumpeni*, the only remaining power able to combat the traditional political patchiness and instability of the region. The political vacuum went hand in hand with a religious vacuum, which led the VOC to implement a convincing conversion policy. In the next sections the VOC policies towards Catholic missions and Islam are discussed, followed by the 'internal' missionary history of the church itself.

TAKING OVER CATHOLIC MISSIONS

The capture of Siau in 1677 marked the end of Catholic missions in eastern Indonesia. The Siau mission, which began with the Portuguese priests (1606–54) and was continued by Spanish priests from Tidore and Manila (1654–77), was completely taken over by the Protestant ministers of the Ternaten Church. The same happened in parts of Sangihe and Kaidipan, and a number of other coastal locations.[17]

Catholic scholars have expressed strong regrets about the final loss of the Catholic flock. C. Wessels S.J.[18] and H. Jacobs, who published all relevant documents in his monumental *Documenta Malucensia*,[19] have negative judgements on Protestantization and idealize the Catholic missions. On the one hand, Jacobs describes the conversions of the *raja*s of Siau and Sangihe as political manoeuvres to escape from Ternaten

[15] ANRI, Ternate, 80, *Memorie van Overgave* Goverrnor Jacob Claasz, 14 July 1710.

[16] J. S. Wigboldus, 'A History of the Minahasa c.1615–1680', *Archipel*, 34 (1987), pp. 63–103.

[17] H. Jacobs, S.J., *Documenta Malucensia*, III, *1606–1682* (Rome, 1984), pp. 17–19.

[18] C. Wessels, *De katholieke missie in de Molukken, Noord-Celebes en de Sangir-eilanden gedurende de Spaansche bestuursperiode 1606–1677* (Tilburg, 1935).

[19] Jacobs, *Documenta Malucensia*.

domination, and points to the long interruptions in the Catholic missions. Curiously enough, he does not fully acknowledge the political dimensions of Catholic conversions and still maintains that the 'the most astonishing fact in the history of that people in the 16th and 17th centuries is their steadfast faithfulness and fidelity to the Christian faith.'[20]

If these and other Catholic scholars had used secular archival materials from the VOC governments, a more realistic picture of the wider process of religious transformation would have emerged. The use of ecclesiastical documents containing protests and apologetic language of both Catholic and Protestant clergy is not enough to reveal the real motives for conversion, which were related mainly to political decisions. The VOC-controlled inauguration of the king of Taruna, Tatanda, for instance, triggered an emotional protest by Father Miguel de Pareja against the disturbance of his Catholic flock in 1670.[21] A few years later, the Reverend Montanus reported in the same partisan language that 'the shameful departure of the Spaniards mean that the village people easily abandon papist idolatries'.[22] Secular VOC reports, however, make clear that conversions were in the first place a consequence of political decision-making. The kings of Taruna were Muslims when ruled by Tidore, Catholic under the Spaniards, and Protestant when the VOC became the strongest. The rulers of Taruna and also nearby Candahar requested a Reformed schoolmaster for purely pragmatic reasons. The Reverend Montanus' observations confirm the great attraction of Islam to many Catholic converts. At a time when new political choices were hard to make, some of the village elite preferred the familiar Islamic path.

The political and religious vacuum, of course, was also observed by Islamic outsiders. A Malay and a Javanese haji took the opportunity to promote Islam on Sangihe in 1673. The people of Manganitu were willing to follow them, but the son of the *segaji* and the *kapita laut* had already become Christians in Ternate; the village of Saluran was also Islamized, together with Saban, where a young *jogugu* resisted the will of his father Philip and became a Muslim. Garuda, the son of the Catholic former king Francisco Gomma and *raja* of the most populous

[20] H. Jacobs, S.J., 'The Insular Kingdom of Siau Under Portuguese and Spanish Impact, 16th and 17th Centuries', in B. Dahm, *Regions and Regional Developments in the Malay-Indonesian World* (Wiesbaden, 1992), pp. 33–43.

[21] Jacobs, *Documenta*, III, p. 646.

[22] ARA, VOC 1294, fos 169r–181r; Church report by Montanus, Oct. 1673.

village of Sangihe, Tabukan, was inclined towards Islam as well. Within five years, the Reverend Montanus wrote, he had removed all signs of Christianity from his kingdom.[23]

This evidence demonstrates that during the important period of political transition, 1663–77, the unstable situation stimulated Catholic 'apostacies' in favour of Islam or Protestantism. Sometimes the *raja*s were directly driven into the arms of the Company. The Muslim king of Kaidipan on the mainland, who was constantly plagued by raids from Sangihese, repeatedly asked to become a Protestant. The Muslims from Sangihe had destroyed the swiddens and sago forests of his village and had kidnapped his daughter. The VOC had enough reasons to pursue this mixture of political and religious desires and aimed at securing the region for a transfer of power, securing the spice monopoly in the peripheries, and stopping the spread of Islam in order to stabilize the region.

CONTAINING ISLAM

In the beginning, the VOC's contracting policy implied strict non-interference in religious matters. The Ternate and Tidore territories, formerly subject to Catholic missions, were guaranteed that they would not be the target of Protestant missions. For political reasons they were recognized and respected as Islamic states. In the renewal of all earlier contracts with the Ternate sultans in 1638, spice trade prohibitions in return for yearly payments were again reaffirmed, and religious liberty granted. The Company representative, Anthonio van Diemen (a devout Calvinist), and the sultan agreed that neither Christians nor Muslims were allowed to make converts amongst each other. A Muslim subject of the sultan was not allowed to become a Christian even if he requested it. The religious sovereignty of Ternate was too sensitive to ignore.[24]

After securing the spice monopoly in the 1660s and 1670s, the VOC faced increasing Islamic resistance, and gradually began to display its aversion to Islam more openly. By 1670 the VOC position in Maluku was stronger than ever, as the sultanates were obliged to eradicate all

[23] For Catholic missions on Sangihe, see S. Stokman, 'De Missies der minderbroeders op de Molukken, Celebes en Sangihe in de XVIe en XVIIe eeuw', *Collectanea Franciscana Neerlandica*, II, pp. 499–556, especially pp. 543–9. Raja Garuda requested Spanish protection and Christianity in 1677; see Jacobs, *Documenta*, III, p. 723.

[24] Fr Valentyn, *Oud- en Nieuw-Oostindien* (Dordrecht, 1724–6), I, p. 272.

clove trees in Malukan territories.[25] But there existed a continuing problem. As elsewhere in the archipelago, it was impossible to separate trade and religious contacts between local kings and their Muslim partners from Java and the Malay world. A typical incident in 1669 in the Ternaten port demonstrates this. Three vessels from Mindanoa anchored in front of the kraton. One of the ships was from Gresik, one of the most firmly Islamic ports on Java's northeast coast, and had sailed from Mindanao to Ternate. It was caught with an 'illegal' cargo and the captain accused of ignoring all VOC trade restrictions. After the confiscation of the cargo, some Ternaten district heads (*bobatos*) were also questioned because the ship also carried an Islamic cargo. They clarified the purpose of the visit of the suspicious vessel. Amongst other things, the ship was carrying a Javanese *mullah*, a pulpit (*mimbar*) for the Friday prayers (*khutbah*) for the main mosque, and a letter from the king of Mindanao for the Ternaten sultan. The Governor decided to detain the Javanese crew until the ship's return to Mindanao. Meanwhile the Islamic cleric was kept under guard to avoid unrest within the Muslim community. These measures supported the policy of the Batavian High Government, the Governor argued. The 'Moorse papen' would only seduce 'the poor heathens of these regions into becoming adherents of their sect', and damage the interests of the Church. The *mullah* seemed to be only a 'wandering spirit who belonged nowhere'.[26]

Despite such incidents, the sultan's religious liberty on the island itself could not be revoked. But in North Sulawesi, where Ternate's political and religious influence had been marginal, a policy of containment was still possible. As early as 1671, the Governor agreed with the sultan to abolish Islamic public worship in Manado. The Governor planned to resettle the few Manadonese Muslim families in nearby Amurang, 'to keep that place clean from the Moors'.[27] Some of the Manado ruling elite, such as the Catholic *kapita laut* Don Andries Cambe, converted to Protestantism in the same year. Two years later, a Muslim *jogugu* converted, together with several people from nearby

[25] After the pacification of the Ambon region in 1656, clove production was entirely concentrated in the Christian Ambonese districts. See G. J. Knaap, *Kruidnagelen en Christenen. De Verenigde Oost-Indische Compagnie en de bevolking van Ambon 1656–1696* (Leiden, 1987).

[26] ARA, VOC 1271, fol. 606, letter from the Political Council of Ternate to Batavia, 24 Aug. 1699.

[27] ARA, VOC 1286, fos 705r–722r, letter from Governor Abraham Verspreet to the cassier Hendrick van den Broeck in Manado, 7 March 1671.

villages. The Reverend Montanus witnessed that the *jogugu* took off his turban in public, and said these words before his baptism:

> I despise and throw away this turban, voluntarily without force, as God and my conscience have moved me to do so; I reject all the dirt of Muhammed, the Lord of Heaven be praised for opening my eyes and heart, now I believe that Jesus Christ has died for me.[28]

The king of Manado, a nominal Muslim, was repeatedly requested to join these nobles in repudiating Islam and accepting the Christian hat.

The beginning of the conversion of Manado demonstrates once more that the VOC openly promoted Christianity in areas where Islam was still weak. The Reverend De Leeuw's report on Sangihe from 1684 shows that the VOC had succeeded in preventing further Islamization and in continuing Christian missionary work on the island. In Taruna, he wrote, 'an extremely high number people is converting from the Moorish religion and being baptized after confession. . . . The king is a good leader for the school and the Church and is also good at singing psalms, and this makes the psalm singing in this place better than elsewhere'.[29] This glimpse of successful Protestant mission work on an island were Islam had been strong finally raises the question how Reformed mission work was organized and how its relative 'internal' success can be explained.

THE PROTESTANT CHURCH OF TERNATE

The Church Council or Consistory of Ternate, comprising a minister, chosen elders, and deacons, was founded in 1626 to serve the colonists and few Asian Christians of the Dutch Fort Oranje. The earliest Consistory letters to Batavia express many complaints about concubines held by the colonists. The Christian Asians, mostly manumitted slaves (the so-called *Mardijkers*) were strongly distrusted. These market-gardeners also sold their food products to the Spaniards. Some of them attended Catholic services and requested baptism from Jesuit priests when Calvinist church membership regulations became too strict.

[28] ARA, VOC 1294, fos 169r–181v, Church report by the Revd Jacobus Montanus, Oct. 1673.

[29] E. C. Godée Molsbergen, *Geschiedenis van de Minahassa tot 1829* (Weltevreden and Batavia, 1928), pp. 47–9 for fragments of this report.

Not surprisingly, the Ternate Church did not show any growth during the first decades of its existence. Pastoral care was in the hands of only one pastor and a few so-called 'comforters of the sick'. Only twelve members participated in the communion celebrations. Dutch Church services in the Dutch fortress were only attended by high ranking Company officials and their wives, while Malay Church services attracted only three 'old native females'. In 1654 all Church services were relocated to a wooden church building, which made the attendance a little more attractive.[30]

AN UNEXPECTED MISSIONARY ROLE

After decades of complaints about immoral lives, conflicts with Company officials, and the 'interfering' activities of successful Jesuit priests throughout the region, the Reformed ministers received a request from the king of Manado for a schoolmaster and catechist. When the end of Spanish presence was apparent, Minahasa rejected the dominance of the nearby kingdom of Bolaang Mongondow, and asked for Company protection. Just before the last Spanish soldiers left Manado, a schoolmaster was sent, in early 1662 or shortly before.[31] Another schoolmaster was send to the island of Tagulandang, which the Makassarese had previously possessed. This was also done at the request of the *raja*, who rejected Islam and turned the local mosque into a Christian prayer house and school.[32] These early conversions in Manado and on Tagulandang unexpectedly pushed the Ternate Consistory into a missionary role.

The response of the Church was not at first adequate, as the only minister of Ternate, the Reverend Joannes à Burum, felt unable to conduct any missionary work. He was characterized as a devout man, but was reported to suffer from 'a melancholic character'. The Governor ordered him to visit Manado and Tagulandang, but instead the minister went back to Batavia.[33] Not surprisingly the Governor reported in 1669 that Christianity on Tagulandang had made little

[30] On the nearby islands of Makian and Bacan, three more simple wooden Reformed churches were found near the Dutch strongholds. Reports on the small Protestant community of Bacan-Labuha (a former Portuguese settlement) near the VOC fortress of Barneveld were usually negative.

[31] ARA, VOC 1240, fol. 799, *Memorie van Overgave* Governor Simon Cos, 23 May 1662.

[32] Ibid., fol. 801.

[33] Ibid., fol. 823. His wife had also died on Ternate.

progress. Regrettably enough, he wrote, conversion had also taken place for 'worldly motives'. The Company did not have any personnel on the island to monitor school attendance, and the islanders probably interpreted the presence of an indigenous schoolmaster as a safeguard against their enemies.[34]

The Reverend à Burum's situation was typical. The Ternaten pastors were often unable to conduct church and school visitations abroad, mainly because they suffered from tropical illnesses. Of the twenty-eight ministers who served the Church of Ternate during the years 1626 to 1700, nine died within two years of arrival. The Reverend Franciscus Dionysius came to Ternate in 1674 but died in the same year in Taruna (Siau) during a church visitation. One year later the Reverend Isaac Huysman was called from the church of Ambon to continue the visitation, but he also fell ill and was buried in a sand grave next to his predecessor. Only eight of the twenty-eight ministers served the Ternate Consistory for more than three years; the rest were quickly re-employed within two or three years on Ambon, Banda, or other places where the same problems of repeated vacancies occurred.[35]

FEATURES OF THE EARLY MISSIONS

Despite these physical hindrances, considerable efforts were made to expand Protestantism among the new allies from 1670 onwards. The Ternaten ministers sailed almost yearly to Manado. Sometimes government expeditions were combined with missionary visitations. Governor Padtbrugge was accompanied by the Reverend Zacharias Caheing during his famous journey of 1677. Several matters concerning the founding of Protestant churches and schools in Manado and Kaidipan (Dauw and Bolaang-Itam) were arranged.[36] During his lengthy journeys throughout the region in 1681, Padtbrugge was assisted by the Reverend Cornelius van der Sluys, and the first permanent minister of Manado, the Reverend Cornelius de Leeuw.[37]

34 ARA, VOC 1271, fol. 593r, *Memorie van Overgave* Governor Maximiliaan de Jongh, 14 May 1669.

35 M. H. Schippers, 'De Christelijke gemeente te Ternate en hare predikanten; Eene bijdrage tot de kennis der geschiedenis van de Indische Kerk', *Mededeelingen vanwege het Nederlandsche Zendelinggenootschap*, 41, pp. 163–301.

36 Leupe, 'Het journaal van Padtbrugge's reis'.

37 ARA, VOC 1366A, fos 640–58.

After the missions, the ministers handed in their reports to the Consistory and the Governor.[38]

The missionary reports from the Reformed ministers offer detailed accounts of five or six month-long voyages around a considerable number of former Catholic or recently converted settlements (see Table 1). The first missionaries usually sailed with a Company vessel to Manado, but ventured on to the outlying villages in indigenous proas (*perahu*) rowed by a few dozen men. During the lengthy trips, the pastor could only stay a few days in each village. He followed a standard visitation procedure. Immediately after arrival, the minister checked the school administration, and asked the schoolmaster to gather all the children in the school. After examining the progress the children had made in reading, writing, and catechism lessons, the inspector ordered the schoolmaster to bring all Christians together in the church. A few collective catechism-examinations were held to prepare adults for baptism. During a special church service, children and adults were baptized and couples married. In the evenings conflicts between Christians or the schoolmasters and village heads were solved. In some villages the Communion was celebrated by the few communicant members, usually including only the *raja* and the schoolmaster.

The Reformed missions depended heavily on indigenous (often Ambonese) schoolmasters and on primary religious education. The system focused on the education of youth in the small bamboo village schools, where catechism classes for adults were also held. This was in accordance with the Reformed ethical tradition, in which children were seen as young plants in need of living water from catechisms, moral conduct books, postils, and Bible stories. According to the Calvinist tradition of the Dutch Republic, basic religious education was the primary task of schoolmasters. It can be argued, however, that

38 Several reports are preserved: the Revd Huisman 1674; the Revd Dionysius 1675; the Revd Montanus 1675; the Revd Peregrinus 1676; the Revd Caheing 1677; the Revd Van der Sluys 1681; the Revd De Leeuw, 1681, 1684 and 1685; the Revd Stampioen 1696. Two such reports were published in the early eighteenth century in the great encyclopedic work on Asia by the Revd François Valentyn: the Revd Jacobus Montanus' report 17 Nov. 1675 and the Revd Gualterus Peregrinus' report, 15 Aug. 1676, in Valentyn, *Oud- en Nieuw Oost-Indiën*, I, part 2, pp. 392–406. Another report from 1684 from the Revd Cornelius de Leeuw was discovered by E. C. Godée Molsbergen; see *Geschiedenis*, pp. 47–9. More original documents can still be discovered in VOC archives; on recent archival discoveries see H. E. Niemeijer *et al.*, 'Nieuwe bronnen tot de geschiedenis van het christendom in Maluku (1605–1935); Vondsten, thema's en oriëntaties, in *Documentatieblad voor de Geschiedenis van de Nederlandse Zending en Overzeese Kerken (DZOK)*, 4–2, pp. 52–90.

this was the only strategy that could be followed in remote island societies, where pastoral visitations from Ternate were rare. Educating children only required the support of the local *raja*, who made agreements with the missionaries about the number of schoolchildren. A well-trained Malukan schoolmaster was sufficient for this basic religious education.

The influence of the schoolmaster, however, was certainly not enough to discipline and teach adult 'pagans' Christian morals. During their visitations, the ministers often complained about the absence of the village population, who went out to the forest for weeks to gather food and products. As Table 1 shows, the numbers reported in a Church visitation in 1696 confirm that mission work was focused on the education and baptism of children. The number of catechized adults and communicant members appears to be extraordinarily low.

To keep this system running, the Reformed ministers of Ternate continuously trained a small class of excellent students (twelve, for instance, in 1682) as schoolmasters, receiving from the Company 1 rixdollar a month for every student.[39] Mission work done by educated indigenous schoolmasters proved to be succesful. At the start of the eighteenth century more than fifty schoolmasters served the Ternaten Church districts. They kept the village school and undertook church administration, and wrote down the names of baptism candidates, communicant members, and schoolchildren in special books. On Sundays the schoolmasters read sermons, during weekdays they beat the drums in the morning and evening to gather the people in the small churches for prayers. The schoolmasters, often the sons of Ambonese *raja*s or local leaders (*orangkaya*), were held in high esteem by the local population, and made Protestantism readily acceptable among their own people.

The earliest missionaries baptized large numbers of people, leaving the villages directly after the church services. The Reverend de Leeuw's report from 1684 gives a number of 1,400 converts (both adults and children) during one visitation to the Sangihe archipelago. The total number of Christians (about five thousand) increased considerably during this one visitation. The conversion of ordinary people made only slow progress. Many were not able to read books, and they learned catechism questions and answers by heart, only to forget them again

[39] ANRI, Ternate, 62, Alfabet PO, fol. 512.

Table 1: *Number of Christians reported in 1696 by the Reverend Joannes Stampioen*

	Christians	Members	Children baptized	Adults baptized	Children	Marriages
Manado	438	-	21	-	35	1
Bulang	135	-	8	15	90	-
Rabonto	59	-	4	16	-	-
Dauw	557	-	18	51	100	3
Buol	370	-	15	33	112	8
Attingola	136	-	10	11	18	-
Kaidipan	?	?	14	-	-	-
Tagulandang	1,107	48	53	-	80	6
Minanga	283	7	12	-	40	5
Ulu (Siau)	?	-	73	-	86	1
Pehe (Siau)	?	-	51	-	68	-
Ondong (Siau)	555	-	18	-	60	-
Lehi (Siau)	359	-	10	-	63	-
Tabukan (Sangir)	2,000	-	52	-	40	97
Kendahe (Sangir)	380	-	21	8	48	14
Kolongan (Sangir)	433	9	31	5	30	8
Taruna (Sangir)	2,070	40	92	-	110	25
Manganitu (Sangir)	2,581	40	69	-	48	-
Tamako (Sangir)	491	-	30	-	38	16
Salurang	296	2	16	-	38	11
Menalu	?	1	20	-	38	11
Coulour	180	-	14	1	-	20
Kuma	295	-	20	4	32	41
Mattani	378	16	28	7	35	15
TOTALS	13,103	163	700	151	1,209	282

shortly after baptism. The occasional visits of the Ternaten ministers and the presence of a schoolmaster could not prevent a syncretistic form of Protestantism emerging.

Most crucial were the conversion and co-operation of the local political leaders. When these were willing to watch over school attendance and daily prayers, conversions went easily. The Reverend De Leeuw was very excited when he saw the elite of Sangihe writing out the Catechism in their Arab script. 'Formerly, these were influential Muslims', he wrote.[40] The Reverend Joannes Stampioen's observations in 1696 give proof of continuous Islamic sympathies on Sangihe. Stampioen had lengthy religious discussions with the king of Candahar, who seems to have favoured a mixture of Islam and paganism. In Taruna, the king walked quickly through the streets, waving his arms, to call people to church for prayers, 'and this for no other reason than to show his vigilance', Stampioen distrustfully wrote.[41] These and other rulers only co-operated when a minister was on the island, Christianity depending on the quality and influence of the schoolmaster.

CONCLUSIONS

Conversions to Dutch Reformed Protestantism were the result of an extraordinary political constellation during the 1660s and 1670s. The VOC was placed in the centre of power, which made it an attractive overlord for local rulers. Political submission naturally implied conversion to 'the strongest religion'. There was no perceived separation between the political and religious spheres. In their expansion efforts, the sultans of Tidore, Ternate, Mindanao, and Makassar had all followed this pattern. Now Catholicism and Islam were left for Protestantism. This sudden demand for conversion surprised the Church Council of Ternate. Despite their limited capacities, the ministers were able to visit the new converts frequently. The system of education, combined with the support of most of the local rulers, stabilized Protestant conversion by the end of the seventeenth century.

University of Leiden

40 ANRI, Ternate, 144, fos 220–2, letter from the Revd Cornelius de Leeuw to the Consistory of Batavia, Manado, 30 July 1685.

41 ARA, VOC 1579, fos 478–511, visitation report, the Revd Joannes Stampioen, 18 Sept. 1696.

THE BELIEFS, ASPIRATIONS AND METHODS OF THE FIRST MISSIONARIES IN BRITISH HONG KONG, 1841–5

by KATE LOWE

THE British phase of Hong Kong's history started when Hong Kong was ceded to Britain on 20 January 1841.[1] The negotiations were carried out by Captain Charles Elliott for the British and the commissioner Ch'i-shan for the Chinese. A small British contingent landed at what came to be known as Possession Point on the northwest of Hong Kong island on 25 January and drank the health of Queen Victoria; on the following day they signalled the taking of possession by hoisting the union flag.[2] Hong Kong had been suggested as a possible British acquisition only on 11 January, when other more acceptable islands, such as Chusan[3] off the northern coast, had been vetoed by the Chinese. Hong Kong was mainly known to sea captains as it had been used as a rendezvous for opium ships for a number of years, but most other people in the area had very little idea about its appearance, population, or potential as a colony.

Representatives from the four groups with most to gain from the acquisition of Hong Kong were quick to explore the new possession. Captain Charles Elliott and the naval commodore J. Gordon Bremer, in effect representing the colonial government and the army and navy,

[1] For the history of Hong Kong in the early 1840s, see E. J. Eitel, *Europe in China* (London and Hong Kong, 1895), pp. 135–252; G. R. Sayer, *Hong Kong: Birth, Adolescence and Coming of Age* (London, New York and Toronto, 1937), pp. 90–161; G. B. Endacott, *A History of Hong Kong* (London, 1958), pp. 14–78; Dafydd Evans, 'Chinatown in Hong Kong: the beginnings of Taipingshan', *Journal of the Hong Kong Branch of the Royal Asiatic Society*, 10 (1970), pp. 69–78; W. K. Chan, *The Making of Hong Kong Society: Three Studies of Class Formation in Early Hong Kong* (Oxford, 1991); Frank Welsh, *A History of Hong Kong* (London, 1993), pp. 132–83; and Jung-fang Tsai, *Hong Kong in Chinese History: Community and Social Unrest in the British Colony, 1842–1913*, pp. 36–51.

[2] Kate Lowe, 'Hong Kong, 26 January 1841: hoisting the flag revisited', *Journal of the Hong Kong Branch of the Royal Asiatic Society*, 29 (1989).

[3] On Chusan, see Robert Montgomery Martin, 'Report on the island of Chusan' [1844], in *British Parliamentary Papers: China, 24: Correspondence, Dispatches, Reports, Ordinances, Memoranda and Other Papers relating to the Affairs of Hong Kong, 1846–60* (Shannon, 1971), pp. 129–42; and Christopher Munn, 'The Chusan episode: Britain's occupation of a Chinese Island, 1840–46', *The Journal of Imperial and Commonwealth History*, 25 (1997), pp. 82–112.

steamed round the island at the first opportunity.[4] James Matheson, of Jardine Matheson and Co., representing colonial mercantile interests, went from Macao to Hong Kong to witness the hoisting of the British flag, and afterwards circumnavigated the island.[5] Finally, and most importantly for the purposes of this article, eight Protestant missionaries hired a lorcha in Macao and sailed to Hong Kong on 8 February for a two-day reconnoitre. These men were the cream of the British and American Protestant missionary field in Southeast Asia, and all of them read Chinese and spoke at least one Chinese dialect. They had arrived in the region at various times between 1817 and 1839, and many of them subsequently continued their missionary careers in China. The eight missionaries were David Abeel (of the American Board for Conducting Foreign Missions), who had been previously at Singapore and Bangkok and who went on to Amoy; W. J. Boone (of the American Episcopal Church), who had been formerly at Batavia and who went on to Shanghai; Samuel R. Brown, a former teacher at the New York Institution for the Deaf and Dumb, who became principal of the Morrison Education Society's School in Hong Kong; Walter H. Medhurst (of the London Missionary Society), who had also worked extensively in Java and Malaya and who went on to Shanghai; W. C. Milne (of the London Missionary Society), who spent some time in Macao and who later went to Ningpo; Issachar J. Roberts (a Baptist who was supported by private or local funds), who subsequently moved to Canton; Jehu Lewis Shuck (of the American Baptist Board of Foreign Missions), who also subsequently went to Canton; and S. Wells Williams (of the American Board for Conducting Foreign Missions) who worked at Macao and Canton.[6]

These men realized immediately the crucial role Hong Kong was to play in the opening up of China to Christianity, and many of them had an enormous impact on missionary work in early Hong Kong itself. Two of them have left accounts of the expedition, containing similar sentiments. Milne's account lies in the London Missionary Society's archive at the School of Oriental and African Studies in London. He

[4] W. D. Bernard, *Narrative of the Voyages and Services of the Nemesis from 1840 to 1843*, 2 vols (London, 1844), 1, p. 304.

[5] Cambridge, University Library, Jardine Matheson Archives, c5/6, 65.

[6] George Smith, *A Narrative of an Exploratory Visit to each of the Consular Cities of China, and to the Islands of Hong Kong and Chusan, on Behalf of the Church Missionary Society in the Years 1844, 1845, 1846* (London, 1847), pp. 530–2, has a list of Protestant missionaries either in China in May 1846 or who had been there within the two previous years.

described Hong Kong as 'a spot which seemed destined to be the seat of an important settlement and to offer facilities for carrying on those operations with advantage, which had either from local inconveniences or from existing prejudices been greatly restricted, if not entirely precluded'. This is the first reference of many to the rivalry and hostility between Catholic and Protestant jurisdictions, which was internalized by the relevant missionaries, and which may be of particular importance to an understanding of the Protestant view of the Chinese. Milne's account of Hong Kong island emphasised the inhospitable nature of its terrain, its scattered and insignificant population and their poor habitations. He described visiting Chekchu (present-day Stanley), the largest village on the island, where the villagers 'were curious to examine the strangers', just as the strangers were keen to examine the villagers. A sub-theme of the trip must have been an evaluation of the strength of attachment to Chinese forms of religion on the island (and therefore of the potential competition), for the missionary party also inspected the temple at Stanley: reassuringly, Milne found that 'every idol and idol-appurtenance was covered with dust and cobwebs, while the keeper himself was in no wise careful to conceal his own vileness nor to hide from view the evidences that he was a devotee of the opium-pipe'. The difference or otherness of Chinese religion was thus exaggerated and derided by reference to non-essential cultural habits and customs. Milne, however, could not contain his general disappointment at the state of the new insular possession ('Hong Kong is an island which, in itself considered, would certainly never have been selected for missionary purposes' – but which colony ever was chosen on this basis?) and its inhabitants, who perhaps totalled 2,500 people and were 'very poor indeed'.[7]

Roberts' report, published in the *Canton Register* on 18 February and in the *Canton Press* on 27 February, also bemoaned the mountainous and barren aspect and small size of the population, but took comfort in the island's new-found Britishness:

> It . . . may form a substantial foundation, in the providence of God, on which to establish, under the auspices of the flag which now waves upon its summits, the true principles of commerce,

[7] London, SOAS, Council for World Missions archive (formerly London Missionary Society archive), South China, incoming, Box 4 (1840–7), included in report of 22/3 March 1841 by several LMS missionaries: J. Robert Morrison, William Lockhart, W. C. Milne, and Benjamin Hobson.

JUSTICE, THE CHRISTIAN RELIGION, where protected these may flourish untrameled, until this nation be enlightened and saved.

So according to this view government by Britain of Hong Kong island would lead inexorably to Chinese salvation. This is a good example of two of the four prior assumptions which Brian Stanley has isolated as being crucial to 'the close association in missionary thinking between Christianity and civilisation': that nineteenth-century Britain constituted a model of Christian culture and society, and that missionaries believed implicitly in human progress, which was one of the legacies of the Enlightenment to Christian thought.[8]

Roberts' account makes mention of a temporary village of twenty to forty houses which had sprung up opposite the anchorage in the two weeks since possession. Hong Kong's temporary feel continued, as the island was not officially ceded until the treaty of Nanking in August 1842, whereby in addition five ports were opened to British trade and residence. This treaty in turn was not ratified until 1843. The first missionaries moved from Macao in advance of the treaty of Nanking, but none of them was British: the American Baptist Issachar Roberts went in February 1842 and his Baptist co-national Jehu Lewis Shuck followed him in March. Both of them quickly started conducting services and preaching in both English and Chinese,[9] trying to attract converts and form a congregation in the time-honoured fashion.

French and Italian Catholics of unknown orders were also reported to be operating on the island by May 1842.[10] As soon as Hong Kong was claimed by the British in January 1841, Theodor Joset from Switzerland,[11] who was the representative in Macao of the Congregation for the Propagation of the Faith (*Propaganda Fide*), the official church body in charge of missions, appealed to Rome for permanent arrangements to be made to establish a mission at the new British settlement. On 22 April 1841 Hong Kong and an area around it was

[8] Brian Stanley, *The Bible and the Flag: Protestant Missions and British Imperialism in the Nineteenth and Twentieth Centuries* (Leicester, 1990), pp. 160–2.

[9] SOAS, LMS archive, South China correspondence, incoming, Box 4 (1840–7), mentioned in letter of 10 July 1842.

[10] Ibid., William Lockhart from Macao, 30 May 1842.

[11] On him see J. Beckmann, 'Msgr. Theodor Joset, Prokurator der *Propaganda* in China und erster Apostolischer Präfekt von Hongkong (1804–1842)', *Zeitschrift für Schweizerische Kirchengeschichte*, 36 (1942), pp. 19–38, 121–39.

constituted a new ecclesiastical prefecture, under Joset, who went immediately to Hong Kong, where he was given a site to build a church at what is now the intersection of Wellington and Pottinger Streets in Central. He also moved his *Propaganda Fide* office and the seminary for the training of Chinese priests to this site. On Joset's early demise in August 1842, he was replaced by an Italian Franciscan, Antonio Feliciani,[12] and it fell to Feliciani to preside over the consecration of the church of the Immaculate Conception and of the seminary on 18 June 1843.[13]

There was no love lost between these two rival groups who set to work on parallel projects. The balance of power had shifted somewhat in favour of the Protestants who had always been in an inferior position in China vis-à-vis the Catholics, who had a longer and more glorious record of missionary activity in the country. A Protestant-controlled Hong Kong offered them a chance to make up some lost ground. Both groups were also attracted by the newness of Hong Kong. Shuck was accompanied to Hong Kong by his wife Henrietta and their young children, and Henrietta can lay claim to the distinction of being the first non-Chinese female to live on the island.[14] A memoir of her life, constructed around a selection of her letters, was published in the nineteenth century and from it one can gain an impression of her strong Baptist faith.[15] Along with her husband she carried out missionary work, starting up schools first of all in Macao and then in Hong Kong, and working also amongst the European poor, mainly soldiers' wives and children. Interestingly, although fully cognizant of the advantages of living under British (and therefore by implication Protestant) rule, as opposed to Portuguese, Catholic rule, as a Virginian she was stung by criticisms of American slavery, and claimed that the British treated soldiers' families as worse than slaves. Like the majority of nineteenth-century missionaries who were stuck inside their own religious and cultural references, she was not ideal material for cross-cultural exchange, and her views on Chinese religion illustrate this well: 'The whole empire [of China] abounds in temples, but they are not dedicated to HIM who justly claims the adoration of all hearts, but

12 Thomas Ryan, *The Story of a Hundred Years* (Hong Kong, 1959), pp. 1–2.

13 Eitel, *Europe in China*, p. 190.

14 For general background, see Susanna Hoe, *The Private Life of Old Hong Kong: Western Women in the British Colony, 1841–1941* (Hong Kong, 1991), pp. 33, 37, 94–5.

15 J. B. Jeter, *An American Woman in China and Her Missionary Work There* (Boston, 1874).

to senseless gods who cannot see, or speak, or feel, or hear.'[16] Not only was Chinese religion 'senseless' or 'stupid', but she perceived striking similarities between Buddhism and Roman Catholicism, thus managing to link up and demonize two of her greatest enemies. An obsession with the horror of idols and idolatry and a categorization of any non-Christian as a heathen impeded any understanding of Chinese culture. Nor was her husband any better of course. When times were difficult, he fell back on the old chestnut: 'I sometimes think that the hearts of the Chinese are farther from God than those of any other people.'[17]

This refusal on the part of the European and American missionaries to acknowledge Chinese cultural values and identity led directly to the failure of the missions to secure significant numbers of converts, for notions of Chineseness and belonging were very strong. The London Missionary Society missionaries in Macao in 1841 characterized these traits as 'peculiarities' and claimed that their degree, at least, was unique. They named the peculiarity of the language (as though there were only one), the singularity of Chinese education, manners, and ideas, and most strikingly, 'that national vanity which excludes every other nation from their own immediate pale as inferior and worthless'.[18] Chinese belief in the superiority of Chinese culture mirrored exactly European and American belief in the superiority of the Christian religion, and for this reason, one was proof against the other.

There were, of course, many 'types' of missionary activity, and all the main ones were attempted in the first few years of Hong Kong's life as a British colony. Preaching and conducting services in Chinese dialects constituted a substantial part of the missionary effort, but it was probably the least successful part. Native Hong Kongers converted by this method were few and far between (although some Chinese converts who were not Hong Kong Chinese accompanied the Western missionaries from earlier postings), and they were usually persuaded to become assistants and translators in the spreading of the word, rather than remaining as ordinary members of the congregation. The first Chinese pastor ordained in Hong Kong, in 1846, Ho Fuk-tong, had in

[16] Mrs Henrietta Shuck, *Scenes in China: or Sketches of the Country, Religion or Customs of the Chinese* (Philadelphia, 1852), p. 38.

[17] Jeter, *An American Woman*, p. 182.

[18] SOAS, LMS archive, South China correspondence, incoming, Box 4 (1840–7), 22/3 March 1841.

fact accompanied James Legge from Malacca in 1843.[19] Reception of the Christian message in Hong Kong itself was not numerically satisfactory, and the quality of the potential recruits was often raised as a drawback to evangelization on the island. Thus Karl Gützlaff,[20] a controversial Pomeranian missionary who had worked up and down the China coast in the 1830s and who spoke a variety of Chinese dialects, organized the Chinese Union in June 1844. It boasted nineteen Chinese members and its purpose was to train people to distribute religious literature and to spread the Christian faith. By 1849 the sincerity of its hundreds of Chinese converts was called into question, and the project effectively failed.[21] Translation of the Bible and preparation of Christian texts were also carried out as a matter of course by many of the missionaries, so that in the future materials for conversion and religious sustenance would be more readily available. The printing of these works was another missionary activity. These tasks, however, were not aimed primarily at the inhabitants of Hong Kong, but would later reap rewards in the greater mission field of China.

Undoubtedly, the most successful missionary work in early Hong Kong occurred when the foreign missionaries offered a service to the Chinese: education, medicine, and care of (mainly female) orphans. The Chinese were prepared to countenance paying lip-service to Christianity, or would appear to accept Christianity if its requirements were merely passive, so long as the rewards they received in return were tangible. Schemes which involved training the Chinese to replace the foreigners in these tasks all foundered, however; obviously, it was acceptable for foreign missionaries to hold certain ideas and perform certain tasks, but much less acceptable for Chinese to be seen to be mimicking them by taking over these tasks. It was all right for the Chinese to be passive recipients but not active providers of missionary education and medicine. Looked at in another way, primary and secondary education for the Chinese were successes, but tertiary and higher education were failures, and this seems to have been true throughout the whole of the early period of Hong Kong's history.

Both Catholics and Protestants were quick to open schools for the

[19] Carl Smith, 'Introduction', in idem, *Chinese Christians: Elites, Middlemen and the Church in Hong Kong* (Hong Kong, 1985), pp. 4, 7.

[20] For some biographical information, see H. Schlyter, *Der China-Missionar Karl Gützlaff und seine Heimatbasis* (Studia Missionalia Upsaliensia XXX) (Uppsala, 1976).

[21] Smith, 'Introduction', p. 8.

Chinese as soon as Hong Kong was legally secured by the Treaty of Nanking. Catholic ones were operating earlier, by April 1842, both from near the church at Pottinger and Wellington Street in Central, and from near the chapel next to the Catholic burial ground off Queen's Road East in Wanchai.[22] Both these were also reputed to have been sites for seminaries training Catholic priests for work in China, which had transferred from Macao.[23] The most famous Protestant school at Hong Kong in this period was the Morrison Education Society School which opened in temporary premises in November 1842, also having transferred from Macao.[24] In 1843 it opened on Morrison Hill to the east of Victoria and had twenty-four pupils. The Society had been formed in 1836 at Canton in memory of Robert Morrison. The school's principal was Samuel Brown, a famous New England educationalist. Brown realized that 'there was a reciprocal relationship between language and basic thought patterns' and by injecting new approaches and new topics into the boys' education, as well as insisting that they continue with their Chinese studies, he believed they would be able to pass on their ideas to other Chinese, to become 'transmitters of western knowledge in Chinese forms'.[25] The boys in the school were used as guinea pigs in this short-lived experiment – Brown returned to America due to ill health in 1846 and the school only continued for a further three years before closing down. They were however very successful guinea pigs, and Brown lived to see his ex-students 'play a direct role in the opening of China to western education, medicine, business methods and technology',[26] and to contribute directly to the policy of self-strengthening initiated after 1861.

The Chinese boys at the school may have continued to learn Chinese, but in every other respect they were seduced away from their own culture. Treated as members of the family, they adopted the attitudes and discourse of their Western, Christian, colonial teachers and 'parents'. This can be very clearly observed in the English

[22] Carl Smith, 'Wan Chai – in search of an identity', in idem, *A Sense of History. Studies in the Social and Urban History of Hong Kong* (Hong Kong, 1995), pp. 112–13, 153.

[23] The histories of these institutions are complicated. See Ryan, *The Story*, pp. 5–6.

[24] Anthony Sweeting, *Education in Hong Kong, pre-1841 to 1941: Fact and Opinion* (Hong Kong, 1990), p. 143.

[25] Carl Smith, 'The Morrison Education Society and the moulding of its students', in idem, *Chinese Christians*, pp. 14–15.

[26] Ibid., p. 16.

compositions written by the students as exams on subjects such as Chinese government, Notions of the Chinese in regard to a future state, Labour, and An imaginary voyage, some of which were later published in local publications, and also in the letters they were encouraged to write to Mr Brown's former pupils at the New York Institution for the Deaf and Dumb. The boys internalized at once (or learnt to parrot) the precepts of the missionary line. One eleven-year old wrote: 'I want to learn the Bible because God spake all these words. I had not Bible in my father's house. My countrymen have no Bible. I want to teach them learn the Bible.'[27] Thus the boy had already imbibed the idea that the West could supply something lacking to the Chinese, and that he could be a conduit for it. Missionary teaching also centred on the superiority of the West and the inferiority of China; therefore, the essays and letters lamented the ignorance, corruption, conservatism, and vileness of China and extolled the virtues of Christian countries. One classic statement of the contrast between the two countries read:

> The great difference between the English and the Chinese is this: the Chinese look back into ancient times, but the English are always looking to the present and the future, to discover the truth, therefore the Chinese are always about the same, while the English become better and better.[28]

In July 1843 Brown's pupils were given as the theme for their compositions 'The history of Hong Kong', and five of these were printed in *The Chinese Repository*, a monthly journal published by the American missionary, Elijah Bridgman. The students once again had internalized Western values and viewpoints, writing of Hong Kong as a safe and just place, of missionaries travelling to every region 'to diffuse sound knowledge among the heathen', and of Hong Kong island becoming 'more dignified by spreading over the country light and knowledge'.[29]

The school's success, measured in terms of what Brown's pupils later achieved, was unfortunately not matched by Dr James Legge's Anglo-Chinese College and later Theological School. The Anglo-Chinese College had been founded at Malacca by Robert Morrison and

[27] Ibid., p. 23.
[28] Ibid., p. 27.
[29] *The Chinese Repository*, 12 (1843), pp. 362–8.

William Milne in 1818, and was moved to Hong Kong in 1843 where it turned from a 'liberal arts college' to a theological seminary.[30] It foundered due to a lack of suitable candidates for advanced instruction, and its former pupils were a disappointment.

As far as missionary medicine was concerned, the Medical Missionary Society's Hospital, which was located close by the Morrison Education Society's school to the east of Victoria, opened under the charge of Dr Benjamin Hobson on 1 June 1843,[31] and proved extremely popular. It was the latest in a long line of institutions that moved from Macao. In its 1844 report, Hobson wrote: 'According to the objects for which I was sent hither by the LMS, I have endeavoured to make the hospital an effective auxiliary in spreading a knowledge of Christianity among the patients.' The hospital rules included compulsory daily attendance at a service, and the Scriptures and religious tracts in Chinese were freely distributed.[32] The Chinese in Hong Kong (and some in neighbouring China who started arriving in junkloads) obviously considered that free medicine warranted very limited participation in foreign rituals. Dr Hobson's plans for a medical school for Chinese students, however, failed due, amongst other things, to a lack of qualified students,[33] mirroring the failure of James Legge's theological school.

The third strand of missionary activity prevalent in Hong Kong in the 1840s was care of female Chinese orphans. Many female children were abandoned to die at birth and there was great need for these institutions. The first three sisters of charity from the Order of St Paul de Chartres arrived in Hong Kong in 1845 (or 1848 – the date is disputed) and set up the first orphanage in Wanchai, along the north side of Queen's Road East.[34]

Hong Kong's early days were marked by an insistence on the principle of religious toleration, which was a major issue at the time. William Tarrant, an infamous Hong Kong journalist who wrote a history celebrating the first twenty-one years of the colony, noted that in 1842 the governor, Sir Henry Pottinger, refused to differentiate

[30] Brian Harrison, *Waiting for China* (Hong Kong, 1979), pp. 109–13.

[31] William Lockhart, *The Medical Missionary in China: A Narrative of Twenty Years' Experience* (London, 1861), p. 202.

[32] *The Chinese Repository*, 13 (1844), pp. 379, 603–4.

[33] Carl Smith, 'The contribution of missionaries to the development of Hong Kong', in idem, *A Sense of History*, pp. 299–301.

[34] Smith, 'Wan Chai', pp. 121–2, Sweeting, *Education in Hong Kong*, p. 145 and Ryan, *The Story*, p. 7.

between gifts of land to Protestant and Roman Catholic religious and charitable institutions.[35] In 1843, in addition to the consecration of the Roman Catholic Church of the Immaculate Conception, Tarrant noted the building of a mosque for the Muslim population and the granting of a cemetery to the Parsee community.[36] Supporters of the new settlement liked to compare it in this respect with China. One editorial in *The Chinese Repository* in October 1843 read: 'The Chinese government is most intolerant, its laws forbidding the practice of certain forms of religion on penalty of death. The British government, on the contrary, tolerates all religions; and it is in this island the dominant power.' But whilst using toleration as a stick with which to beat China, the Protestants could not contain their hatred of Catholics; the same journal ran an article in several issues of 1844 on Catholics, in which it virtually accused all former Catholic missionaries to China of lying.[37]

The emperor of China in fact issued a rescript on religious toleration at the five treaty ports in response to a memorial from the governor of Guangdong and Guangxi in the first months of 1845. A translation of Keying's original memorial circulating in Hong Kong in April contained the following: 'I have taken it on me to examine into the sect of the Lord of Heaven, and find its doctrines are honoured and reverenced by the various nations of the west, their principal object being to exhort to virtue and re[ject?] vice'. Missionaries in the region saw this opening up of limited parts of China to Christianity as the most important development to have taken place for some time. The level of Protestant paranoia can be gauged by the fact that a rumour gained ground in Hong Kong that toleration would only be extended to Catholics, 'to those Chinese christians who honoured the religion of the west by worshipping the crucifix, images etc.'; they were reassured only when it was clarified that toleration would extend to all forms of the Christian religion.[38] Increased opportunity for mission work in China meant increased competition between various denominations.

According to George Smith, who was sent out by the Church

35 William Tarrant, *Hong Kong: Part I, 1839–44* (Canton, 1861), p. 37.

36 Ibid., p. 75. Many others noted the building of the mosque: see Eitel, *Europe in China*, p. 190, and *The Chinese Repository*, 12 (1843), p. 549.

37 *The Chinese Repository*, 13 (1844), p. 596.

38 SOAS, LMS archive, South China correspondence, incoming, Box 4 (1840–7), letters of James Legge of 21 April 1845 and of William Gillespie of 27 December 1845.

Missionary Society in 1844–6 to tour the treaty ports, Hong Kong and Chusan, and to assess their viability as mission centres, it was just this jealous rivalry that had made Protestant missionary work difficult in Macao prior to the acquisition of Hong Kong.

> On the one hand was a popish priesthood, intimately connected with the local government, narrowly watching the measures of missionaries, and ready to crush, at the earliest stage, any attempts to make converts to Protestantism. . . . Added to which there was a mixed authority, in Macao itself, of the Portuguese and Chinese governments.[39]

Lacking access to Catholic missionary reports on the British government of early Hong Kong, it is difficult to make meaningful comparisons, except to note that most of the Catholic organizations (such as the Jesuit seminary) also moved to Hong Kong in those heady days.

George Smith gives some interesting accounts of missionary excursions in the company of Karl Gützlaff to Chinese villages on Hong Kong island and on Kowloon in 1844. Gützlaff and two Chinese assistants gave short speeches and prayers and handed tracts to any Chinese they encountered (although virtually everyone was illiterate), with Gützlaff apparently compelling the reluctant to hear him out.[40] Smith examined any traces of Chinese religion he found: 'I saw two or three ugly idols, black in appearance, and only about six inches in height.' At Shamshuipo in Kowloon, Smith described the images in a Buddhist temple dedicated to the 'goddess of mercy' or 'queen of heaven'.[41] But these belittling descriptions led him nowhere, and his inability to accept the validity of other religions caused him always to seek unsuccessfully in their practices for traces of his own: 'The people appeared to take delight in showing us the various sacred objects; but there was an entire absence of any indications of religious awe.'[42]

George Smith's general reflections on the opening up of China to Christianity are worth repeating. He shared the common belief that the missionary's primary objective was the evangelization of the heathen and that empire provided him with the means to do it.

[39] George Smith, *A Narrative*, p. 69.

[40] Ibid., pp. 72–9.

[41] Ibid., p. 79. See also Carl Smith, 'Sham Shui Po: from proprietary village to industrial-urban complex', in idem, *A Sense of History*, p. 191.

[42] Smith, *A Narrative*, p. 79.

> Believing that his country has been honoured by God as the chosen instrument for diffusing the pure light of christianity through the world, and that the permanency of her laws, institutions and empire is closely connected with the diffusion of evangelical truth, a British missionary feels jealous for the faithfulness of his country to her high vocation, and 'rejoices with trembling' at the extension of her colonial empire.[43]

Smith makes it clear, however, that sites other than Hong Kong would have been preferable as mission bases in China. This is slightly paradoxical, as Hong Kong was a British colony whereas the treaty ports were not British territory. Smith cites the low moral and social character of the Chinese on the island as a particular disadvantage. It has often been argued that Hong Kong was not typically Chinese in its demographic formation because its population was composed of transient, poor, single males rather than respectable families, which made conversion more difficult, although some have seen this as a reason why a few Chinese, already marginalized and cast out from normal Chinese society, were willing to convert as they had nothing to lose.[44]

Smith here seems unable to separate missionary work at Hong Kong from missionary work in the rest of China, a common failing at the time. Many missionaries wanted Hong Kong to serve a dual function: to provide Christian converts, and to act as a base for China. Endless arguments went round and round on these two issues, with every Protestant missionary expressing an opinion. In 1843 there was in fact a conference of seven LMS missionaries in Hong Kong[45] (a conference of missionaries rather than a conference on missionaries) to discuss the future location of the Anglo-Chinese College. The majority opted for Shanghai or Ningpo, as the students in the north were supposedly of a 'better class' than the ones in Hong Kong, and teaching could be in Mandarin rather than Cantonese (this seems to ignore the dialect spoken in Shanghai, for example). However, a minority of one (William Milne) believed Hong Kong to be the best bet, due to the

[43] On Christianity's collaboration with imperialism in China, see Stanley, *The Bible and the Flag*, p. 109.

[44] Carl Smith, 'The Hong Kong situation as it influenced the Protestant church', in idem, *Chinese Christian*, pp. 182–7.

[45] Samuel Dyer, Benjamin Hobson, James Legge, Walter Medhurst, William Milne, and Alexander and John Stronach.

insecurity of the situation in the north of China and to the fact that the Catholics were already well established in Shanghai and would plot against them.

Of Smith's other reasons for not believing Hong Kong to be the best missionary station, the first is related to dialects and the second two to the colonial situation. Hong Kong was also different from much of China because of the variety of dialects spoken by its inhabitants. Although the vast majority were Cantonese speakers (who were themselves divided into different linguistic sub-groupings), there were significant numbers of Hakka, Hoklo, and Chiu Chau. As these dialects were so difficult for Westerners to master, it was argued that it would be better to be based in a community with only one dialect. This does not seem much of an argument, because missionaries to different parts of China needed to learn different dialects. Missionaries in Hong Kong attached themselves to distinct dialect groups (for example, the Baptist William Dean worked with a Chiu Chau congregation). The two colonial drawbacks are 'the frequent spectacle of European irreligion' (that is, acquaintance with colonists and soldiers behaving badly) and the discriminatory treatment of the Chinese by the colonial government and individual colonists.[46] Both sets of behaviour remained characteristic of Hong Kong throughout the nineteenth century, and both were directly linked to the attitude of superiority attached to Western imperialism, whereas discriminatory treatment of non-whites was also a feature of evangelical Christianity.

The first few years of British Hong Kong saw a great rush of missionary activity and much heart-searching over the best way forward to the Christianizing of China. Although toleration had become the official policy by 1845, incomprehension, rivalry, and uncertainty characterized relations between Protestant and Catholic, colonist and colonized, Christian and non-Christian, China and the European powers. The new British settlement offered great opportunities to large groups of Chinese and non-Chinese alike, some of which were taken up by the missionary establishments. But the newness of Hong Kong could not change the minds and attitudes of the missionaries, nor in a short period of time convince many Chinese of the value of Christianity. In the course of the nineteenth century, Hong Kong would come to occupy a niche as a stepping-off point for Chinese Christianization, but in the 1840s all was in flux. James Legge

[46] Smith, *A Narrative*, pp. 511–14.

expressed it well: 'Ultimately the island will become a hive, and I hope that many a christian swarm will be thrown from it to settle on the adjoining continent.'[47]

Goldsmiths' College, University of London

[47] SOAS, LMS archive, Ultra Ganges, Malacca, incoming, Box 3 (1830–59), letter of James Legge of 31 August 1843.

CIVILIZING THE KINGDOM: MISSIONARY OBJECTIVES AND THE DUTCH PUBLIC SPHERE AROUND 1800

by JORIS VAN EIJNATTEN

INTRODUCTION

REFLECTING trends in international scholarship, recent explanations of the rise of Dutch missionary activity and thought in the period around 1800 tend to draw on a revised image of the Dutch eighteenth century as a period of Enlightenment. This revised image is based on the twofold claim that there was an Enlightenment in the Netherlands and that this Enlightenment was Christian or Protestant in character. At the turn of the eighteenth century, it is maintained, the strong influence of revivalism and pietism led to widespread missionary fervour, and this newly-found enthusiasm was able to bear fruit because it was spread through the private societies and social activism developed during, and characteristic of, the Dutch Enlightenment. Thus in recent accounts the positive connotations of the Enlightenment and the emancipatory significance of the new missionary enterprises have been strongly emphasised.[1]

The prolific growth of missionary activity in the period around 1800 was unprecedented. In England alone three missionary societies were founded in the final decade of the eighteenth century: the Baptist Missionary Society (1792), the London Missionary Society (1795), and the Church Missionary Society (1799). The Dutch established their society in 1797, as the *Nederlandsch Zendeling Genootschap ter voortplanting en bevordering van het Christendom, bijzonder onder de Heidenen.*[2] Similar societies sprang up in the first half of the nineteenth century in Switzerland, Germany, France, Denmark, Sweden, Norway, and the

[1] J. Boneschansker, *Het Nederlandsch Zendeling Genootschap in zijn eerste periode. Een studie over opwekking in de Bataafse en Franse Tijd* (Leeuwarden, 1987), pp. 180–5; I. H. Enklaar, 'De aanvangsperiode van de nieuwere Nederlandse zending. Motieven, doelstelling en internationale verbondenheid', in idem, *Kom over en help ons! Twaalf opstellen over de Nederlandse zending in de negentiende eeuw* (The Hague, 1981), pp. 16–22; P. N. Holtrop, *Tussen piëtisme en Réveil. Het 'Deutsche Christentumgesellschaft' in Nederland, 1784–1833* (Amsterdam, 1975), pp. 152–70.

[2] E. F. Kruijf, *Geschiedenis van het Nederlandsche Zendelinggenootschap* (Groningen, 1894); I. H. Enklaar, *Life and Work of Dr. J.Th. van der Kemp 1747–1811. Missionary Pioneer and Protagonist of Racial Equality in South Africa* (Cape Town and Rotterdam, 1988).

United States.[3] This remarkable growth certainly requires an explanation. Contemporary discussions – including the recent Dutch literature – of nineteenth-century mission often reflect on the various currents that influenced missionary activity: patristic, medieval, and Reformation traditions, but above all pietism in its various forms and the (Protestant) Enlightenment.[4] These currents mingled in various ways to create different but related missionary visions. The driving force behind the nineteenth-century rise of mission itself is, however, still described as a 'release of new Christian energy',[5] 'a new zeal to make the world full of justice and truth',[6] the sudden ascent of 'forces of renewal' and a new 'spirit of enterprise',[7] the final 'great breakthrough' of 'the long repressed idea of missions' in a period of 'awakening', characterized by eschatological expectations and fevered activity.[8] Such explanations are evidently either indebted to or modelled after the accounts provided by those who, within the nineteenth-century missionary movement itself, regarded their work as a sign of providential guidance, as an extraordinary divine blessing bestowed upon the modern world. In 1894 the leading Dutch historian of missions, E. F. Kruijf, for example, characteristically observed that a century of memorable missionary work had been instigated and sustained by a new verve, inspired by the grace of God, and leading to a wholesale revitalization of the Christian spirit.[9]

The explanations given or (as is often the case) implied by recent accounts of the Protestant missionary expansion of the nineteenth century are not particularly convincing from the historian's point of view. To be sure, the attempts to unravel various strands of thought and activity, ranging from Lutheran pietism and Moravianism to

[3] S. Neill, *A History of Christian Missions* (Harmondsworth, 1964), pp. 243–60; for references to recent literature, see above all K. Cracknell, *Justice, Courtesy and Love. Theologians and Missionaries Encountering World Religions, 1846–1914* (London, 1995), Chapter 1.

[4] E.g. D. J. Bosch, *Transforming Mission. Paradigm Shifts in Theology of Mission* (Maryknoll, NY, 1991); J. van den Berg, *Constrained by Jesus' Love. An Inquiry into the Motives of the Missionary Awakening in Great Britain in the Period Between 1698 and 1815* (Kampen, 1956). For a discussion of the literature, cf. B. Stanley, 'Enlightenment and Mission: A Re-Evaluation', unpublished paper written for the North Atlantic Missiology Project Consultation on the Evangelical Revival and the Missionary Movement, Cambridge, 1996.

[5] Neill, *A History of Christian Missions*, p. 252.

[6] Cracknell, *Justice, Courtesy and Love*, p. 3.

[7] Bosch, *Transforming Mission*, pp. 277, 327–34.

[8] Van den Berg, *Constrained by Jesus' Love*, p. 106.

[9] Kruijf, *Geschiedenis van het Nederlandsche Zendelinggenootschap*, pp. 3–7.

English evangelicalism and Enlightened society culture, or to distinguish different 'paradigm shifts' in missiology, shed a welcome light on the religious and cultural baggage of the missionaries, and on the different views they developed over time on the principles, preconditions, and strategies involved in missionary work. But the explanatory factor underlying contemporary analyses of the missionary take-off around 1800 is to all appearances still the *deus ex machina* of a sudden and unprecedented awakening of the Christian spirit. Whether this Christian spirit is subsequently described as evangelical, pietist, Enlightened, or simply modern, is immaterial to the point that a sudden and prolonged outburst of spiritual energy does not really get us very far in explaining the rise of nineteenth-century Protestant mission.

This paper attempts another explanation.[10] Instead of discussing the role of the Reformation, pietism, or the Enlightenment in the missionary take-off around 1800, I shall focus on the *public* status of early-modern missions. My aim in this paper is to demonstrate that the eighteenth century witnessed a transformation in the public status of missionary activity, and that this transformation was a factor of primary importance in bringing about the prolific growth of missionary thought and work in the decades around 1800. In the following I shall not only emphasise the public status of ostensibly private undertakings, but also interpret missionary objectives as an effort to redefine the public sphere. To do this, I shall concentrate on the various ways in which missionary objectives were discussed, taking the biblical idea of the Kingdom of God as my point of reference.

Efforts to redefine the public sphere imply an attempt to control it. The emphasis put by the missionaries on 'civilization' was precisely an attempt to define and hence control the limits of 'publicity'.[11] This paper is concerned with such limits. Its focus is therefore on the social and political function of ideas, rather than on their status as pietist or

[10] My approach is partly based on my thesis 'God, Nederland en Oranje. Dutch Calvinism and the Search for the Social Centre' (Kampen, 1993), but is particularly indebted in its focus on missions to Peter T. van Rooden's chapter on missions and national consciousness in his *Religieuze regimes. Over godsdienst en maatschappij in Nederland 1570–1990* (Amsterdam, 1996), pp. 121–46 (ch. 4: 'Beelden van bekering. Religieus nationalisme en de opkomst van de zending').

[11] The term 'publicity' is derived from Jürgen Habermas's conception of *Öffentlichkeit*; for its enduring applicability to the eighteenth century, see e.g. A. J. La Vopa, 'Conceiving a Public: Ideas and Society in Eighteenth-Century Europe', in *JMH* 64 (1992), pp. 79–116.

Enlightened – which is not, of course, to disqualify either of these categories as useful tools for historical analysis.

I shall begin by discussing the relations between early modern missionary thought and the public sphere, addressing first the traditional Calvinist establishment and subsequently its early eighteenth-century critics. My goal in these first two sections is to provide an explanation for the restricted possibilities for private missionary enterprise during the Dutch old regime. I shall then focus on the way in which the public status of missionary activity was affirmed and legitimized in the decades around 1800. I shall generally argue that the missionary objectives of the time reflect a new conception of civilization and nationhood. The structure of this paper, then, is roughly chronological. Three conceptions of the 'public' Kingdom of God will be distinguished, each of which predominated during a certain time, though none can be rigidly restricted to a specific period.

THE MAGISTERIAL KINGDOM

The amplification of the glory of God through the expansion of His Kingdom has always been a primary motive of missionary activity. Throughout the early modern period it was widely recognized that the expansion of the Kingdom was not just a matter of religious zeal or ecclesiastical policy, but also one that had public, and therefore political, implications. In territories with more than one religion, this meant that not everyone was entitled to spread publicly the Word of God, at home or in the colonies. In the Netherlands, missionary activity was a monopoly of the privileged church of the Dutch Republic. This privileged, public church was the Reformed Church. Although the religious policy of the seventeenth-century Republic was relatively lenient, granting minority denominations the freedom to worship in private, the Reformed Church possessed the exclusive right to proselytize in public and establish churches in the colonies. In other words, prospects for an expansion of the Kingdom of God depended on the way in which the public sphere was defined. In theory, if not always in practice, the early modern public sphere was controlled by a religious and political establishment that retained, and closely protected, certain exclusive rights.

As far as the Netherlands are concerned, the second half of the seventeenth century, though far from having been a period of unlimited toleration, was one in which the right of other Protestant denominations to play a part in the public organization of religion had increasingly been recognized. Peter T. van Rooden has aptly described this state of limited legitimacy – of semi-publicness, as it were – in terms of a hierarchical structure.[12] In his view, the Dutch public sphere of the late seventeenth century was characterized by the fact that religion was 'localized' in a hierarchy of denominations. The Reformed Church as it had been defined at the Synod of Dordrecht in 1618–19 was at the top of this public hierarchy; beneath it were the dissenting Protestant groups, the Lutherans, the Remonstrants, and the Mennonites; right at the bottom were the Roman Catholics. Van Rooden not only claims that this hierarchical structure remained in place until at least the 1770s, but also argues that it was given due support by the various denominations which held a position within it. I would agree with the former claim, but not necessarily with the latter. As I shall argue in the next section, forceful alternative conceptions of the public sphere had been circulating among dissenters and critics of ecclesiastical policy since at least the beginning of the eighteenth century.

The point is that for a good part of the eighteenth century, 'publicity' was defined, not necessarily in terms of the Synod of Dordrecht (as Van Rooden emphasises), but in terms of state-sanctioned confessionalism. Confessions defined what was public within the Kingdom of God; and to the religious authorities (ranging from theologians and university faculties to consistories and synods) confessions were not subject to change. However, because missionary activity was a means of disseminating one interpretation of Christian truth at the cost of another,[13] it was also an obvious means of bringing about religious change. Religious change was regarded as a main source of social unrest – Calvinist divines often reminded the magistrate of the religious conflicts that had led up to the Synod of Dort and brought the country into civil war. Hence the exclusive right of the Reformed Church to pursue missionary goals was jealously guarded by both the Church and the government. Missionary activity undertaken

[12] Van Rooden, *Religieuze regimes*, pp. 78–120.

[13] Cf. L. J. Joosse, *'Scoone dingen sijn swaere dingen'. Een onderzoek naar de moetieven en activiteiten in de Nederlanden tot verbreiding van de gereformeerde religie gedurende de eerste helft van de zeventiende eeuw* (Leiden, 1992), pp. 528–81, on the motives of seventeenth-century mission. These motives were doxological (spreading the *true* religion so as to further the glory of God), christocratic (but allowing for connections between the *regnum Christi* and the magistrate), and soteriological (with, again, an emphasis on the true religion, as defined in officially and publicly recognized confessions).

by any religious denomination other than the Reformed Church was regarded as a veiled attempt to attain control of the public sphere, provoke an overthrow of the existing regime, and supplant truth with falsity. The Kingdom of God was, in this sense, a magisterial Kingdom, a spiritual Kingdom involving the authority of the magistrate.

This state of affairs was exemplified by the way in which the Dutch received the German Moravians or Herrnhuters, who formed the strongest missionary force within early modern Protestantism. The reception in the Dutch Republic of the irenical ideals and missionary zeal of this evangelical brotherhood has often surprised church historians. The Moravian movement was condemned by virtually the whole Reformed establishment. The disregard for denominational boundaries exhibited by the Moravians was perceived as a threat to the delicate status quo among the various religious groups; and their endeavour to spread the Kingdom of God was seen as a menace to the Reformed monopoly. Not surprisingly, the Moravians mainly found support among pietistic Dutch Mennonites, whose own potential as a source of religious and civil unrest was never underestimated. Thus the Moravians, for all the Christian inspiration of their missionary aims, were rejected. And they were not rejected because they so ardently believed in the diffusion of the Kingdom of God, but because they failed to respect the way in which the Dutch public sphere was organized. The Reformed Church immediately understood that Herrnhuter activity undermined the stability of the existing religious-political order.

Interestingly, the Moravians were not the only group who, unintentionally or otherwise, undermined that religious order. From the early decades of the eighteenth century, the dominant status of the Calvinist Church, and the influence of the clergy on public religious policy, had been criticized incisively by writers from dissenting denominations. Given this early eighteenth-century critique of the traditional public sphere, one would expect the dissenters of the period to have supported the missionary objectives of the Moravians. Support for the latter would have been an obvious way for critics to express their dissent. Surprisingly however, the critical minds of the early eighteenth century joined the Reformed establishment in rejecting the Moravian movement. How do we explain this?

THE KINGDOM OF LIBERTY

The question is best answered by examining the alternative public sphere put forward by the critical dissenters of the early eighteenth century. Rejecting the dominant status of the Calvinist Church, they proposed certain far-reaching changes to the religious structure of Dutch society. They argued, in effect, for complete religious freedom. This brings us to a second conception of the Kingdom of God. In the first half of the eighteenth century the Kingdom of God in its relation to the public sphere began to be perceived, not as a magisterial Kingdom, a confession-based Kingdom supervised by the Reformed magistrate, but as a Kingdom of liberty.

The difference between the traditional hierarchic definition of the public sphere and the new one proposed by radical dissenters is illustrated by a subscription controversy that raged in the Netherlands between 1740 and 1743.[14] The interesting point about this particular debate is that the various participants extensively discussed the nature of the Kingdom of God and its relations to the public sphere. Most texts that entered into the debate were concerned with the freedom of the private conscience in relation to the obligation to subscribe to a public confession of faith. The main participants were Johannes Stinstra (1708–90), a preacher among the Frisian Mennonites who in due course was suspended from his office on suspicion of heresy, and his main opponent, the leading Calvinist theologian and Leiden professor, Johannes van den Honert (1693–1758).

Stinstra wrote a number of sermons *On the Nature and Constitution of Christ's Kingdom, Subjects, Church and Worship*, a book that was duly answered by Van den Honert with a collection of sermons on exactly the same texts and published under exactly the same title. Both divines emphasised that freedom of conscience was an indefeasible human right. Stinstra, however, argued that subscription to a confession of faith should never be obligatory. In conformity with the position of other radical dissenters, he suggested that all confessions and formularies of faith should be abolished, so that a single universal Church could be established to which all Christians belonged. The Kingdom of God, he claimed, was a free Kingdom, which recognized Christ, rather

[14] See my *De Mutua Christianorum Tolerantia. Irenicism and Toleration in the Netherlands: The Stinstra Affair, 1740–1745* (*Studi e testi per la storia della tolleranza in Europa nei secoli XVI–XVIII* 2) (Firenze, 1998).

than a synod of fallible theologians, as its only head and lawgiver. Thus in Stinstra's view, religious equality and freedom ought to reign in the Kingdom of God as a public Kingdom. Van den Honert, on the other hand, tried to put forward a more equitable version of the magisterial, hierarchic version of the public sphere. He believed that a universal Church would only lead to discord and strife. Like-minded Christians, he said, ought to convene within a particular church. The religious beliefs on which such a church was based should be made public, so that the magistrate could recognize its legitimacy, and other citizens might be convinced of the truths it defends. Anyone who sincerely follows his conscience is bound to end up in the Church best suited to his own religious beliefs. To Van den Honert, then, the Kingdom of God was a divided one.

According to both Stinstra and Van den Honert, the Kingdom of God was a realm inhabited by sincere and conscientious Christians. But while Stinstra claimed that the freedom to make public and defend private beliefs was a right possessed by all individual Christians, Van den Honert restricted this right to those religious societies officially recognized by the magistrate. Both divines defined the Kingdom of God as a Kingdom of liberty, as a Kingdom presided over by Jesus Christ as the only judge of men and the sole head of the Church. Interestingly, both referred to a famous and controversial sermon by the Anglican bishop Benjamin Hoadly (1676–1761), which had first been published in 1717 and was translated into Dutch in 1734. 'It appears that the *Kingdom* of *Christ*', claimed Hoadly, 'is the *Number* of Persons who are sincerely and willingly *Subjects to Him*, as *Law-giver* and *Judge* in all Matters truly relating to Conscience, or Eternal Salvation.' Stinstra and Van den Honert subscribed to this definition of the Kingdom of Christ.[15]

The conceptual shift in the relationship between the Kingdom of God and the public sphere, from a magisterial Kingdom to a Kingdom of liberty, implied that missionary activity could in principle no longer be limited to the Reformed Church. Even according to some leading Calvinist theologians, each denomination ought to be allowed, not

[15] B. Hoadly, *The Nature of the Kingdom or Church of Christ, or a Sermon Preach'd before the King, at the Royal Chapel of St. James's, on Sunday, March 31st, 1717* (London and Edinburgh, 1717), p. 13; J. Stinstra, *De natuure en gesteldheid van Christus Koningrijk, onderdaanen, kerk en godsdienst afgeschetst in vijf predicatien* (Harlingen, 1742), pp. 13–43; J. van den Honert, 'Academische redenvoering over de onderlinge verdraagsaamheid der christenen', in idem, *Derde versameling van heilige mengelstoffen* (Leiden, 1747), p. 322, note (i).

only to worship in public, but also to put forward its views publicly and vie for religious ascendancy on the basis of sound argumentation. It is not surprising, however, that the Calvinist establishment continued to reject the Herrnhuter movement. The Moravians showed a principled disregard for denominational distinctions and, therefore, endangered public peace. It is more remarkable to find that even the radical dissenters firmly rejected the Moravians. Stinstra himself was, in fact, the author of a highly influential Dutch book on 'enthusiasm' in which the Herrnhuter movement was castigated, and which was immediately translated into German, French, and English. This repudiation of the Moravians is important because it shows that eighteenth-century dissent – or, if you will, Enlightenment criticism – was highly ambivalent. The criticism levelled at the Calvinist establishment by radical dissenters was accompanied by an attempt to achieve cultural and social hegemony at the expense of other groups. In their view the subjectivism of the Moravians or, for that matter, any other pietistic group, was highly dangerous because it undermined the objective rational basis of the Kingdom of God as a Kingdom of liberty.

THE BOOK OF CIVILIZATION

Although spirited pleas for missionary activity were put forward from time to time throughout the eighteenth century, there was no boom in missionary endeavour comparable to that of the period around 1800. This lack of large-scale missionary enterprises during the eighteenth century can be explained by analyzing the kinds of discourse used to defend religious activity within the public sphere. To those early eighteenth-century minds concerned with defining the extent of freedom and delimiting the exercise of power, missionary activity was simply not a matter of primary interest. Radical dissenters were concerned with freedom from subscription and freedom from magisterial tutelage, not with the spread of the gospel. Moreover, to most parties missionary activity was an issue compromised by the religious 'enthusiasm' or 'fanaticism' of the Moravians. Theirs was a static view, not a dynamic one.

Missionary activity was, however, bound to come to the fore as a legitimate and inoffensive enterprise when the subscription controversies were over. For missionary activity required that the public sphere itself was seen to be constituted by individuals who were not only wholly free from magisterial tutelage, but also susceptible to being educated as free individuals. These conditions were met in the Netherlands, as elsewhere, around 1800.

To come to an understanding of the relations between mission and the public sphere around 1800, it is necessary to glance at the way in which missionary activity was legitimized at the time. Representative of this new missionary discourse are the sermons and pamphlets written by the founders of the 'Dutch Missionary Society for the Propagation and Advancement of Christianity, in Particular among Heathens'. Established by some twenty gentlemen convening in Rotterdam in December 1797, the Dutch Missionary Society was intended to function as a sister organization to the pioneering London Missionary Society (which itself was founded in 1795). Membership of the Dutch society was open to Christians belonging to all denominations. And this ecumenical principle was, typically, combined with an appreciation of the missionary fieldwork done by the eighteenth-century Moravians.

A characteristic pamphlet is 'A Lecture on the Necessity and Salutariness of Converting Heathen Peoples', published anonymously in 1801.[16] In this concise and irenic essay the writer argues that the conversion of heathens has to be pursued because Christians are obliged to demonstrate their love of Christ and their neighbour. But the conversion of heathens is also salutary, claims the author. Conversion, he observes, is both useful and advantageous. Which are the advantages that accrue to conversion? The main benefit, according to the author, is the growth of 'true civilization' (*beschaving*). The Bible is not only a source of pure and excellent morality; it also contains 'the true grounds and rules of civilization'. In fact, the Bible is indisputably 'the Book of true civilization', because it teaches us godliness, righteousness, equity, moderation, humility, kind-heartedness, diligence, honesty, loyalty, love for humankind, and decorum. Since the Apostles themselves had not been particularly well educated in 'true enlightenment and civilization', this proves the Bible's more than human status. 'It is indisputable that *moral civilization*, exercised in all activities worthy of being called virtuous, has to be established through education in, and the exercise of, the Christian Religion: similarly,

[16] 'Eene voordragt, van het noodzaakelijke en heilzaame der bekeering van heidensche volken' (1801), in: *Gedenkschriften van het Nederlandsch Zendeling-Genootschap*, 2 vols (Rotterdam, 1801–5), I, pp. 57–99.

the direction and perfection of the true civilisation of the *mind* is due to the same [Christian Religion].' The Christian nations of Protestant Europe are 'the principal members of the great household of humanity'; they are the 'schools' into which heathens must be enrolled if they wish to participate in the Kingdom of truth and virtue, which is the Kingdom of God. The author argues at length that only the Gospel is able to bring into full blossom the small traces of civilization still extant in primitive heathen cultures. The means proposed by the Gospel are education and instruction. Moral perfection is an attribute of civilization, and civilization a fruit of the Gospel. Hence it is unnecessary to civilize heathens first before converting them.[17] Indeed, it is impossible to separate civilization from conversion. Only the Gospel can bring true civilization to any given society and enable its inner potential to flourish.

A well-known Dutch poet wrote a book on the subject called *Preach the Gospel to Every Creature! A Political Maxim of the Kingdom of Truth and Virtue* (1801).[18] The title is interesting in that it emphasises the public nature of missionary activity by suggesting an analogy with public ethics and politics. Freedom, equality, and brotherhood, declares the writer, are signs of the true civilization taught by Christianity. 'A nation in which the Gospel is preached in purity, believed with respect, and experienced with vigour, has, by virtue of this moral improvement alone, become ripe for the preaching of true civil freedom; as well as for [the preaching of] a well-determined liberty and sincere brotherhood.' The general trend of this lecture was elaborated on in many other sermons and pamphlets. In the decades around 1800, cultural refinement and religious creed had become two sides of the same coin. The Bible was a book of conversion as much as it was a book of

[17] The discussion in the nineteenth-century Netherlands on the question of what comes first, civilization or the gospel, was analogous to the debate on the topic in England and elsewhere. The supporters of the Dutch Mission Society had to contend with critics who stressed that bringing civilization was a precondition to spreading the Word. In 1808 one critic even argued that it is impossible to supplant deep-rooted non-western cultures by western civilization, and tried to demonstrate that two centuries of missions had, in fact, changed very little; see J. Haafner, 'Antwoord op de vraag: welken dienst hebben de zendelingen in de twee jongst-verlopene eeuwen aan de voortplanting des waren christendoms gedaan, en welk eene vrucht heeft men van de tegenwoordig werkzame zendings-genootschappen ten dezen opzigte te wachten?', in *Verhandelingen, raakende den natuurlyken en geopenbaarden godsdienst, uitgegeeven door Teyler's Godgeleerd Genootschap*, 22 (Haarlem, 1807), pp. 1–296.

[18] [H. van Alphen], *Predikt het Euangelium allen creaturen! Eene staatsmaxime in het rijk van waarheid en deugd. Uit de papieren van den Christelijken Spectator* (Den Haag, 1801).

civilization, a book as necessary to spiritual salvation as it was to moral, cultural, and social improvement. It was this belief that now legitimized private missionary activity. Far from undermining the legal or rational foundations of the public order, private missionary activity was now seen to conduce to its maintenance. By educating individual Christians convinced of the moral and religious significance of Christian civilization, missionaries belonging to all denominations could be regarded as contributing to public peace and social stability.

THE KINGDOM OF IMPROVEMENT

This brings us to a third conception of the Kingdom of God. After the magisterial Kingdom and the Kingdom of liberty, the period around 1800 witnessed the development of a Kingdom of improvement. In this Kingdom, conversion and civilization were inseparably intertwined. The Kingdom of improvement was a public Kingdom requiring of its subjects that they subscribe, not to one of the various religious convictions formally recognized during the old regime, but to the moral code that now formed the basis of Dutch nationhood.

In this respect the development, during the latter half of the eighteenth century, of private societies is a highly relevant issue. As I suggested previously, the so-called 'Dutch Enlightenment' is usually valued for, or interpreted in terms of, its emancipatory character: its optimistic view of man, its belief in social progress, its emphasis on right and utility rather than licence and privilege. These Enlightened ideals were disseminated in private societies, among other circles. But the importance of these private societies lies not so much in the fact that they were private, but in the fact that together they constituted a new public sphere. The societies that mushroomed during the second half of the eighteenth century were founded for the benefit and education of mankind in general and the Dutch nation in particular. They devoted themselves towards the creation of a public sphere in which they could realize their pedagogic aspirations. They were devoted, that is, to a Kingdom of improvement.

As repositories of the Enlightenment, the new societies harboured emancipatory ideals; but at the same time they were part and parcel of a broader development towards new forms of social constraint. Within this newly-established Kingdom of improvement, exclusion was no longer based on the refusal to subscribe to a particular confession, or on the rejection of rationality; exclusion now resulted from a disavowal of the principles of Christian civilization, which by all accounts meant Protestant civilization. Adherence to civilized principles was a prerequisite to participation in the public sphere. To illustrate the contention that the new missionary aims also involved an attempt to participate in, and hence gain control of, the public sphere, I shall briefly review some of the motives expressed by the founders and supporters of the Dutch Missionary Society. These motives are charity, ecumenism, and obligation.[19]

It goes without saying that the new missionary activities were induced by religious ideals, that they were inspired, for example, by Christian charity. However, the point is that the idea of Christian charity functioned differently in each of the various conceptions of the Kingdom of God as a *public* realm. For example, the eighteenth-century subscription controversies had focused on Christian brotherhood as a manifestation of charity. Yet on each side of the debate brotherhood was interpreted differently. The Calvinist establishment restricted Christian brotherhood to the Reformed and the Lutherans, thus ensuring the continued dominance of the traditional, magisterial establishment. The radical dissenters, justifying a Kingdom of liberty, emphasised a universal Christian brotherhood based on rationality and therefore excluded Moravians, pietists, and other 'enthusiasts'. In terms of public discourse, then, the idea of Christian charity has not always been straightforwardly charitable.

Similarly, around 1800 the idea of Christian charity took on a specific function within the new conception of the Kingdom of God as a Kingdom of improvement. Christian charity was now centred, not on the need to tolerate or respect fellow Christians, but on the need to elevate fallen Christians and unbelievers. Most of the authors concerned with legitimizing missionary activity were convinced that unbelief was rampant throughout Europe. Now, it is hardly certain that unbelief was, indeed, so much more popular in 1800 than it had been in, say, 1740. But given the redefinition of the Kingdom of God as a Kingdom of improvement, the discovery of widespread unbelief was as logical as it was welcome. There was no need now to convince deviant believers of a particular truth, or underline the rational basis

[19] Cf. Bosch, *Transforming Mission*, pp. 285–345, on the various motifs within the 'modern Enlightenment paradigm', including the glory of God, Christian charity, culture, and Manifest Destiny; Boneschansker, *Het Nederlandsch Zendeling Genootschap*, pp. 53–9, on commiseration for pagans, eschatology, Christian charity, ecumenism, and civilization. The motive of charity is discussed broadly in Van den Berg, *Constrained by Jesus' Love*.

of such a truth; unbelievers could be approached as if they were *tabulae rasae*, as so many educable individuals who could be instructed in Christian morality and Christian civilization. Given the changes in 'publicity', the real or imagined prevalence of unbelief offered an opportunity to mould citizens into subjects of the modern nation state.

Another characteristic objective expressed by the missionaries in the years around 1800 was the wish to encourage the unity of Christians. This ecumenical desire was again closely connected to the idea that the public Kingdom of God was, above all, a Kingdom of individual and educable Christians. While during the eighteenth century ecumenical ideals had been discussed from the point of view of religious freedom, spiritual freedom was now regarded as a result of Christian education. A spiritually free society is a civilized one; that is, it is a society in which a basic knowledge of elementary Christian truths is both widespread and ingrained. This is why European societies are free and democratic and pagan societies are oppressive and dictatorial. Ecumenical ideals were a natural concomitant to the emphasis on those truths basic to Christian civilization. It is not surprising, moreover, that the educational ideals of the Herrnhuters now found large support.

A third motive expressed by the early missionaries was the desire to contribute to the efficacy of the Holy Spirit by fulfilling one's Christian duty. Again, this desire fitted in perfectly with the dynamism inherent in the expansion of the Kingdom of God, defined as a Kingdom of improvement. It is not difficult to interpret the concern with pneumatology as an attempt to legitimize in theological terms the subjection of heathen colonies to the Protestant culture of the nineteenth-century Netherlands. The culture nourished by the Gospel in the heart of Europe was, so the early missionaries believed, an evident sign of higher civilization signalling the efficacious work of the Holy Spirit. Are not the Protestant nations of Christian Europe 'the principal members of the great household of humanity'? Are they not the 'schools' into which heathens must be enrolled if they wish to participate in the Kingdom of truth and virtue, which is the Kingdom of God?[20] The beliefs that inspired missionaries to risk their careers and sometimes their lives in bringing the light of the Gospel to the nations were connected to a modern conception of a public Kingdom of God, a conception eminently suited to civilizing and improving

[20] Van Alphen, *Predikt het Euangelium*, pp. 1, 70–1, 171.

both the lower classes at home and the coloured populations abroad by providing for an education in national Protestant values.

CONCLUSION

The eighteenth century thus witnessed a transformation in the public status of missionary activity. This change is illustrated by the various ways in which, in the Netherlands, the Kingdom of God was related to the public sphere. In the magisterial Kingdom presided over by the Calvinist establishment, mission was regarded as the exclusive right of a particular group. In the Kingdom of liberty defended by radical dissenters of the early eighteenth century, mission was compromised by pietist irrationality. In the decades around 1800, the public status of mission was affirmed and legitimized in terms of the civilizing power of the Gospel. The Kingdom of God was now conceived as a Kingdom of improvement, as a realm of individual and educable Christians who subscribed to a basic Protestant moral code. From this perspective there is no need to take recourse to a release of spiritual energy as an explanation for 'the great missionary break-through'. What seems like a sudden burst of energy inspired by evangelicalism and Enlightenment was the concomitant effect of a fundamental change in the way in which the public sphere was defined. Missionary enterprise did not suddenly come into its own in an unprecedented and enduring release of Christian fervour, but bloomed because it achieved public legitimacy by being incorporated into a Kingdom of improvement. Missionary work was only one of many activities that contributed to the creation of this new moral order based on education and civilization. The transformation in the public status of missions entailed the integration of missionary activity into a national public sphere comprised of individuals whose ability properly to exercise their rights and freedoms depended on their being sufficiently instructed in Christian morality.

Thus the religious and moral void created by the decline of the established churches of the old regime was filled with a forceful conception of Christian nationhood. In this paper I have emphasised the pedagogic ideal that went into the formation of this new discourse. The idea that the sinful human self required magisterial tutelage to come into its own, or that it could only do so by virtue of its ability to reason in freedom, was supplanted by the idea that the human self is constituted first and foremost by education, instruction, and refinement – in short, by civilization. The missionary spirit that flowered in the Netherlands at the turn of the eighteenth century reflected this modern ideal. And to all appearances it was bound up with a conception of Protestant nationhood that in some ways contradicted the emancipatory ideals of the Enlightenment.

Free University of Amsterdam

LANGUAGE, 'NATIVE AGENCY', AND MISSIONARY CONTROL: RUFUS ANDERSON'S JOURNEY TO INDIA, 1854–5

by ANDREW PORTER

IN the early years of the modern missionary movement there were many influences which turned minds towards support for the general principle and practice of reliance on 'native agency'. Strategies of conversion such as those of the London Missionary Society and the American Board of Commissioners for Foreign Missions at work in the Pacific,[1] which aimed at kings or other influential local leaders, at least implicitly allotted important roles to the leadership and example of highly-placed converts. Awareness of the scale of the missionary task in densely-populated regions, contrasted with the limits of the western missionary input, pointed to the need for delegation as quickly as possible. The Serampore missionaries, Alexander Duff and Charles Gutzlaff, all travelled early down that road.[2] Financial crisis – manifested either locally as Dr John Philip found in South Africa, or centrally as when the Church Missionary Society decided in the early 1840s to withdraw from the West Indies – prompted inevitable questions about the possibilities for deployment of local agents, who were far cheaper than Europeans.[3] Mortality among white missionaries, notably in West Africa, which threatened shortages of another kind, also raised the possibility that acclimatized indigenous agents were the only reliable missionaries for the future.[4] A more active policy of promoting indigenous agents was a consequence both of increasing awareness among society organizers of the European missionaries' tendency to hang on to power and

[1] From an enormous literature, see, for example, Niel Gunson, *Messengers of Grace: Evangelical Missionaries in the South Seas 1797–1860* (Melbourne, 1978); John Garrett, *To Live Among the Stars: Christian Origins in Oceania* (Geneva, 1982); Andrew Porter, 'British Missions, the Pacific and the American Connection: the career of William Ellis', in Alan Frost and Jane Samson, eds, *Pacific Empires: Essays in honour of Glyndwr Williams* (Melbourne, 1999), pp. 193–214, 308–13.

[2] M. A. Laird, *Missionaries and Education in Bengal 1793–1837* (Oxford, 1972).

[3] Andrew Ross, *John Philip (1775–1851): Missions, Race and Politics in South Africa* (Aberdeen, 1986).

[4] C. Peter Williams, *The Ideal of the Self-Governing Church: A Study in Victorian Missionary Strategy* (Leiden, 1990), p. 4.

responsibility, and of their growing familiarity with the practices of the early Christian Church. There was also a range of domestic British developments, including the growth of powerful humanitarian and philanthropic movements, which pushed missionary thinking in a similar direction.[5]

These haphazard coincidences of metropolitan diagnoses with local practical need were of course encompassed by the variously rational, romantic, and millennarian but always optimistic visions of world-wide conversion and global Christianity. It gradually became clear that the route from individual conversion to a world-wide Church lay via the creation, in some form, of local indigenous churches. In recent years, much light has been thrown on the evolution of contemporary thinking about the integration and development of those churches and forms of native agency.[6]

Crucial to the working out of these principles of missionary strategy was the gradual elaboration both of the distinct roles of missionary and local pastor, and the place of bishops in the missionary enterprise. Our knowledge of this process has been shaped above all by research into Anglican practice, through the examination of Henry Venn's career and the subsequent fortunes of his ideas about indigenous episcopates within the operations of the Church Missionary Society (hereafter CMS). This paper, by contrast, suggests that in order to advance understanding of the missionary movement's approaches to the question of Native Agency, something may still be gained from examining the debates being carried on within the non-episcopal churches.[7] Using material chiefly from the Archive of the American Board of Commissioners for Foreign Missions (hereafter ABCFM), it considers the significance of a series of events touching India in the mid-1850s which caused leading members of several Protestant missionary societies to share their thoughts on the role of indigenous Christians in the extension of the Christian Church.

[5] C. Peter Williams, *The Ideal of the Self-Governing Church*, pp. 10–11.

[6] Charles W. Forman, 'A History of Foreign Mission Theory in America', in R. Pierce Beaver, ed., *American Missions in Bicentennial Perspective* (Pasadena, 1977), pp. 69–140; William R. Hutchison, *Errand to the World: American Protestant Thought and Foreign Missions* (Chicago, 1987); T. E. Yates, *Venn and Victorian Bishops Abroad* (Uppsala and London, 1978); Wilbert R. Shenk, *Henry Venn – Missionary Statesman* (Mary Knoll, New York, 1983); Williams, *Ideal of the Self-Governing Church.*

[7] For a related argument, see David M. Thompson, 'British Missionary Policy on the Indigenous Church: The Influence of Developments in Domestic Ecclesiology and Politics, *North Atlantic Missiology Project [NAMP] Position Paper 38* (Cambridge, 1997).

I

On 16 August 1854, the Foreign Secretary of the American Board, Rufus Anderson, called at Church Missionary House to find the Reverend Henry Venn, the Society's Clerical Secretary, out of his office. Only Mr Graham, the Lay Secretary, was at home. In response to Venn's letter of apology a few hours later, Anderson visited Venn again the following day and also dined with him at his home in Islington that evening.[8]

Whether the meetings of these two notable figures were of particular significance may be doubted in the light of Anderson's recollections in his journal. At the Church Missionary House meeting, he found the presence of the Bishop of Sierra Leone a source of 'some embarrassment'; he felt conscious of his official position and, both then and later at dinner, found himself talking at length, not least about the American Board's work. The extended company at dinner was nevertheless congenial and relaxing, somewhat to Anderson's surprise. 'Is it possible that we were among none but Episcopal clergymen, Van Schnop[?] excepted? How the missionary work and spirit break down the sectarian barriers! Nothing could be more cordial than their manner.'[9] However, neither occasion was suited to detailed business, and Anderson was asked by Venn to put in writing the questions about missionary strategy on which he really wished to hear the latter's opinion. Three weeks later, Venn again invited Anderson, this time to the monthly CMS Parent Committee meeting; this he found 'most instructive', especially for the Committee's mode of questioning recently returned missionaries, and CMS policy towards missionaries' children.[10] Subsequently, despite later encounters, Anderson's personal contact with Venn seems to have led to no extended correspondence of the sort that he happily engaged in

[8] This meeting was first examined by Wilbert R. Shenk in his article, 'Rufus Anderson and Henry Venn: a special relationship?', *IBMR*, 5, 4 (1981), pp. 168–72; Harvard University, Houghton Library, ABCFM Archive [hereafter ABC], ABC 30/12, Rufus Anderson's Journal of a Visit to India 1854–5 (3 vols), 1, entries 16–17 August 1854. Publication of documents in this archive is by permission of the Houghton Library, Harvard University.

[9] ABC 30/12, Anderson's Journal, I, 17 August 1854. Besides Venn, Anderson, and the latter's colleague, the Revd A. C. Thompson, present at the dinner were Mr Bowen (probably T. H. Bowen, missionary to West Africa), Mr Ridgeway (editor of CMS periodicals), Mr Bishop, Mr Van Schnop 'from Smyrna', Mr F. E. Schneider (CMS missionary, Agra), 'and another, name not recollected'.

[10] Ibid., 11 September 1854.

with William Ellis, Arthur Tidman, and Joseph Mullens, successively Secretaries at the London Missionary Society (hereafter LMS), or even with E. B. Underhill, Secretary of the Baptist Missionary Society, 1849–76 (hereafter BMS).[11]

In assessing the significance of Anderson's introduction to Venn, however, it is necessary to recall what had brought him to Britain in the first place. For at least a decade, dissatisfaction had been growing at the ABCFM about the mounting costs of their missions while the numbers of converts increased only slowly. In considering how to reverse this position, Anderson and his colleagues in Boston had begun to question the Board's practice of supporting sizeable missionary establishments and English-language secondary education, with their emphasis on social transformation. Financial economy and evangelistic efficiency might be better served by methods which gave pride of place to vernacular languages and indigenous agents. Along with his fellow Prudential Committee member, the Revd A. C. Thompson, Anderson was therefore on his way to India in 1854 as a deputation to inspect the work of the Board's missions there. Their tour and subsequent Report were decisive in precipitating far-reaching changes in the Board's Indian operations. Written in the context not only of the Board's general concerns, but of Anderson's personal preference for and an American domestic reassertion of the value of preaching over schooling, they brought about an extensive retreat from the conventional emphasis placed on English-language education.[12]

Intending to travel to India by the shortest – Suez – route to Bombay, the two Americans arrived in London on 14 August and embarked at Southampton on the next stage of their outward journey on 20 September. As Anderson's diary shows, the six intervening weeks in England and Scotland were very full. Sightseeing was not neglected. Notable preachers were listened to with varying degrees of admiration. In Cambridge, en route for Scotland, he relished a visit to Holy Trinity

[11] For Anderson and Ellis, see Porter, 'Career of William Ellis'; for Underhill, Brian Stanley, *The History of the Baptist Missionary Society 1792–1992* (Edinburgh, 1992), esp. pp. 148–54.

[12] For the fullest analyses of these changes, Hutchison, *Errand to the World*, chs 3–4, and R. Pierce Beaver, *To Advance the Gospel. Selections from the Writings of Rufus Anderson* (Grand Rapids, MI, 1967). For the origins of Anderson's critical approach to English-language education in his Levant deputation of 1843, see Paul Harris, 'Denominationalism and democracy: ecclesiastical issues underlying Rufus Anderson's Three Self Program', *NAMP Position Paper 43* (Cambridge, 1997).

Church 'where Simeon long preached', but found his pleasure at Queen's College offset by fatigue.

> There for the first time in my life I heard . . . the Church of England service chanted . . . it was beautifully done, but . . . we had to stand during the greater part of an hour and a half. . . . I tired exceedingly, and was never so grateful to our fathers for the reform they effected in the mode of public worship.

York, Edinburgh, and Chester were all enjoyed, unlike Newcastle, which was 'literally filled and covered with smoke'.[13]

However, business naturally predominated. Anderson spent his time above all in talking to experts on missions, apparently with the intention of gathering evidence and opinions to support his own views on the radical reshaping of Indian missions which he had no doubt was necessary. His questions focused particularly on the best ways of obtaining dedicated and effective native agents. Could this be most readily achieved through the English-medium schools, or by preaching and teaching in the vernacular, or by some other means? Anderson seems to have had little doubt that the reluctance of missionaries to bring on native converts (which he at once discovered on reaching London was equally a feature of LMS operations) lay in their preoccupation with English schooling and other aspects of Western culture.[14]

It was supposedly to explore, but in effect to confirm, these ideas that Anderson went to Scotland, source of great support in the Free Church for the tradition of English education vigorously advocated by Alexander Duff.[15] Meeting the Free Church's General Secretary and the chairman of its Foreign Missions Committee, he dismissed their support for the prevailing policy. 'Mere echoes of Duff', he wrote.[16] More helpful was the convenor of the established Church's Foreign Missions Committee, who, although supporting the school system, acknowledged that results so far remained few and the future looked uncertain. It was enough for Anderson to conclude that 'The Duff school rests as yet upon theory.'[17]

13 ABC 30/12, Anderson's Journal, 1, entries 27 August–4 September 1854.
14 Ibid., 15 August, conversation with Arthur Tidman (LMS Secretary).
15 Laird, *Missionaries and Education*, *passim*.
16 ABC 30/12, Anderson's Journal, 1, entry 30 August.
17 Ibid.

Most instructive of all was a chance meeting with Dr William Brown, author of a standard history of missions and long-serving Secretary of the Scottish Missionary Society. Anderson's account is worth quoting at length.

> Found the worthy Doctor, & had a very profitable interview. He is not a believer in the Duff scheme, & never has been. Says it is contrary to Scripture & reason, & he believes it will fail; but says the Scotch people must have another five-&-twenty years to try it. He would have gone against it in his history but for his personal friendship towards Dr. Duff. In the long run, he believes that far greater results will follow from a main reliance in India upon preaching. – When Dr. Duff started his plan, it was objected to by many, but the Doctor's eloquence finally carried all before him. Dr. Tweedie goes for it, & so do their missionaries in India. – This interview repays for our visit to Scotland . . . [and] is of great importance to us, & would hardly have been possible had we not been disappointed in seeing Dr. Tweedie, which was of far less importance.[18]

Back in London, Anderson went to see William Beecham, Secretary of the Wesleyan Methodist Missionary Society. 'Found Dr. B.'s views strongly tending in the direction of our own, as to the use of schools & the English language. A common sense man.'[19] A subsequent visit to the Reverend George Candy, Corresponding Secretary for the CMS Committee at Bombay, tended in the same direction. Anderson found that, as elsewhere, the social nature of the occasion meant that 'we could not enter deeply into any matter, nor talk freely & confidentially.' However, the other visitor 'showed much interest in my inquiries, & his strong common sense & piety inclined him in every sense to verge very decidedly towards our own views.' Candy's own comments and reservations about the English schools left Anderson with the sense that 'our English brethren have been forced into these high English Schools, & not willingly'; he felt the meeting had been a

[18] ABC 30/12, Anderson's Journal, 1, entry 30 August. William Brown, *The History of the Propagation of Christianity Among the Heathen Since the Reformation*, 3 vols (Edinburgh and London, 1854); William Tweedie was convenor of the Free Church's Foreign Missions Committee, 1848–62; see entries in Nigel M. de S. Cameron, ed., *Dictionary of Scottish Church History and Theology* (Edinburgh, 1993).

[19] ABC 30/12, Anderson's Journal, 1, entry 12 September 1854.

useful preparation for his encounter with the Board missionaries in Bombay.[20]

Finance, Anderson's other preoccupation, encouraged his thinking to move in the same direction. He made detailed enquiries about costs and welcomed every sign that Western ways only served to raise the costs of the missions. If English-language schooling were associated with excessive cost as well as meagre results, the case for a 'preaching' strategy was clearly strengthened. At the CMS he was struck by official concern over the generous levels of support provided for missionaries' children. 'Their making such a fund for this purpose, and saying so much about it, have long seemed to me to be ominous of evil. Let us beware!'[21] He had a 'very agreeable and profitable conversation' with the LMS Secretary, in which he learned how the Society was passing costs on to local converts and cutting provision for its own missionaries. Similar information came from the Reverend N. J. Moody from Madras, including an account of the disposal of the CMS's local press 'because it had become . . . an incubus upon the operations of the Society'. Notwithstanding Moody's very brief experience of India, this was, Anderson recorded, 'a most profitable conference'; Moody's views were 'strikingly accordant with our own'.[22]

Before he left for India Anderson received a long letter from Venn with answers to the nine questions he had put to him several weeks before.[23] The American Secretary's queries reflected the severely practical concerns evident elsewhere in his British discussions. He wished to know, for example, the CMS's 'reasons for excluding the English language from our Seminary at Copay in Ceylon & the effect of that measure'. 'How far would you be in favour of excluding the English language, as a medium of instruction from schools sustained by Missionary Societies?'; was 'training from boyhood in missionary schools . . . found to be the most effective way of obtaining Native Preachers and Pastors'?; should there be a rule 'that no school should be

[20] Ibid. For Candy, see List I, no. 411, *Church Missionary Society. Register of Missionaries and Native Clergy from 1804 to 1904* (privately printed, London, nd).

[21] Ibid., entry 16 August 1854.

[22] Ibid., entry 19 September 1854. Moody had gone out in October 1852, as Secretary of the Madras Corresponding Committee, returning with failing health in March 1854: List I, no. 448, *Church Missionary Society Register.*

[23] ABC 14/3 no.506, Venn to Anderson, 6 September 1854. Shenk, 'Rufus Anderson', pp. 169–70, refers to the copy of this letter now preserved in the CMS Archive, Birmingham University Library.

sustained in which the vernacular language is not made the grand medium of instruction'?; and could missionaries 'be much more forward, than they have been, to throw responsibility upon their native converts & Preachers'?

Venn's answers, framed with India in mind, were guarded, reflecting his own awareness of varied circumstances and a cautious distrust of regulations and standardization.[24] Although his general outlook was broadly supportive of Anderson, Venn ended his letter with an implicit reminder to him of the need to avoid hasty conclusions.

> In conclusion I will only remark that while the present era is one for the development of Missionary Principles of action, it is also one of incompetent theorizing and with a tinge of Missionary romance. It is most important to remember that principles which may apply to one Mission will often be inapplicable to a different field, as well as different stages of advancement in the same field. And beyond any principles, as we call them, we must never forget that some of the most signal successes of modern Missions have been granted not to measures devised by wisdom and skill, but to individual zeal following at the leadings of divine Providence, without regard to fixed principles of action. Whatever rules or principles we may lay down we must never lose sight of 'the glorious footsteps of divine Providence'. . . . For my own part I am more and more disposed to follow this providence than to trust to my Rules.

Anderson's encounter with Venn thus seems to have been shaped above all by concerns about missionary progress in India. These not only provided the reason for Anderson's journey; they also chimed in with the British debate then taking place among government officials as well as missionaries as to the wisdom of continuing to favour English-language higher education. The imperial government's policy set out in Sir Charles Wood's Education Despatch of 1854, which opened the way to government grants-in-aid for a wide range of private and Indian-run schools and for secular elementary education, involved a move away from the earlier policies established in the 1830s. British missions thus found themselves under pressure, not only from the doubts prompted by their own restricted successes but from the

[24] For Venn's sense of Africa's differences, see his answer to Anderson's Qu.7 about the employment of converts, and ABC 14/3 no. 509, Venn to Anderson, 2 March 1858.

actions of their own government, to reconsider their strategies.[25] Anderson's questions helped to concentrate the minds of several British missionary organizers, at the same time as their own uncertainties strongly reinforced his own scepticism about current fashions.

The conversations stimulated by the American visitor in the late summer of 1854 have a further dimension. They not only illustrate how Indian circumstances were shaping debate on the nature of 'native agency'. They demonstrate how much of that discussion focused not on questions of ecclesiastical polity or episcopacy, but on an altogether lower level of native agency and evangelization. They also reveal the extent to which mission organizers were pushed along by the pressures of finance and by popular perceptions of their methods, irrespective of the implications these might have for the structure of emergent churches.

II

Anderson arrived in Bombay on 3 November 1854. Mixing with the Free Church of Scotland and CMS missionaries as well as those of the American Board, he very soon found his worst suspicions confirmed. Conversions associated with the English schools seemed negligible, yet teaching in English remained essentially unquestioned. 'What an infatuation on this subject has come over the minds of missionaries in India!'[26] Reaching the American station at Ahmadnagar – 'the centre for many years of much interest to my thoughts and feelings' – where the Board's missionaries were all assembled, Anderson found conditions very discouraging. In addition to 'the backwardness exhibited by some brethren to come into necessary reforms', 'we find very little attempt at organization in these missions, with a view to the future independence of these churches.' The extent to which mission funds were used for temporal aid to Indian converts was 'painfully disheartening'.[27]

After several days of preliminary meetings, Anderson spent the last

[25] Andrew Porter, 'Scottish Missions and Education in Nineteenth-Century India: The Changing Face of Trusteeship', in Andrew Porter and Robert Holland, eds, *Theory and Practice in the History of European Expansion overseas* (London, 1988), pp. 35–57; David W. Savage, 'Evangelical Education Policy in Britain and India, 1857–60', *Journal of Imperial and Commonwealth History*, 22, 3 (1994), pp. 432–61.

[26] ABC 30/12, Anderson's Journal, II, entry 12 November 1854.

[27] Ibid., entries 20–2 November, 4–13 December 1854.

week of November touring the district. There then followed a month of often painful argument and discussion. This finally brought the results Anderson wanted. It was decided to do away with mission compounds as fast as possible, and to abandon any school 'in which the vernacular was not the general medium of instruction'.[28] The general meeting begun on 20 November finally wound up on Christmas Day, leaving Anderson exhausted but pleased that self-support, vernacular training, and evangelism by preaching were at last in the ascendant.

This was a process to be repeated at successive mission centres. At Satara, the large mission house, he felt, was 'a sad specimen of thoughtless missionary extravagance'. 'The sooner this is sold the better.' An encounter there with a missionary of the Scottish Free Church left him quite bemused. 'A most singular missionary. He has no confidence in preaching, and does not preach. Has a school. Very eccentric.'[29] Even as Anderson left Bombay and journeyed south, meeting missionaries everywhere along the way, there were no longer any doubts in his mind. 'Alas, what mischief has grown in India out of the schools system! The *success* is most of it fictitious and deceptive.' 'My patience is all gone with the use of the English language in attempting to convey a knowledge of the Gospel to the poor degraded [people?] of this country.'[30]

His next general meeting, at the Madura mission from 20 February to 17 March, followed the same pattern, as did that sitting at Jaffna for three weeks in April and May. Anderson found himself time and again confronted with 'English – English – English!' In the seminary at Jaffna, a good man like the Principal was being wasted because the 'native teachers and pupils have managed to throw almost every book not English out of use. Their whole object is to acquire the English language in order to better their circumstances.' However, although Anderson regarded the 'nature and magnitude of the evil' as only too obvious, he was less confident of a remedy beyond removing from any responsibility those missionaries whose influence was 'too much in the direction of science and English'.[31] Finding missionaries disheartened by existing policies, not least among those he encountered belonging to the CMS, he stuck to his agenda. At Jaffna, for example, on the subject

[28] ABC 30/12, Anderson's Journal, II, entry 15 December 1854.
[29] Ibid., entry 29 December 1854.
[30] Ibid., entries 29–30 December 1854.
[31] Ibid., III, entry 6 April 1855.

of schools, Anderson opened with a speech 'to show that their present system was destructive of all village operations; that too many were educated beyond the village demand, so that they had to emigrate for a market and none returned; that such a proportionate number of academics in New England would be ruinous; etc.'[32] Thus his message and his remedy became standardized. He called for modest missionary establishments, for an end to boarding schools and the reduction of seminaries, for vernacular education to be provided in village schools, and for catechists and congregations to be quite distinct from the schools, part of a separate 'evangelical system'.

After bringing the Jaffna meetings to a close, Anderson summed up his conclusions.

> Experience has shown that it is by means of village churches and pastors, chiefly, that the gospel becomes rooted in the soil, and makes them belong not to the mission but to the people. With them stands connected the village vernacular school, for the children of the church, where the rising generation will learn to connect gospel ideas and sentiments with their mother tongue. . . . Here too will be the house of worship in native style. . . . All native, yet all christian. How much better this plain building . . . than the lofty wall and vaulted roof and vast dimensions, Gothic, Grecian, Roman, of which so many have been erected in former times, and serve generally as monuments of disappointed expectations of the wonders to be wrought through schools.'[33]

III

While there is something of the iconoclast's pursuit in Anderson's record of his Indian journey, he took no delight in that aspect of his work. The meetings were not only very laborious, but 'in some respects very unpleasant. I shrink from so much fault-finding with the missionary plans and proceedings of my brethren.'[34] However, his deputation is the more notable in retrospect, and was almost certainly the more bearable for him, because it coincided with similar investigations by several British missionary societies of their own Indian operations.

32 Ibid., entry 4 May 1855.
33 Ibid., entry 24 May 1855.
34 Ibid., entry 11 March 1855.

On the ship to Bombay, 'a sort of Noah's ark as to the variety of characters on board',[35] Anderson found himself a fellow passenger not only with Marshman, son of the famous Serampore missionary, but also E. B. Underhill, Secretary of the Baptist Missionary Society in charge of foreign affairs.[36] As part of his determination to revive BMS activity in India, Underhill's starting point was to put the missionary affairs of Calcutta in order. Major aspects of this were to reduce the significance of the Serampore press which had become a commercial enterprise dominating the mission's activities, and to encourage the local election and support of Indian pastors. BMS troubles with the press evoked precisely the kind of situation which alarmed Anderson, who subsequently felt that in the Board's own mission at Bombay he had not done enough to curtail their commercial printing operations.[37] He was no less dispirited to learn from Underhill of the tendency for missionaries in India to be diverted into preaching to European congregations. In this he saw a problem for all the societies, exacerbated by missionaries being drawn into English schooling and congregating together in the cities.[38]

Anderson got on well with Underhill, who in turn appears to have valued the American's views. In May and June 1855, when both men were in Ceylon, Underhill wrote to the two Americans, anxious to share impressions and thoughts with them before he wrote his Report home.[39] Later he sent on to Anderson copies of his Calcutta Reports, including that in which he decided after all not to break up the Serampore press. After staying at Serampore, he emerged far more ready than Anderson to preserve a place for English in the training of native preachers.[40] In other respects, however, his views chimed in with Anderson's. Worried by the schools, he waxed enthusiastic about the 'most novel result' of his meetings, namely 'the proposal to employ some of the best native preachers as missionaries'.

[35] IABC 30/12, Anderson's Journal, II, entry 17 October 1854.

[36] For Underhill and India, see Stanley, *History of the Baptist Missionary Society*, pp. 149–54.

[37] ABC 30/12, Anderson's Journal, III, entry 14–18 May 1855, at Jaffna, where he noted 'Letters from Bombay. The mission there still in great danger from the press.'

[38] Ibid., 2, entry 29 September 1854. For a contrary view, see Stock's defence in E. T. Stock, *The History of the Church Missionary Society*, 3 vols (London, 1899), 2, p. 520.

[39] ABC 14/3, nos 494–5, Underhill to Anderson, 21 May, and to Thompson, 9 June 1855.

[40] ABC 14/3, no. 497, Underhill to Anderson, 7 August 1856.

I have begun to act upon it . . . as opening the way for the independent action of the native church. I am more and more convinced that many evils follow the state of dependence in which they have hitherto been kept. Very many of the complaints of the character of converts originate in this. We have all the faults and results of pauperism, without getting one step towards independency; indeed only rendering it impossible.[41]

This was a correspondence and friendship which both continued after they had returned home, and it was renewed when Underhill was able to visit Boston in 1860 on the way back to London from a deputation visit to the West Indies.[42]

Shortly after leaving Ceylon, Anderson met in Madras the Reverend William Knight, one of Venn's Secretarial colleagues in the CMS, who had already 'been some time in India'. Knight had been sent out to resolve the problems afflicting the Society's Ceylon Corresponding Committee. Pleased to discover 'Our experiences singularly harmonious with that of the Church Miss. Society', Anderson gave Knight copies of his first Report on the Mahratta mission.[43] When Anderson subsequently supplied further material, Knight not only reciprocated in kind but provided him with introductions to CMS men in Bengal, including the Reverend James Long. Long, wrote Knight, 'is all for the vernacular', and knew more of the natives at Calcutta than anyone else. Knight described his experience in India as very similar to Anderson's own, and to those of Underhill with whom he too had had contact.[44]

Along with Underhill and Knight, Anderson found another valuable informant in Joseph Mullens, a member of the LMS's Bhowanipore mission at Calcutta since his arrival in India in 1844, and later the Society's Foreign Secretary. He later recalled how he was 'somewhat intimate with Drs Mullens and Ewart', discussing with them at length the problems of evangelizing the large cities and what was needed for this purpose in addition to the schools, a question 'not then answered

[41] Ibid., no. 496, Underhill to Anderson, 26 October 1855.

[42] See ibid., nos 498–501, Underhill to Anderson, 5 April 1859, 14 July, 14 August, and 12 December 1860. See also later correspondence (1861–70) in ABC 14/4.

[43] ABC 30/12, Anderson's Journal, III, entries 11–16 June 1855; Stock, 2, p. 283.

[44] ABC 14/3, no. 271, Knight to Anderson, 5 July 1855. For Long, see *CMS Register*, List I Entry 301; and G. A. Oddie, *Social Protest in India: British Missionaries and Social Reforms, 1850–1900* (Delhi, 1979). For Long's views on vernacular education, see Savage, 'Evangelical education policy', p. 443.

to my satisfaction'.[45] After Anderson left India for home, Mullens sent after him details of the proceedings of the LMS's own local conference on education. Dismissing the dissenting minority, Mullens emphasised how 'the great *majority* held vernacular preaching to be *the* most important branch of missionary labour. . . .'[46] As with Underhill so with Mullens, discussion in India were continued in correspondence; again, the two men apparently reinforced each other's views as to the priority of vernacular rural missions and the limited place for English education in the cities.[47] Mullens clearly felt the growth of a consensus which embraced the American Board, the London Missionary Society and the Baptist Missionary Society on these issues of missionary strategy, native agency and training.[48]

These exchanges may be regarded as a part of the rethinking which led Henry Venn, under the further prompting of the Indian Mutiny in 1857, to take the initiative which led to the establishment of the Christian Vernacular Education Society in 1858.[49] It was a venture which Anderson, along with the other Missionary Society secretaries in London, was happy to support, both for the assistance which it gave to selected schools and for its concern to promote 'a cheap, efficient Native Christian Agency'.[50]

CONCLUSION

What was the significance of these Indian questions for mid-nineteenth-century missionary strategy? Some contemporary debates about missionary strategy were evidently of little relevance to Indian circumstances. In missionary eyes, the possibility of linking commerce with Christianity, which to David Livingstone and others seemed to hold out great hopes in Africa, had in India demonstrated little

[45] Anderson to Dr John Wilson, 24 November 1868, ABC 30/18,2, fos 178–81; for Mullens, J. Sibree, ed., *London Missionary Society: A Register of Missionaries, Deputations, etc., from 1796 to 1923* (London, 1923), no. 459.

[46] ABC 14/3, no. 323, Mullens to Anderson, 22 September 1855.

[47] ABC 14/3 no. 325, Mullens to Anderson, 8 December 1856.

[48] Ibid., no. 326, Mullens to Anderson, 9 September 1857. Correspondence continued steadily thereafter (see ABC 14/4; and ABC 30/18, Anderson, Private Letters 1867–71), and Anderson eventually arranged for Mullens to receive a D.D. from Williams College: see ABC 14/4 no. 219, Mullens to Anderson, 17 October 1861.

[49] ABC 14/3, nos 269–70, letters from Knight to Anderson, both 31 May 1858.

[50] Ibid., nos 485–6, H. Carre Tucker (Secretary, CVES) to Anderson, 18 September 1858, and 22 January 1859. For the formation of the CVES and its early difficulties, Savage, 'Evangelical education policy', pp. 444–5.

attraction or transforming power. The debate about native agency in India in the 1850s was also not one for which worries about episcopacy had much significance. The established Anglican Church already had bishops in place; even among its supporters the idea of a 'missionary bishop' was not regarded as appropriate for India.

As we have seen, much missionary discussion was therefore concentrated at a lower and more immediately practical level. The challenge to English language education which one can see developing in Anderson's tour of the Board's Indian stations, reflected a broader disquiet which had been growing in the missionary community with the meagre results of 'the Bengal system'. It would of course be impossible to claim that Anderson's initiatives alone brought this process to a head, any more than that Joseph Mullens's compilation in 1851 of what became a standard statistical survey of Indian mission progress first alerted missionaries to the problem.[51] However, it seems highly likely that the American Secretary's determined advocacy of change, and his views on the direction it should take, helped other missionaries and society organizers to crystallize their own views. Perhaps he even helped sustain Venn's own commitment to vernacular training in the face of the earlier English tide.[52] Certainly Anderson found his own thoughts clarified by his growing awareness and encouragement of the misgivings which others, not least missionaries on the ground, were experiencing.

With the passage of another decade after Anderson's return to Boston, attitudes on all sides seemed to mellow. At Bombay early in 1855, Anderson had written of his 'impression that the Scotch brethren have a rather sad feeling connected with our visit to this country, though they are kind and polite – Dr. Wilson especially so, no wonder. We do certainly object to copying their example.'[53] Recalling those views in a letter to Joseph Mullens, now LMS Foreign Secretary, as he sat down to follow up his recent lectures on missions with a history of the American Board's work, Anderson seemed perhaps less single-minded.

[51] Joseph Mullens, *The Results of Missionary Labour in India* (London, 1852).

[52] Cf. Williams, *Ideal of the Self-Governing Church*, pp. 19–20.

[53] ABC 30/12, Anderson's Journal, II, entry 5 January 1855. Dr John Wilson (1804–75), outstanding Free Church missionary along with Duff, who ended his career as Vice-Chancellor of the University of Bombay: see George Smith, *The Life of John Wilson, D.D. F.R.S.* (London, 1878).

> You are aware that I did not take, when in India, and I have never taken, ground against great English schools in great Indian cities. On the contrary, I have regarded them as among the desirable agencies for planting the Gospel in such cities. Still I feel, and, as at present advised, much urge, that the reliance upon them has been too great, *comparatively*, at Bombay, and that there should have been in our own Bombay mission, a far greater direct effort to make converts, and plant and build up *selfgoverned, selfsupporting, self-propagating native churches, with native pastors in each church.*[54]

Anderson also wrote directly to Dr Wilson in Bombay in a similarly more flexible and conciliatory vein.[55] Anderson by this time seems to have moved closer to the view advocated by Underhill in 1856 after spending almost two years in India. Underhill was by then more inclined than when he and Anderson had travelled out to India together to argue against any resolute rejection of the English language. This he did on the grounds that vernacular Bengali was now 'being rapidly reduced to elegance and literary power by the transfusion into it of English thought and English science, and this by the hands of Bengalis who owe their culture to the acquisition of the English language'. The way to improve the preaching of missionaries and evangelists lay not in relying on their knowledge of the vernacular, but in obliging them to study 'the popular books which are everywhere in the hands of the people'.[56] Effective evangelism and local church growth required both languages.

Anderson's argument nevertheless remained in essence that English education as the principal means of instruction was inimical to the development of viable local churches. In his reply, Mullens, after expressing pleasure at the publication of Anderson's lectures, noted that even the Scots were now shifting their ground in the direction of vernacular training and evangelization. Duff, in lecturing to the Free Church students in Edinburgh, like Anderson at Andover Theological Seminary, was 'embracing within his course the Evangelising System both at home and abroad'. Evidently, felt Mullens, 'missionary plans and agencies [have] now acquired an experience which may now be

[54] ABC 30/18, 2, Private Letters 1867–71, fos 188–90, Anderson to Mullens, 12 December 1868. Rufus Anderson, *Foreign Missions: Their Relations and Claims* (Boston, 1869).

[55] ABC 30/18, 2, fos 178–81, Anderson to Dr John Wilson, 24 November 1868.

[56] ABC 14/3, no. 497, Underhill to Anderson, 7 August 1856 (from Serampore).

systematised and freely discussed with a view to render our entire work more efficient.'[57]

The implications of this mid-century debate about language and schooling for the nature of the Church and the spread of Christianity were clear and important. Agents and the local churches were to be kept in touch with their people through exploitation of the vernacular, the restriction of the mission's material support for agents' work, and insistence on a suitably modest scale for missionary establishments. The villages were to become a much more important target than they had been, and the limited contribution of English language education even to the evangelization of the large cities like Bombay was to be admitted. Examination of Anderson's deputation of 1854–5 reveals missionaries who understood that, especially perhaps for non-episcopal churches, the key to a vigorous native agency and threats to the local advancement of the Christian Church might lie less in the nature of ecclesiastical structures, than in the language of evangelism. In local wishes to acquire English, and in British or American missionaries' uneasiness with the vernacular languages, lay two important roots of continued missionary control.[58]

King's College, London

[57] ABC 14/4, unnumbered, Mullens to Anderson, 30 January 1869.

[58] For a different interpretation of Anderson's views and ABCFM policy, in which their concern with financial economy and self-support drove out self-government and perpetuated missionary control, see Harris, 'Denominationalism and democracy'.

WHY PROTESTANT CHURCHES? THE AMERICAN BOARD AND THE EASTERN CHURCHES: MISSION AMONG 'NOMINAL' CHRISTIANS (1820–70)

by H. L. MURRE-VAN DEN BERG

INTRODUCTION

> In Palestine, Syria, the provinces of Asia Minor, Armenia, Georgia, and Persia, though Mohammedan countries, there are many thousands of Jews, and many thousands of Christians, at least in name. But the whole mingled population is in a state of deplorable ignorance and degradation, – destitute of the means of divine knowledge, and bewildered with vain imaginations and strong delusions.

THUS wrote Rufus Anderson, in his *History of the Missions to the Oriental Churches*, when he looked back on the start of mission work in 1819.[1] Anderson had been the foreign secretary of the American Board of Commissioners for Foreign Missions for more than thirty years (1832–66), and his words illustrate the opinions held by many of the missionaries as well as administrators of the American Board. Such opinions inspired the American Board, consisting mainly of Congregationalists and Presbyterians, to start mission work among the Christians and Jews in Western Asia. It is their work among the Eastern Christians that this paper examines.[2]

Earlier research into the history of Protestant mission work among the Eastern Churches usually stressed that despite the fact that this mission work was inspired by a rather negative evaluation of the state in which the Eastern Churches found themselves, its missionaries at the same

[1] Rufus Anderson, *History of the Missions of the American Board of Commissioners for Foreign Missions to the Oriental Churches* (Boston, 1873 [I], 1872 [II]; 2nd edn Boston, 1875 [III and IV], same pagination).

[2] In the following I will use the designation 'Eastern' to refer to all ancient Christian Churches of Western Asia, including the Chalcedonian Churches of the Greek tradition as well as the non-Chalcedonian 'Oriental' Churches, like the Armenian and Syrian-Orthodox Church. The Church of the East, representing a separate non-Chalcedonian tradition, is included too.

time strongly believed in the possibility of reform. It is somewhat surprising, therefore, that such authors as Mary Walker in her article of 1976 and Peter Kawerau in his fundamental work, *Amerika und die orientalischen Kirchen*, of 1958, single out the missionaries' negative opinions of the Eastern Churches as being the primary reason for the emergence of separate Protestant Churches. David Kerr, in his well-balanced article on proselytism in West Asia, argues along the same lines, although he clearly is aware of other elements which played a role.[3] Recent research by Habib Badr on the American Board Mission in Beirut gives a much more detailed picture of the developments leading to a separate Protestant Church. He describes a range of other elements which might have influenced this process.[4] His findings in many ways are confirmed by my own research into the history of the mission in Urmia in northwestern Persia, and I was therefore encouraged to reconsider the matter of the emergence of Protestant Churches alongside the Eastern Churches.

In the following I will present an overview of three missions of the American Board in Western Asia: in Beirut, Constantinople (as Istanbul was consistently called by missionaries and Eastern Christians alike), and Urmia. I hope to shed some new light on the factors that gave rise to the formation of Protestant Churches in Western Asia, and in this way to contribute to the history of Protestantism in the Middle East within the context of the history of Protestant missions on the one hand and of the Eastern Churches on the other.

BEIRUT

After the American Board was established in 1810 and missionaries had been sent to India and the Sandwich Islands (Hawaii), the mission in Syria, then part of the Ottoman Empire, became the first of the Board's missions in Western Asia. Its missionaries arrived in 1819, worked in Jerusalem for a while, and after a few years decided to settle in Beirut.

[3] Mary A. Walker, 'The American Board and the Oriental Churches. A Brief Survey of Policy Based on Official Documents', in *International Review of Mission*, 56 (1976), pp. 214–23; Peter Kawerau, *Amerika und die orientalischen Kirchen. Ursprung und Anfang der Amerikanischen Mission unter den Nationalkirchen Westasiens* (Berlin, 1958); and David A. Kerr, 'Mission and Proselytism: A Middle East Perspective', *IBMR*, 20/1 (1996), pp. 12–22.

[4] Habib Badr, 'Mission to "Nominal Christians": The Policy and Practice of the American Board of Commissioners for Foreign Missions and its Missionaries Concerning Eastern Churches which led to the Organization of a Protestant Church in Beirut (1819–1848)' (Ph.D. thesis, Princeton, NJ, 1992).

It was here that they were able to establish good relations with some local clergy and with other members of the various Eastern Christian communities present in this city. The missionaries set up an educational system, distributed religious pamphlets, started translation work, and set up a printing press. The actual evangelizing work was done mainly by what they called 'conversational preaching', that is, informal exposition of the Scriptures in the missionaries' homes or in other meeting places.[5]

Almost all the Eastern Churches were represented in Beirut. The missionaries met with Greek Orthodox of the Chalcedonian patriarchate of Antioch, Greek Catholics, also called Melkites, Maronites, Armenians, and Roman Catholics of the Latin rite. They further came in contact with the Arabic-speaking Muslim population and with Druze communities.

Some of the missionaries had some previous knowledge of the history and doctrines of the Eastern Churches. William Gooddell, who started work in Beirut in 1823 and later was transferred to Constantinople, had written a paper on the Armenian Church in 1819, while he was still a student in Andover Theological Seminary.[6] Later missionaries among the Eastern Christians could make use of the work of Eli Smith and H. G. O. Dwight, who published their *Missionary Researches in Armenia* in 1834.[7] Naturally, the first generations of missionaries had had hardly any personal encounters with Eastern Christians before leaving America.

In Beirut, opposition to Protestant mission work arose almost immediately. This opposition was located mainly within Churches with Roman Catholic connections, such as the Maronite and Melkite Churches.[8] In 1825, Jonas King, one of the American missionaries, had his strongly anti-Roman-Catholic 'Farewell Letter' translated into

[5] For the history of this mission, including further biographical references, see Badr, 'Mission to "Nominal Christians"'; Kawerau, *Amerika*; and A. L. Tibawi, *American Interests in Syria, 1800–1901. A Study of Educational, Literary and Religious Work* (Oxford, 1966).

[6] E. D. G. Prime, *Forty Years in the Turkish Empire; or, Memoirs of Rev. William Goodell, D.D., Late Missionary of the A.B.C.F.M. at Constantinople* (New York, 1876), pp. 64–5: 'The History and Present State of Armenia as a Missionary Field'.

[7] Eli Smith and H. G. O. Dwight, *Missionary Researches in Armenia: Including a Journey through Asia Minor, and into Georgia and Persia, with a Visit to the Nestorian and Chaldean Christians of Oormiah and Salmas* (London, 1834). For this work, Smith and Dwight made use of the work of the Maronite scholar J. S. Assemani, *Bibliotheca Orientalis* (Rome, 1719), which was one of the most extensive studies on Eastern Christianity then available.

[8] Badr, 'Mission to "Nominal Christians"', pp. 90–4; Julius Richter, *A History of Protestant Missions in the Near East* (New York, 1910 [repr. New York, 1970]), p. 187.

Arabic. In a rather polemical tone King separated himself from the Roman Catholic, Maronite, and other Eastern Churches. Hereafter, opposition from these quarters increased. In later years, especially after 1834, a decidedly less polemical tone was assumed by missionaries such as Eli Smith, cited above. Opposition, however, did not cease.[9] In the thirties, one of the early converts, the Maronite priest Asad as-Shidyak, was put in prison by the Maronite patriarch and subsequently died in the dungeon of a monastery in 1839.[10] In 1909, Julius Richter, in one of the earliest works on the Protestant missions in Western Asia, saw this incident as a clear step on the way to the formation of Protestant Churches. He concluded his historical description: 'This experience had the advantage or disadvantage, according to one's point of view, of leaving the Protestant Mission in no doubt as to whether a reformation of these Oriental Churches from within, with the help of their authorities, was possible.'[11] However, this interpretation is not without its difficulties. Since Shidyak died in 1839 and a separate church did not come into existence until 1848, it clearly was not the death of Shidyak, nor, for that matter, other measures that the Eastern clergy took, which made the missionaries change their mind about the formation of Protestant Churches. For that, we have to look in another direction.

In 1827, a mission church had been established in Beirut. This body was intended to function as the church of the missionaries themselves, not as a church for local Christians. Surprisingly, however, one of the reasons for converting the missionaries' fellowship into a regular church had been the request of two Armenian converts to be admitted to the Protestant worship.[12] What made their case peculiar was the fact that they had left the Armenian Church well before the missionaries had arrived in the country. Their admittance to the mission church, therefore, was not seen as a deviation from the earlier policy of working towards reform of the Eastern Churches. In the same period, the missionaries advised other converts, or potential converts, to stay in their original Churches as long as possible. In the eyes of the missionaries, these early converts were to be the initiators of reform within the Eastern Churches. None but the Easterners themselves could effectively challenge these old institutions. In the early thirties,

[9] Badr, 'Mission to "Nominal Christians"', pp. 119–25.

[10] Kawerau, *Amerika*, pp. 488–91.

[11] Richter, *History*, pp. 188–9.

[12] Badr, 'Mission to "Nominal Christians"', pp. 100–3.

this policy was further developed by the missionaries Smith and Goodell. At that time it was supported also by foreign secretary Rufus Anderson in Boston, on behalf of the Prudential Committee of the American Board. He agreed that it was not the missionaries' duty to attack ecclesiastical structures or practices, that is, the 'outward forms' of the Christians amongst whom they were working. Such a method would only incite opposition. Rather, the missionaries should labour towards a revival of the heart, a revival worked by the Holy Spirit. A reform of the outer forms would follow in due time. Ecclesiology was made subservenient to soteriology – so Badr summarizes the opinions of the missionaries.[13]

Before these idealistic ideas could be put into practice, the missionaries were overtaken by the events of the early forties. In a politically unstable situation, Druze communities were exploring the possibilities of conversion to Christianity. The missionaries were very reluctant to accede to their wishes, because they feared that other than purely spiritual reasons were at stake. And while the missionaries tried to keep the Druzes from associating themselves too much with the Protestant missionaries, they hardly could report any succesful conversions from the side of the Eastern Christians. Similar difficulties in the Greek mission made Anderson want to visit the mission fields in Western Asia in person. This visit took place in the years 1843 and 1844. By that time, Anderson's ideas on mission policy had ripened. Although he still held to the possibility of reform, he more and more began to equate the missions to Eastern Churches with those in other places, to the missions among the 'heathen'. This included a growing emphasis on a 'native' church of 'native' converts, led by a 'native' ministry. Ultimately, the implementation of such a policy would lead to Protestant Churches being formed alongside the Eastern Churches. If that perhaps was not feasible for the time being, at least something like what Anderson called 'formal preaching' (in a public place, with a congregation – thus: opposed to the 'conversational' preaching current in Beirut) should be introduced. He further stressed that preaching and evangelization should always have priority over other activities of a mission, such as education and printing. Educational and literary activities were allowed only as far as they contributed to the education of a local Protestant clergy.[14]

[13] Badr, 'Mission to "Nominal Christians"', p. 167.

[14] Rufus Anderson, 'Report to the Prudential Committee of a Visit to the Missions in the

Anderson's visit to Beirut convinced both himself and the missionaries that *here* the time for reform was over:

> It was agreed, that the grand aim of our mission is of course the converting of men to God; that the preaching of the gospel is the great, divinely appointed means to this end; that whenever and wherever there are small companies of natives ready to make a credible profession of piety, they are to be recognized as churches.[15]

Thus the way was paved for the formation of a Protestant Church in Syria. Political disturbances and lack of potential church members, that is, of people 'truly converted', however, made the missionaries hesitate to take further steps. It was only in 1848 that a small church of about sixteen members was constituted. Badr suggests that without further pressure from the Board and the foreign secretary the formation of a Protestant church in Beirut probably would have taken place even later than that.[16] Ussama Makdisi, in an interesting article on the introduction of 'Evangelical Modernity' in Syria, suggests that the missionaries' reluctance to form 'native' churches should be explained by their distrust of the Syrian converts. Although it cannot be denied that the missionaries in Beirut were rather cautious about the supposed conversions of their followers, I would say that Badr's work clearly shows that the missionaries' sincere wish for reformation of the Eastern Churches must be considered to be of at least equal importance in the formation of Protestant Churches.[17]

In summary, I would suggest that in the case of Beirut, it was the policy of the Board on the Eastern Churches, as advocated by Anderson, which played a decisive role in the formation of a Protestant Church. Opposition from the Eastern Churches did not so much stimulate the formation of a separate church, as effectively limit the number of potential converts. The opinions of the missionaries

Levant', also 'A Letter to the Committee from the Rev. Dr. Hawes' (Boston, 1844). On Anderson and the influence of his mission policy, see R. Pierce Beaver, 'Rufus Anderson 1796–1880. To Evangelize, Not Civilize', in Gerald H. Anderson, Robert T. Coote *et al.*, *Mission Legacies. Biographical Studies of Leaders of the Modern Missionary Movement* (Maryknoll, NY, 1994), pp. 548–53, and William R. Hutchison, *Errand to the World: American Protestant Thought and Foreign Missions* (Chicago, 1987), pp. 62–90.

15 Anderson, 'Report', p. 25.

16 Badr, 'Mission to "Nominal Christians"', pp. 275–80.

17 Ussama Makdisi, 'Reclaiming the Land of the Bible: Missionaries, Secularism, and Evangelical Modernity', *AHR*, 102–3 (1997), pp. 680–713.

themselves probably would have allowed for working amidst the Eastern Churches for some time longer.

CONSTANTINOPLE

The mission among the Armenians of Constantinople started in 1831, when William Goodell, one of the missionaries of Beirut, was transferred to that town. At that time, a strong reform movement within the Armenian community had taken hold of clergy and lay people alike. This explains why the proposals by the American missionaries to establish schools and a printing establishment were warmly welcomed. Under Patriarch Stepan III (1831–9 and 1840–1) the Protestant missionaries in general were allowed to proceed undisturbed. The number of Armenians interested in the American activities steadily grew, and the missionaries looked forward to the day when the Armenian Church would undergo a more thorough reform.[18]

However, Patriarch Stepan's successors, Asduadsadur II (1841–4) and especially Matteos (1844–8), began to oppose the mission work. During his 1843–4 trip, Anderson also visited the missionaries in Constantinople. He concluded: 'The reformation among the Armenians is eminently *evangelical*.'[19] Despite this positive judgement, he was not entirely convinced that the formation of a separate church could be avoided: 'these questions in all their relations and bearing appear not to have been fully settled in the minds of the missionaries even up to the time of our arrival among them'[20] – and neither, apparently, were these questions settled *during* Anderson's visit. Whether indeed the

[18] For a recent evaluation of the influence of ABCFM policy on the mission among the Armenians, see Paul Harris, 'Denominationalism and democracy: ecclesiastical issues underlying Rufus Anderson's Three Self Program' (unpublished paper presented at the North Atlantic Missiology Project Consultation in Madison, Wisconsin, 2–4 November, 1997, *NAMP Position Papers*, 43). For an overview of the start of the mission work, up to the establishment of a separate Protestant Church in Constantinople, see Thomas Otakar Kutvirt, 'The Emergence and Acceptance of Armenia as a Legitimate American Missionary Field', *Armenian Review* 37 (1984), no. 3–147, pp. 7–32 and 'The Development of the Mission to the Armenians at Constantinople through 1846', *Armenian Review*, 37 (1984), 4–148, pp. 31–62. For older overviews of the history of this mission, see Prime, *Forty Years*, and Leon Arpee, *The Armenian Awakening. A History of the Armenian Church, 1820–1860* (Chicago and London, 1909). The chapters in the latter book concerning Armenian Protestantism were later re-published as Leon Arpee, *A Century of Armenian Protestantism, 1846–1946* (New York, 1946).

[19] Anderson, 'Report', p. 14.

[20] Ibid., p. 26.

missionaries in Constantinople, like those in Beirut, began to reckon with the necessity of establishing a separate Protestant Church after Anderson's visit, is a matter of uncertainty, but it seems clear that, contrary to Beirut, where almost no converts were available, in Constantinople a church could have been formed right away. Further study of archival material should reveal whether the missionaries just waited for a better opportunity to do so, or were still reluctant in view of their hopes for a reformation of the Armenian community as a whole.[21] Whatever might have been the private opinions of the missionaries on the formation of a Protestant Church, a change in policy became apparent only after Patriarch Matteos, who became patriarch in 1844, set himself to bring the evangelically-influenced Armenians – said to number about 8,000! – back into his fold. Although he succeeded in bringing back the majority of them, some refused. Early in 1846, Matteos decided to excommunicate these members.[22]

This had severe consequences on the daily lives of the Armenians, since excommunication from the Armenian Church implied exclusion from the Armenian millet as well. Those who were excommunicated lost their legal status in the Ottoman Empire and with this, most ways of earning a living. When this happened to the early converts, the missionaries decided to form a Protestant church, which began with forty members. They then proceeded to help them to obtain official status. They succeeded in this, thanks to the efforts of the English ambassador, Lord Stratford Canning. The latter had some influence at the Sultan's court and had been interested in religious policy matters for some time. In 1846, he succeeded in obtaining official recognition for the Protestants. This was followed in 1850 by recognition of the Protestant millet, and in 1856 by the Hatti Humayun in which freedom of religion was granted to all subjects of the Sultan.[23]

What is interesting about the mission among the Armenians is that for quite a long period reform seemed to be a real possibility. This made the missionaries rather careful in their contacts with the

[21] On this issue, see Kutvirt, 'The Mission to Armenians', p. 58. According to Kutvirt, the missionaries from 1844 onwards began to work towards a separate Protestant Church, even if no concrete steps were taken before 1846. The same is suggested by Arpee, *The Armenian Awakening*, pp. 161–3.

[22] Kawerau, *Amerika*, pp. 535–40.

[23] Prime, *Forty Years*, pp. 315–22.

Armenian clergy. Even Anderson, who expressed a clear preference for separate churches, did not force the missionaries into a separatist policy. That reform seemed possible was at least partly due to the fact that at the time of the missionaries' arrival reform was already going on. The Armenians had been searching for ways to modernize and reform their community, for which the American missionaries readily offered their assistance. In hindsight, it seems highly unlikely that such reform would have been possible without schism, but one can hardly blame the missionaries for having hoped to avoid a rupture. It certainly is telling that as soon as the number of 'Evangelicals' began to rise, opposition too began to increase.

URMIA

In 1835, the missionaries Justin Perkins and Asahel Grant, and their wives, Charlotte Bass and Judith S. Campbell, started a mission in Urmia, in northeastern Iran.[24] This mission was directed at the 'Nestorians' who lived in this region. The Nestorian Church, or better, the Church of the East, shares the Syriac heritage with the Syrian Orthodox and the Maronites, and therefore often is called 'East-Syrian'. Since the late nineteenth century the designation 'Assyrian' has been generally preferred to 'East-Syrian' or 'Nestorian'. During most of its existence the Church of the East was separated from the Western Church dogmatically and geographically, and after Tamerlane's destructive campaigns of the fourteenth century lived a rather isolated existence in the northeastern parts of the Ottoman and the northwestern parts of the Persian empires.

The Assyrians of Persia warmly welcomed the missionaries, and for almost ten years they were able to proceed with their work practically unhindered. The missionaries founded schools for boys and for girls, translated the Bible into the modern vernacular, were invited to preach in Assyrian churches, established a printing press, and distributed religious and educational literature. Assyrian clergy – deacons, priests, and bishops – were employed by the mission and assisted in most of

[24] On the history of this mission, see John Joseph, *The Nestorians and their Muslim Neighbors. A Study of Western Influence on their Relations* (Princeton, New Jersey, 1961), and H. L. Murre-van den Berg, *From a Spoken to a Written Language. The Introduction and Development of Literary Urmia Aramaic in the Nineteenth Century* (Leiden, 1999). On the early period, see in particular Justin Perkins, *A Residence of Eight Years in Persia among the Nestorian Christians with Notices of the Muhammedans* (Andover, 1843).

the work. However, despite all the sympathy the missionaries experienced from the Assyrians, and despite the good progress of their educational and literary work, they could point to barely two or three persons who in their opinion had become 'truly converted' as a result of their labour.

In 1844, after nearly ten years of undisturbed mission work, this period came to an end. The Patriarch and his family, who represented the religious and political power of the Assyrians, began to oppose the missionaries. In order to prevent repercussions for Assyrians who worked with the mission, the missionaries decided to discontinue most of their activities. The opposition forced them to face a number of issues of mission politics that had not been adequately dealt with before. The opposition of the patriarchal family, which initially was caused by socio-political circumstances, was further fueled by a discussion between the Patriarch and the missionaries concerning financial support for the family and the employment of certain bishops. This matter became rather complicated and caused heated discussion among the missionaries themselves. In the same year, the latter were also accused of proselytism by the Persian government, probably at the instigation of French diplomats who were trying to act for French Roman Catholic missionaries in the same region. The Protestants were able to refute this accusation. They were supported in this by the Assyrians, who confirmed that so far the Protestants had not made one proselyte and had never even tried to make one. The missionaries expressly promised the Persian government that they would not do so in the future either. After about a year, opposition decreased, probably because the patriarchal family did not succeed in gaining enough support among the Assyrians. In 1845, the missionaries resumed most of their activities.

Anderson had not visited Persia in the mid-forties, but he was closely watching the developments in this mission. He was rather worried about the lack of converts and about the employment of Assyrian bishops. The missionaries' policy of non-proselytism bothered him most. Contrary to the missionaries' intentions, he explained their behaviour to himself and to the American public as a tactical move due to local circumstances. At that time, it was probably the extensive preaching activities in Assyrian churches that made Anderson give the Urmia missionaries the benefit of the doubt. Anderson always had stressed the importance of 'formal preaching', preferring it to the informal, conversational preaching which most missions in Western

Asia had to confine themselves to. This he might have found sufficient reason to let the missionaries in Urmia continue their policy.[25]

In 1846, the discussion on mission policy took a decidedly different turn when, for the first time in a Western Asian mission, a fully-fledged revival took place. About fifty Assyrians experienced a classical pietistic conversion. The revival started almost simultaneously among the teenage girls of the 'Female' and the boys of the 'Male' seminaries.[26] The students of both these seminaries took the revivalist fervour to their home villages. In the next ten years, bouts of revival occurred from time to time.[27] During the fifties, as a result of these revivals a number of local Assyrian churches took on a definitely 'Protestant' character. The liturgical parts of the service were shortened, preaching was given greater attention, new songs were introduced (many of them translated from English) and communion services acquired greater weight. Assyrian priests and deacons began to imitate the missionaries' preaching. Not long after, the mission church which, as in Beirut, served the missionaries and their families, was opened to Assyrians at special occasions. During these special services 'new converts' (although the term 'convert' in Urmia was usually avoided) made their profession of faith and took part in the communion services. Bishops, priests, and deacons of the Church of the East were among the participants.

In the sixties, relationships between the 'Evangelical' and the 'Old Church' party within the Church of the East started to worsen, but it was not until 1871 that the Evangelical Assyrians formally separated themselves from the Church of the East. The missionaries attributed the problems of the sixties mainly to the new patriarch who was consecrated in 1861, but the final separation from the Church of the East might be attributed also to changes among the Protestant

[25] On this period, see H. L. Murre-van den Berg, 'Geldelijk of Geestelijk Gewin? Assyrische Bisschoppen op de Loonlijst van een Amerikaanse Zendingspost', *Nederlands Archief voor Kerkgeschiedenis*, 77–2 (1997), pp. 241–57, and 'The American Board and the Eastern Churches: the Nestorian Mission (1844–1846)', *Orientalia Christiana Periodica*, 65 (1999), pp. 117–38.

[26] The female seminary was headed by the missionary Fidelia Fiske. On her role in the context of the American missionary enterprise of the mid-nineteenth century, see the recent studies of Dana L. Robert, *American Women in Mission: A Social History of Their Thought and Practice* (Macon, GA, 1997), and Amanda Porterfield, *Mary Lyon and the Mount Holyoke Missionaries* (New York and Oxford, 1997).

[27] By far the most interesting published source on this period of revival is D. T. Laurie, *Women and her Saviour in Persia* (Boston, 1863). Laurie, a former missionary to Mesopotamia, composed the book in close co-operation with Fidelia Fiske. He included a considerable number of texts written by the early Assyrian converts.

missionaries themselves. In 1869 the 'senior brother', the oldest missionary Justin Perkins, left the field after a stay of almost thirty-five years. He is said always to have opposed a formal separation. When other missionaries took his place, the mission as a whole probably became less scrupulous about the separation from the Church of the East. Another element that should be taken into account was the transfer of the mission to the Presbyterian Board of Missions in 1871. Not only did the Presbyterian Board hold stricter views in this regard, but they also intended to enlarge the scope of the mission to the Moslems of Persia. Converts from this group would inevitably lead to separate Protestant Churches. Lastly, British and Anglican influence on the 'Old Church' Assyrians grew considerably, which in all likelihood further stimulated the formation of a separate Protestant Church.[28]

Despite these later developments, the history of the Urmia Mission shows that there was a third option open to the missionaries of the American Board: to co-operate with the clergy of an Eastern Church while keeping the potential 'Protestants' within the bounds of an Eastern Church. Although the missionaries and the Evangelical Assyrians did not succeed in maintaining this policy throughout the nineteenth century, they managed to do it for twenty years longer than the other missions in Western Asia. A good relationship with the Assyrian clergy probably was the main factor in this, a relationship which, among other things, was maintained by the amiable character of senior missionary Justin Perkins. Outward circumstances, like the initial prohibition of proselytizing by the Persian government and the rather isolated position of the Assyrians in northwestern Persia, may have further stimulated the Assyrians' openness to the message of the missionaries as well as their willingness to accept diversion within their fold. These circumstances at the same time induced the missionaries to go all the way in working *with* the Church of the East rather than against it.

CONCLUDING REMARKS

In the three missions discussed here, different causes led to the formation of Protestant Churches. To different degrees, the opinions of the missionaries on the Churches of the East, the attitude of the local clergy towards the missionaries, Protestant-Roman Catholic

[28] See Murre-van den Berg, *From a Spoken to a Written Language*, pp. 66–70.

tensions, the policy of the Board in Boston as represented by Rufus Anderson,[29] and socio-economic and political circumstances in the countries where mission work was done all played a role. The interplay of these factors determined when and how Protestant Churches came into existence in Western Asia. To describe the emergence of Protestant Churches as due solely to the attitudes of the missionaries towards the Eastern Churches is in my opinion an undue simplification.

The mission in Urmia brings to light another aspect that needs attention. At first, the American Board allowed the missionaries in Persia to continue their 'conservative policy' of co-operation with the Assyrian Church thanks to the fact that the missionaries were allowed to preach in the Assyrian Churches. However, their arguments for this 'conservative' policy were greatly strengthened by the fact that it was in Urmia that for the first time in Western Asia a series of revivals took place which clearly followed the North-American model. If it had not been for these revivals, I doubt whether the Board would have allowed the missionaries in Urmia to proceed much longer with their dissident policy.

These revivals should remind us that among American Evangelicals of the mid-nineteenth century, conversion experience was thought to be the basic experience of a Christian life. Evidence of piety, of true conversion of the heart, of spiritual regeneration, allowed someone to be acknowledged as a true Christian. When such a conversion had taken place, it no longer mattered whether one belonged to a North American or an Eastern Church. In the early years of missionary work in Western Asia, this type of conversion was hardly encountered among the Eastern Christians. This made the missionaries fear that the large majority of these Christians were heading towards eternal damnation. The very moment these Eastern Christians experienced the same type of pietistic conversions as they had experienced themselves, being in one church or another became of secondary importance. This brings us back to Badr's opinion that the mission-

[29] In this article, I have not paid attention to what might have been behind Anderson's policy in these matters. Harris, 'Denominationalism and democracy', suggests that Anderson's views were influenced at least by two other factors: internal American discussions on ecclesiology ('denominationalism'), and financial worries. These financial worries became all the more pressing when no 'tangible results' (compare also Arpee, *The Armenian Awakening*, pp. 162–3) could be reported, making fundraising increasingly difficult.

aries' ranking of soteriology above ecclesiology, that is, their valuing 'conversion of the heart' above all 'outward forms', is fundamental for understanding their mission work among the Eastern Christians.[30] This ranking might not explain why Anderson insisted so much on the formation of separate Protestant churches in Beirut and Constantinople, but it certainly does explain the long years in which the missionaries in Urmia were allowed to continue their work within the Church of the East. As long as the Evangelical Assyrians were accepted by the majority of the Assyrian clergy and the missionaries could work alongside bishops and priests to make their influence felt in the community as a whole rather than in a separatist group, there was no theological need for a separate Protestant Church. Anderson might have wanted it otherwise, considering his emphasis on local Protestant congregations, but the missionaries in Urmia effectively defended their position with the help of this Evangelical paradigm of the fundamental importance of the conversion experience.

University of Leiden

[30] Badr, 'Mission to "Nominal Christians"', pp. 308–12.

MODERNISM AND MISSION: THE INFLUENCE OF DUTCH MODERN THEOLOGY ON MISSIONARY PRACTICE IN THE EAST INDIES IN THE NINETEENTH CENTURY

By GUUS BOONE

INTRODUCTION

IN 1866, the Dutch missionary Jan Nannes Wiersma decided it was necessary to teach the Muslim heads in the place where he was working about the life of the prophet Muhammad – rather a peculiar thing for a messenger of Christianity to do. The Board of the Nederlandsch Zendelinggenootschap [Dutch Missionary Society; DMS], who had sent him, therefore reprimanded him. Wiersma, however, defended himself by stating that if the chiefs knew more about what Islam really was, they would have reached a higher level of intellectual development, and they would be closer to conversion to Christianity. This opinion was not uncommon among adherents of the so called Modern Theology or Modernism.

In this article I will focus on the impact of Modernism on missionary practice in the Dutch East Indies. First, I will give an overview of Dutch missions in the first half of the nineteenth century. Second, I will focus on the three most outspoken Modernist missionaries, Theodoor August Ferdinand van der Valk, Samuel Eliza Harthoorn, and Wiersma himself, and show the influence of their theological and missionary ideas on the organization of Christian mission in the Netherlands and on missionary practice in the East Indies.

PROTESTANT THEOLOGY AND MISSIONS IN THE NETHERLANDS

Modern Christian missions in the Netherlands began with the establishment of the DMS in 1797. Before that time the Dutch Reformed Church, not voluntary societies, was responsible for the conversion of the heathen. Apart from the bankruptcy of the Dutch East India Company in 1792 and the termination of the privileged position of the Reformed religion in 1796, this shift towards para-church organization was caused by a change in the localization of religion in society. The Christian faith had become the belief of individuals who could contribute to the well-being of the Dutch commonwealth, instead of being considered to be the legal foundation of the state. Christian mission therefore had to aim at the conversion of individuals, instead of at the creation of Christian communities. This model of mission emphasised the role of education.[1] All founders of the DMS could more or less agree with this approach, although there were some differences in outlook between members who came from an Evangelical pietist tradition and those who were more influenced by the Enlightenment.[2]

After a promising start in 1797 missionary fervour in the Netherlands slowed down in the first quarter of the nineteenth century. The Liberal so-called Groningers and the Orthodox Réveil both fostered missionary enthusiasm in the 1830s and 1840s.[3] Both movements claimed to be the true representation of the Dutch national character and tried to elevate the religious and moral standards of the common man and woman, though they differed in their theological presuppositions. The Réveil wanted to return to seventeenth-century Calvinist doctrine and can be seen as the heirs to the Reformed Pietist tradition, while the Groningers were influenced by Schleiermacher's theology and pleaded for a open attitude in the tradition of Erasmus and the Dutch Enlightenment.[4]

For some time both movements were able to co-operate within the DMS, agreeing that both Western civilization and Christianity had to be spread among the pagans. However, the adherents of the Réveil were reluctant to acknowledge the activities of the Groningers as true

[1] Peter van Rooden, 'Nineteenth-century representations of missionary conversion and the transformation of Western Christianity', in Peter van der Veer, ed., *Conversion to Modernities: The Globalization of Christianity* (New York, 1996), pp. 65–87. Joris van Eijnatten, 'Beschaafd Koninkrijk. Het NZG en de motivering van de zending omstreeks 1800', in Th. van den End et al., eds, *Twee eeuwen Nederlandse zending 1797–1997. Twaalf opstellen* (Zoetermeer, 1997), pp. 25–45.

[2] J. Boneschansker, *Het Nederlandsch Zendeling Genootschap in zijn eerste periode. Een studie over opwekking in de Bataafse en Franse tijd* (Leeuwarden, 1987); P. N. Holtrop, *Tussen Piëtisme en Réveil. Het 'Deutsche Christentumsgesellschaft' in Nederland, 1784–1833* (Amsterdam, 1975), pp. 154–70. Guus Boone, 'Moderniteit en moderne zending. Het ontstaan van de genootschappelijke zending in Nederland', *Wereld en zending*, 26–3 (1997), pp. 3–11.

[3] H. Reenders, *Alternatieve zending. Ottho Gerhard Heldring (1804–1876) en de verbreiding van het christendom in Nederlands-Indië* (Kampen, 1991), pp. 25–39.

[4] A. J. Rasker, *De Nederlandse Hervormde Kerk vanaf 1795. Geschiedenis, theologische ontwikkelingen en de verhouding tot haar zusterkerken in de negentiende en twintigste eeuw* (Kampen, 1986; 3rd enlarged edn), pp. 45–54 and 89–99.

Christian mission. Instead of defining conversion as a radical departure from a sinful past, the Groningers stated that conversion was a pedagogical process, as God himself educated humanity during history. For the Orthodox Calvinists this was unacceptable, since it denied man's salvation by faith in Jesus Christ alone. Consequently, adherents of the Réveil tried, with little success, to initiate new missionary activities to avoid supporting the DMS during the 1840s.

The rise of the so-called Modern Theology increased the tensions between orthodox and liberal friends of missions. Modernists such as C. W. Opzoomer (1821–92), J. H. Scholten (1811–85), Allard Pierson (1831–96), and S. Hoekstra (1822–98) maintained that theology should follow the most recent developments in the natural and historical sciences, lest Christianity should lose its appeal to the cultural elite.[5] They used the methods of analogy and causality as the sole criteria for finding historical truth, and rejected the possibility of supernatural interference in the laws of nature, characterizing themselves as anti-supernaturalists. Leyden professor J. H. Scholten exerted great influence with his book, *The Teachings of the Reformed Church*, in which he redefined the classic Calvinist doctrines to fit into the schemes of positivist science. For example, the dogma of providence was explained in an evolutionist, determinist sense in accordance with the optimistic spirit of the mid-nineteenth century. He believed that all mankind in the future would grow to 'the new heaven and the new earth'. Sin was not personal guilt but a stage on the road to the restitution of all things. The progress of mankind was inevitable.[6]

Most Modernists ignored mission. They directed their activities more to the elite than to the uneducated masses.[7] At the 1866 annual meeting of Modernist preachers the Mennonite professor of theology, S. Hoekstra, formulated some conditions for missionary societies in order to gain the support of the Modernists. The word 'mission' alone, referring to a supernatural sender, did not agree with their anti-supernaturalism. However, Hoekstra was convinced that Modernism was the most likely option for the future religion of

[5] Eldred C. Vanderlaan, *Protestant Modernism in Holland* (London, 1924), pp. 23–5; K. H. Roessingh, *Het modernisme in Nederland* (Haarlem, 1922), pp. 32–41; Rasker, *De Nederlandse Hervormde Kerk*, pp. 113–24.

[6] J. H. Scholten, *De Leer der Hervormde Kerk, in hare grondbeginselen uit de bronnen voorgesteld* (Leyden, 1848–50); Rasker, *De Nederlandse Hervormde Kerk*, pp. 117–18.

[7] Jan van Miert, *Wars van clubgeest & partijzucht. Liberalen, natie en verzuiling, Tiel en Winschoten 1850–1920* (Amsterdam, 1994), pp. 38–43.

all humankind, as it rejected doctrine and miracles and was the only religion consistent with the Christian principles of love of mankind and belief in human potential. The domination of the missionary societies by adherents of supernaturalism precluded the participation of Modernists. The aim of mission should be 'the propagation of truth and justice in a Christian spirit and on a broad foundation'. J. Herderscheê, a historian of Dutch Modernism, added that respect for other religions and denial of the claim that Christianity was the only road to salvation removed the need for missionary endeavours. Modernists would only support Christian mission if it consisted mainly of civilizing activities.[8]

ON THE BORDER OF CHRISTIANITY: THEODOOR AUGUST FERDINAND VAN DER VALK

The theological development of T. A. F. van der Valk (1828–74), a former Amsterdam school teacher, triggered the conflict between the Orthodox and Modernist supporters of missions.[9] Van der Valk was a missionary in East Java, where the DMS had worked since 1848. The Society sent its more intellectual students to this field as they considered the Muslim Javanese to be more elevated than the animists of the outer islands of the Indonesian archipelago. Those missionaries tended to have more interest in academic theology, which became the battlefield of the Modernists and their adversaries around 1850. During his studies at the mission school the orthodox van der Valk developed a taste for the work of J. H. Scholten, much to the dislike of his teacher, H. Hiebink (1809–89), who himself was an adherent of the Groninger theology.[10]

Initially van der Valk's budding Modernist ideas did not interfere with his work as a missionary. He criticized the training school of his colleague Jelle Eeltjes Jellesma (1816–1858), the first missionary on

[8] J. Herderscheê, *De modern-godsdienstige richting in Nederland* (Amsterdam, 1904), pp. 378–82.

[9] A. Th. Boone, 'Moderne zendelingen 1850–1855', *Documentatieblad voor de geschiedenis van de Nederlandse zending en overzeese kerken*, 5–2 (1997), pp. 24–7, and *Bekering en beschaving. De agogische activiteiten van het Nederlandsch Zendelinggenootschap in Oost-Java (1840–1865)* (Zoetermeer, 1997), p. 82 n. 42, and p. 168; A. J. van den Berg, *Kerkelijke strijd en zendingsorganisatie. De scheuring in het Nederlands Zendelinggenootschap rond het midden van de negentiende eeuw* (Zoetermeer, 1997), pp. 31–4.

[10] *Biographisch Woordenboek van Protestantsche Godgeleerden in Nederland* 4, pp. 29–30.

Java,[11] for its purely religious contents. He wanted to introduce more practical subjects, such as handicraft and economics, in order to advance the chances of his Javanese students. He saw a direct connection between the growth of prosperity and intellectual development, a combination which would create better opportunities for the introduction of Christianity.[12] This view was rather common in nineteenth-century missionary thought, and was shared by many Evangelicals.[13] Van der Valk also changed the method of teaching. He emphasised understanding, instead of learning by heart.[14] More outspokenly Modernist was his opinion that it was not necessary that all missionaries taught the Javanese the same doctrine. Through the exposure to different opinions the Javanese were expected to think for themselves and not just to copy the ideas of their religious instructors.[15] Critical thinking, however, was less valued by the board of the DMS, because they thought the Javanese Christians were not mature enough.

Hiebink did not like the opinions of his pupil, but he did not have to act against him, as van der Valk decided in 1855 that he could no longer work as a missionary. He had rejected the Christian faith and had become a libertarian.[16] Van der Valk's resignation fell like a thunderbolt: the anomaly of a missionary, who was trained to spread the gospel and no longer believed it. The Orthodox concluded that their suspicions about the theology of the DMS were justified and that the Society could not be trusted, for van der Valk had resigned and had not been sacked by the board. The DMS tolerated not only moderate Groningers, but also radical Modernists. This was too much. In the years 1858 and 1859 the adherents of the Réveil established three new missionary societies: the Dutch Missionary Union, the Utrecht Missionary Union, and the Dutch Reformed Missionary Union. Each

[11] Chr. G. F. de Jong, '"Vrede door het bloed des kruises". Zendeling J.E. Jellesma's interpretatie van het devies van het Nederlands Zendeling Genootschap', in Th. van den End, ed., *Twee eeuwen*, pp. 71–90; Boone, *Bekering en beschaving*, pp. 75–119.

[12] Utrecht, Archives of the Board of Missions of the Dutch Reformed Church [hereafter ABM] 44–1: T. A. F. van der Valk to J. C. Neurdenburg, Surabaya, 20 December 1853, and Sidokari, 5 December 1854; ABM 29–2A: T. A. F. van der Valk, 'Overzigt van mijne ontmoetingen en bevindingen gdurende mijn eerst verblijf op Java (van 6 december 1852 tot 31 october 1853)', note f.

[13] Brian Stanley, *Enlightenment and Mission: A Re-evaluation [=North Atlantic Missiology Project Position Paper 11]* (Cambridge, 1996), pp. 25–6.

[14] ABM 29–2A: Diary, Van der Valk, 26 January and 14 March 1854.

[15] ABM 29–2A: Diary, Van der Valk, 16 and 17 September 1854.

[16] ABM 44–1: Van der Valk to Revd P. J. Bouman, Sidokare, 20 January 1855.

of them represented a different strand of the Réveil movement, and had its own method of combatting Liberal theology. The Dutch Missionary Union demanded that its members refuse any co-operation with those who denied Jesus Christ's true and eternal divinity. The Dutch Reformed Missionary Union stricly maintained the Calvinist creeds, while the Utrecht Missionary Union expected that membership by co-option would guarantee the exclusion of Liberals.[17]

The DMS was far from content with these developments. As a consequence, Hiebink decided to give up his position, because he felt he was no longer able to fulfil his task. The fact that van der Valk's apostasy was mainly attributed to his teaching played an important role in his decision. The DMS used the vacancy to restore the confidence of the Orthodox by appointing H. C. Voorhoeve (1818–1903), a brother of J. Voorhoeve, founder of the Dutch Missionary Union. However, this did not end the debate about Modernism and mission, especially since soon another missionary in Java fell 'victim' to Modern theology: S. E. Harthoorn.

THE IMPOSSIBILITY OF CONVERSION: SAMUEL ELIZA HARTHOORN

Samuel Eliza Harthoorn (1831–1883) had worked in a bookshop before he was trained as a missionary.[18] His preference for reading and studying was a constant factor in his life. He concentrated on the special nature of missionary work, which he saw as bridging the gap between Western Christian and – in his case – Javanese culture. After his arrival in Java in 1855, he first considered the training of indigenous preachers and teachers as the best way to reach this goal. Supervision of the Javanese helpers was one of the pillars of this method, as they were uncivilized and had only limited intellectual powers. However, the missionary could not exert this guidance without knowledge of Javanese culture and literature.[19]

As a result of his studies Harthoorn reached the conclusion that despite Muslim influences many traditional Javanese religious beliefs

[17] Van den Berg, *Kerkelijke strijd*; E. F. Kruijf, *De geschiedenis van het Nederlandsche Zendelinggenootschap en zijne zendingsposten* (Groningen, 1894), pp. 478–9.

[18] Boone, *Bekering en beschaving*, pp. 120–83.

[19] ABM 29-2D: S. E. Harthoorn, 'Enkele gedachten over het werk, den persoon en de opleiding des Zendelings'; S. E. Harthoorn to Board of the DMS, Malang, 1 October 1857; I. H. Enklaar, 'De vereisten voor een zendeling. O.G. Heldrings zendeling-werklieden afgewezen', in *Kom over en help ons! Twaalf opstellen over de Nederlandse zending in de negentiende eeuw* (The Hague, 1981), pp. 101–5.

had remained intact.[20] He saw no reason why this process of 'javanization' could not have taken place in the Christian community.[21] His low opinion of Javanese Christians decreased even further in theory, but in practice he tolerated more doctrinal and moral deviations than his colleagues did. This was due to his evolutionist thinking. He believed that before the Javanese could become Christians they should go through an inevitable mixed phase, which had repercussions for his missionary method. Instead of bringing the Bible to his pupils he had to bring them to the Bible.[22] Harthoorn decided to javanize his method of working. He modelled his training school on the *pesantren*,[23] the traditional Indonesian Quran school, and decided to tolerate customs and values of a mixed socio-religious nature, such as circumcision, the *selametan* – a meal to celebrate communal harmony – and the traditional views on marriage.[24] His refusal to exert church discipline in these cases brought him into conflict with his board and his colleagues, as they stressed the religious nature of these ceremonies.[25]

From 1858 on he reviewed the Java mission in the light of his knowledge of Javanism and came to a devastating conclusion. Christian mission had changed nothing in the Javanese. The Christians were Javanists who spoke a Christian language but did not think as Christians should. The missionaries knew too little about Javanism to work fruitfully among the Javanese. Harthoorn called for a moratorium on mission until a new missionary method, which took into account the Javanese world of thought and understanding, had been developed. Missionaries could then control the synthesis of Christianity and Javanism and correct deviations that might lead the young Christians astray. For the moment, however, there were too few points of contact to justify efforts to convert the Javanese. They had to be better educated before any new attempts could be made.[26]

20 S. E. Harthoorn, 'De zending op Java en meer bepaald die van Malang', *Mededeelingen van wege het Nederlandsch Zendelinggenootschap*, 4 (1860), pp. 103–37 and 212–52.

21 ABM 29–2D: Diary, Harthoorn, 1 and 4 April 1858.

22 ABM 29–2D: Harthoorn, Annual Report over 1856.

23 ABM 29–2D: Diary, Harthoorn, 1 April 1859.

24 ABM 29–2D: Diary, Harthoorn, 22 August 1857, 22 November, 30 December 1858; Harthoorn to Board DMS, Malang, 20 November 1858.

25 ABM 18–12: H. Hiebink to Harthoorn, Cleves, 17 September 1858; ABM 24–3C: Acts of the Conference of Missionaries on Java, Malang, 28 September to 3 October 1860.

26 ABM 29–2D: Harthoorn, Diary for 1860. This diary will be published in 1999 in the 'Kleine Reeks' of The Society for the History of Dutch Missions and Overseas Churches.

The DMS refused to comply with Harthoorn's request that he be allowed to abandon work in the field and concentrate on studying Javanese culture. Because he threatened the heart of the DMS the difference in opinion could not be bridged. The board interpreted Harthoorn's problems with the Javanese Christians as a result of his imposing too high demands on them. It was not feasible to require that they understand everything about Christianity, although they acknowledged some of Harthoorn's criticisms. They also disagreed with his opinion that the people had to be civilized before they could be converted. Although the DMS in general adhered to the idea that higher education would lead to a better faith, it did not consider intellectual development a prerequisite for conversion. The board pointed to the conversion of northwestern Europe in the early Middle Ages where Christianity had advanced civilization and not the other way round.[27]

Harthoorn's ideas were partly the result of his Modernist opinions. As he was himself an adherent of the most progressive theology, which stressed the importance of uniting Christianity with advanced scientific thought, he had many difficulties with the supranaturalist thinking of the Javanese. On the one hand it made him extremely sensitive to cultural differences, on the other it instilled in him a pessimism about the possibilities of effective missionary work. When he shifted his attention completely to scientific work and wanted to start an immense investigation of ancient Javanese culture and literature, instead of doing work in the field, as the DMS had suggested as a temporary solution to the problems, the board suspended him.[28] Harthoorn went to the Netherlands to defend his case, but since he had done this without the required permission he was sacked.[29]

Harthoorn defended his views in 1863 in a book entitled *The Evangelical Mission and East Java. A Critique.*[30] As it was introduced and edited by the Modernist preacher Allard Pierson it triggered a debate not only on the possibility of Christian mission but also on the role of Modernism in missions. Most Modernists did not support Harthoorn's

[27] *Extract-Acten van het Nederlandsch Zendelinggenootschap*, 1861, pp. 78–89, and 1863, pp. 91–105.

[28] *Extract-Acten*, 1861, pp. 176–82, and 1862, pp. 65–70; ABM 29–2D: Harthoorn to Board DMS, Malang, 3 January 1862.

[29] *Extract-Acten* 1863, pp. 105–10 and 225–7.

[30] S. E. Harthoorn, *De Evangelische zending en Oost-Java. Eene kritische bijdrage* (Haarlem, 1863).

plea that mission should temporarily be replaced by education and civilizing work, but they shared his criticisms of the imposition of doctrine and the negative attitude towards other religions. They also promoted the development of more scientific methods of missionary work and better training of missionaries. The DMS maintained its double goal of spreading the gospel and Western civilization and continued to tolerate Modernist opinions to a certain extent.[31]

The annual meeting of the DMS in 1864 revived the battle against Modernism. The main speaker, J. C. Zaalberg, had announced at the beginning of the year that he had become a Modernist.[32] This was no reason for the board to cancel his speaking engagement, although many Orthodox members requested this. Zaalberg himself decided that it was not in the best interests of the DMS for him to deliver the address, and he refused the invitation. However, this was not sufficient to restore peace. Some Orthodox members requested a more precise statement about the doctrinal base of the DMS, in order to exclude Modernists from membership. The Society remained loyal to its former point of view and decided not to change a word. A new exodus of Orthodox members, among them director H. C. Voorhoeve, was the result.[33] A year later a Modernist attempt to broaden the doctrinal base failed as well.[34] Since almost all Orthodox members had left the DMS and the Modernists never felt comfortable, the dominant position in the Society was left to the Groningers.

MODERNIST MISSIONARY PRACTICE: JAN NANNES WIERSMA

The difficult position of the Modernists within the DMS is best illustrated by the experiences of Jan Nannes Wiersma (1833–1907).[35] Of all post-1864 missionaries he was the most outspoken supporter of Modernism. Before he was accepted as a candidate missionary he had worked as a daily labourer. He was considered less intelligent than many of his colleagues and therefore he was sent against his wish to the Minahasa instead of to Java in 1862. Wiersma was less negative than

[31] Boone, *Bekering en beschaving*, pp. 181–3.

[32] C. J. Toebes, *Dominees-drama (Dr. J.C. Zaalberg Pz. 1828–1885)* (The Hague, 1983), pp. 153–64; Van den Berg, *Kerkelijke strijd*, pp. 51–6.

[33] Van den Berg, *Kerkelijke strijd*, pp. 56–68; Kruijf, *Geschiedenis*, pp. 485–501.

[34] Kruijf, *Geschiedenis*, pp. 501–3.

[35] A. Th. Boone, '"In het belang van zedelijkheid en recht". J.N. Wiersma (1833–1907) als modernistisch zendeling te Ratahan (Minahassa)', in Van den End, ed., *Twee eeuwen*, pp. 91–113; J. J. Kalma, *Dit wienen ek Friezen*, 4 (Leeuwarden, 1971), pp. 91–7.

Harthoorn about the possibilities for mission from a Modernist point of view. He focused more on the opportunities for religious and intellectual development than on the difficulties of bridging the cultural gap.

In the Minahasa Wiersma was the only Modernist among the missionaries. His colleagues adhered either to Orthodoxy or to the Groningers. He was placed in Ratahan, a new station, that was split off from the districts of two Orthodox missionaries, C. J. van de Liefde and A. O. Schaafsma.[36]

Wiersma's method of working was rather conventional. He preached, taught, catechized, supervised his preachers and teachers, baptized, served communion, and exerted church discipline. Yet he made some changes to match his Modernism. Like Harthoorn he thought that his congregations were not able to understand Christianity well. His conclusion was similar to the young Harthoorn's: adaptation to his hearers. He wanted to change their behaviour and free them from superstition. Instead of preaching about Bible texts and explaining Christian doctrine, he told edifying stories. Much detail and liveliness was necessary, because children and child-like people ought to be treated similarly.[37] The curbing of sinful behavior should be done by concrete commands and not by outlining general principles of conduct.[38] Wiersma remained vague in his explanation of Christian doctrine. Not only did he consider it unfit for the Minahasans, but he also wanted to keep a low doctrinal profile to avoid conflicts with his colleagues.

The prosperity of society was one of Wiersma's main interests. Like van der Valk he considered this to be one of the main tasks of the missionaries. Wiersma stressed the importance of education and even taught Dutch at his school, which the board of the DMS considered to be superfluous for the Minahasans. In contrast, the Dutch Indies government subsidized a Malay-Dutch textbook he wrote.[39] The value attached by Wiersma to education is best illustrated by the fact that he taught the Muslim population about the good aspects of Islam. He thought that elevated Muslims would more easily convert to Christianity, as they had travelled on the road

[36] ABM 44–2: Acts of the Union of Missionaries in the Minahasa, Tanawangko, 26 and 27 June 1861.

[37] ABM 29–1B: J. N. Wiersma to Board DMS, Ratahan, 13 December 1865.

[38] ABM 29–1B: Wiersma to Board DMS, Ratahan, February 1864.

[39] ABM 29–1B: Wiersma to Board DMS, Ratahan, 21 December 1869.

to advanced religion.[40] However, most of his colleagues believed that the more Muslims knew about Islam, the less open they would be to the gospel.[41] More directly aimed at the prosperity of the people in Ratahan was Wiersma's plea for liberalization of the economy. This would create a class of traders and artisans. He expected this middle class to become the backbone of the new Christian community. He became a small entrepreneur himself, employing several craftsmen in order to advance this development.[42]

Although Wiersma tried to keep a low profile, he was so outspoken in his opinions that conflict with his colleagues was almost inevitable. The conflict at the 1864 annual meeting of the DMS had an enormous impact on the Orthodox missionaries in the Minahasa. They felt isolated. At the half-yearly conference of the Union of Missionaries in the Minahasa, van de Liefde and Schaafsma, assisted by S. Ulfers, attacked Wiersma in his own house. They felt responsible for the Christians in Wiersma's district, because they had formerly worked there, and they also feared the spread of Modernism into their own stations. Wiersma had to agree with most of the charges held against him. He indeed denied the divinity of Jesus Christ, the resurrection of the body, eternal punishment, and the existence of the devil, as well as the historical truth of most of the New Testament. He defended himself by stating that the points mentioned were not fundamentals of the Christian faith and that he did not openly combat Orthodox opinions! The matter remained undecided, and the DMS reprimanded the three missionaries who had accused Wiersma. The board did not want doctrinal fights on the mission field.[43]

However, one of the complaints stuck. Wiersma was accused of not wholeheartedly subscribing to the doctrinal regulations of the DMS. He was asked to confirm his adherence, but in the first instance he declined, referring to the freedom of opinion that the DMS in 1864 granted its missionaries.[44] The board delivered an ultimatum after

[40] ABM 29–1B: Wiersma to Board DMS, 25 April 1866.

[41] W. Smit, *De islam binnen de horizon. Een missiologische studie over de benadering van de islam door vier Nederlandse zendingscorporaties (1797–1951)* (Zoetermeer, 1995), pp. 75–9 and 116–18.

[42] J. N. Wiersma, *Ervaringen gedurende mijn twaalfjarig zendingsleven* (Rotterdam, 1876), pp. 186–210.

[43] ABM 44–2: Acts of the Union of Missionaries in the Minahasa, Ratahan, 14 and 15 September 1864; ABM 25: Board DMS to S. Ulfers, 4 August and 28 October 1865.

[44] ABM 29–1B: Wiersma to Board DMS, Ratahan, 1 June 1866; ABM 25: Board DMS to Wiersma, 21 March 1866.

having tried to convince him that his Modernism was wrong and that his interpretation of the decision of 1864 was incorrect. If Wiersma did not sign a declaration of allegiance to the general regulations of the DMS he would be fired. Prodded by his wife, Wiersma reluctantly signed the document in order to be able to continue his work, although he explicitly stated that it was against his own notion of Christian mission and freedom within the DMS. As long as Modernists could remain on the board of the Society, he had to be able to work as its missionary.[45] His colleagues were not convinced of the truthfulness of Wiersma's pledge and the conflicts at the meetings of the Union of Missionaries in the Minahasa continued. The board of the DMS therefore tried several times to transfer Wiersma to another mission field, but failed as a result of his attachment to his own district and their own fear of losing the support of the Modernists.[46] As it became clear that Modernism, because of language barriers, remained within Wiersma's district, his colleagues tolerated him.[47]

In 1873 Wiersma asked permission to leave because he was very depressed after the death of his second wife and wanted to visit his family and to find a new spouse.[48] During his leave he strengthened his connections with the Modernists, who considered him as their man on the mission field. Their sympathy boosted his confidence and it also made clear that Modernists could still be important supporters of the missionary cause. As Hoekstra had done in 1866, Wiersma spoke at the meeting of Modernist ministers in April 1875. He claimed that Modernists were the best possible missionaries because of their undogmatic attitude and openness to other opinions.[49] The DMS did not like these remarks and reprimanded Wiersma. When it became clear that he had only wanted to gather support for the DMS no further action was taken against him.[50]

Upon his return in 1876 Wiersma was confronted with a complete reorganization of the Minahasa mission. Due to the bad state of its finances the board of the DMS decided to transfer the congregations to

[45] ABM 25: Board DMS to Wiersma, 4 November 1868; ABM 29–1B: Wiersma to Board DMS, Ratahan, 25 February and 1 July 1869.

[46] *Extract-Acten*, 1870, pp. 133–37, and 1871, p. 173; ABM 29–1B: Wiersma to Board DMS, Ratahan, 28 April 1873.

[47] ABM 44–2: Acts of the Union of Missionaries in the Minahasa, Sonder, 23 and 24 April 1873.

[48] ABM 29–1B: Wiersma to Board DMS, Ratahan, 20 June 1873.

[49] *De Hervorming*, 22 April 1875.

[50] *Extract-Acten*, 1875, pp. 22 and 25.

the Indische Kerk, the church funded by the Indies government. Missionary work in the Minahasa was considered to be almost completed and could well be transferred to the government, which had to maintain religious neutrality. The schools would remain under the supervision of the DMS.[51] Wiersma wanted to keep the congregations and transfer the schools. He had less difficulty with handing over the schools to the government, which excluded any form of religious education from the curriculum. As a Modernist he found it more important that the government maintained a higher standard of education than the mission had done. Better education would eventually lead to better religion.[52]

Wiersma fostered stronger objections to the transfer of his own district. He considered his churches not yet ready for the transfer since most people were still heathen or Muslim. It was more a mission field than a settled church. Furthermore, the missionaries would become assistant ministers paid by the government. He did not want to become a government official as he did not expect any good from the government,[53] since he had frequently clashed with the authorities following publications about misconduct by Dutch and native officials.[54] Being himself of humble origins, he reacted vehemently to injustice done by the high and mighty. The DMS insisted that he become an assistant minister, and threatened to oust him. After losing the support of his Modernist friends, who in the end considered his conscientious objections unfounded,[55] Wiersma once again was forced to act against his own conviction and in 1881 became an assistant minister.[56]

His suspicion of the government proved justified. In 1883 he was appointed to Waay on Amboina.[57] He was the only one of the former missionaries in the Minahasa who was removed from his post. The reason for the transfer was that he once again had published evidence of the corruption and abuse of power by a native chief. In the *Indische*

[51] Kruijf, *Geschiedenis*, pp. 415–24.

[52] ABM 29–1B: Wiersma to Board DMS, Ratahan, 16 January, 25 May, 1 September 1878.

[53] ABM 29–1B: Wiersma to Board DMS, Ratahan, 4 May 1878.

[54] Wiersma, *Ervaringen*, pp. 148–85.

[55] *De Hervorming*, 2 October 1880.

[56] *Extract-Acten*, 1881, pp. 11 and 14.

[57] The Hague, General Archives, Ministerie van Koloniën, inv. no. 7829: 'Notulen der Besluiten van den Gouverneur-Generaal van Nederlandsch-Indië', 14 September 1883, no. 25.

Gids Wiersma had insinuated that this chief only kept his position because he was backed by the Dutch controller of Ratahan, who maintained good relations with the daughters of the native chief.[58] Wiersma was first reprimanded for not filing his complaints in conformity with government regulations. He replied that he had done this in vain and that his conscience urged him in the interests of decency and justice to make this affair public. He placed the freedom of his conscience above the laws of the government, as he had done with the creeds of the Church. The government was lenient and transferred him, but also warned him that repeating this offence would lead to his final discharge. Wiersma wisely requested a leave of absence for two years at his own expense.[59] He returned to the Netherlands and succeeded in finding a new position as minister in the Mennonite Fraternity. He remained loyal to the DMS and became one of its many directors. However, his wish that other outspoken Modernists would become missionaries for the DMS was not fulfilled during his lifetime.

CONCLUSION

Modern theology as such did not inspire missionary fervour, yet it influenced missionary practice in three distinct ways.

First, it caused the break-up of the DMS into four missionary organizations. In fact, Orthodox Christians broke the unity, but they reacted to the increasing rationalization and secularization of theology by the Modernists. The reason for their separation was not missionary practice but Christian doctrine. Modernist theology rejected fundamental Christian doctrines. A missionary who denied or ignored these fundamental beliefs could not be considered as a messenger of the true Gospel. Co-operation on the mission field was no longer possible. The fact that some missionaries could become adherents of Modernism was due to its claim to be the culturally and scientifically most advanced phase of Christianity. It appealed both to their intellect and to their wish to be part of an elite.

Secondly, the Modernist Harthoorn provocatively stated the main problem of Christian mission: could native Christians really understand the gospel? The fact that a former missionary questioned the

[58] J. N. Wiersma, 'Minahassa-toestanden', *Indische Gids*, 5–2 (1883), pp. 109–20.

[59] J. N. Wiersma, *Slaafsche onderworpenheid van het protestantsch kerkbestuur in Nederlandsch Indië aan den staat aangetoond* (Rotterdam, 1889).

validity of Christian missions from a radical evolutionist point of view launched the most intense debate on missionary methodology in the Netherlands during the nineteenth century. The leadership of the DMS rejected his view of civilization and conversion as two consecutive stages. For most Christians, however, civilization, and especially education, remained one of the main tasks of the missionaries. The DMS reacted to Harthoorn's critique of Christian mission by intensifying the supervision of indigenous Christians, and encouraging the study of Indonesian religion and culture. No longer were the missionaries content with hearing the echo of Christian formulae from their converts, they wanted to know what they really meant when they used the words.

In everyday practice the Modernist missionaries did not differ much from their colleagues, except in their sympathy for secular aspects of education, which they considered crucial in preparing the way to Christianity. Their preaching was more moral than doctrinal and they were rather tolerant towards adherents of other religions. However, this did not stop them from making very negative comments about these religions when they wrote to fellow-Christians. They were lenient in their exercise of church discipline against indigenous customs or practices influenced by European elite culture, such as plays, dancing, and working on Sundays. They pointed out that members of their congregations needed some time to adjust to the new standards. But with regard to morality they were certainly not more pliant than their colleagues, and moral transgressors such as adulterers and drunks were disciplined. These differences were not fundamental.

Wiersma's appeals and the adjustments made by the DMS in answer to Harthoorn's critique did not result in large-scale support by the Modernists for Christian missions. They never felt really at home in the most important missionary society that tolerated them, but they had no alternative, since projects to start a separate Modernist missionary society failed due to lack of support.

Free University of Amsterdam

'HUNTING FOR SOULS': THE MISSIONARY PILGRIMAGE OF GEORGE SHERWOOD EDDY[1]

by BRIAN STANLEY

> As I look back upon life it seems one glorious adventure. From early boyhood days of camping in what we loved to think of as the 'wild West', to shooting elephant and tiger in the jungles of my own mission station in India, and on into that bigger and greater hunt for men, life has seemed one long adventure.[2]

THESE words were written on his eighty-fourth birthday on 19 January 1955 by George Sherwood Eddy as part of the foreword to his autobiography and thirty-sixth book, *Eighty Adventurous Years*. They encapsulate the spirit of muscular evangelical activism which characterized his long career as one of the most influential Protestant mission leaders of the twentieth century. Although he died as recently as 1963, his memory has faded in comparison with his associates in the missionary and student movements, John R. Mott and Robert E. Speer. His lengthy pilgrimage through successive stages of missionary enthusiasm is in many respects typical of trends in the missionary movement as a whole, and the recent appearance of a biography of Eddy offers confirmation that he is a figure who deserves renewed attention.[3]

George Sherwood Eddy grew up in the frontier town of Leavenworth in the state of Kansas, and was proud to affirm that 'not only the West but the wild West' was in his blood: his mother, Margaret Louise Eddy, had gone to school with Buffalo Bill Cody.[4] Eddy attributed to his mother's influence the reforming zeal and spiritual

[1] Research for this paper was conducted under the auspices of the North Atlantic Missiology Project, co-ordinated by the University of Cambridge and financed by The Pew Charitable Trusts. The opinions expressed are those of the author and do not necessarily reflect the views of The Pew Charitable Trusts. I am grateful to Martha L. Smalley and Joan Duffy of the Day Missions Library, Yale Divinity School, for their assistance in giving me access to the Eddy and Mott papers.

[2] [G.] Sherwood Eddy, *Eighty Adventurous Years: An Autobiography* (New York, 1955), pp. 13–14.

[3] Rick L. Nutt, *The Whole Gospel for the Whole World: Sherwood Eddy and the American Protestant Mission* (Macon, GA, 1997).

[4] Eddy, *Eighty Adventurous Years*, p. 17.

intensity which so marked his own career. His father, George A. Eddy, owned a pharmaceutical business, and later made his fortune through restoring to solvency and profitability the Missouri, Kansas and Texas Railway. On his death in 1894, Sherwood was left to enjoy a substantial private income. His parents were keen Congregationalists, but Christian belief for Sherwood became a personal reality only as a student at Yale, when he was taken to one of D. L. Moody's Northfield student conferences.[5] Fired by his new-found evangelical faith, Eddy, on leaving Yale, went to New York for a year to work for the YMCA before entering Union Theological Seminary in 1892 to prepare for missionary service. During his two years at Union, Eddy took the pledge of the Student Volunteer Movement for Foreign Missions, affirming his purpose, 'if God permit, to become a foreign missionary'. He then devoted a year to working for the movement as a travelling secretary before a final year of study at Princeton Theological Seminary. While at Princeton, Eddy and his friend, Henry Luce (father of the famous publisher), rose at five every morning to devote themselves for two hours to the 'Morning Watch'.[6] This discipline of daily prayer and Bible study was formalized at Ridley Hall in Cambridge in the 1880s through the Morning Watch Union. The practice of the Morning Watch was endorsed by the Principal of Ridley, Handley Moule, who commended the discipline to John R. Mott on his first visit to Cambridge in June 1894. In a neat example of the transatlantic character of nineteenth-century evangelicalism, the same visit of Mott which introduced many Cambridge students to the American watchword of the Student Volunteer Movement – 'the evangelization of the world in this generation' – was apparently responsible also for transmitting the 'Morning Watch' in the reverse direction.[7] The Watch and the Watchword were symbiotic: the first article to appear in the opening number of *The Student Volunteer*, the journal of the British arm of the Student Volunteer Movement, drew an explicit connection between the hope of the evangelization of the world in this generation and the Morning Watch, when Student Volunteers could plead in secret with 'the Lord of the Harvest' on

[5] Eddy, *Eighty Adventurous Years*, p. 27.

[6] Nutt, *The Whole Gospel*, pp. 27–8.

[7] John Pollock, *A Cambridge Movement* (London, 1953), pp. 99, 131; J. B. Harford and F. C. MacDonald, *Handley Carr Glyn Moule Bishop of Durham: A Biography* (London, nd), p. 124; Eddy, *Eighty Adventurous Years*, p. 39.

behalf of the world.[8] For all the frenetic activism of the Anglo-American student missionary movement, it was, among its most committed adherents, underpinned by a rigorous ascetic and spiritual discipline, which in Eddy's case lasted throughout his life. Eddy himself compared the spiritual power of the Student Volunteer Movement to that of the Catholic religious orders, which made similar, but, more formal, demands of sacrificial obedience.[9] As a Student Volunteer he vowed to give away all of his private income that was surplus to his personal needs, and later waived his right to a salary from the Young Men's Christian Association (YMCA).[10] He also took a vow of celibacy, although this failed to survive his first encounter in India with Maud Arden, daughter of A. H. Arden, a former CMS missionary, whom he married in November 1898.[11]

At the end of December 1895 Eddy left the United States for the first time to attend an international conference in Liverpool from 1 to 5 January 1896 organized by the Student Volunteer Missionary Union of Great Britain. Eddy made it to Liverpool only by divine providence. His ship struck rocks off Holyhead and sank, though all aboard escaped in the lifeboats. Eddy treasured both shipwreck and conference as part of the grandest adventure he had yet sampled: 'As I came into contact with the British and Continental leaders of this student uprising, the conference was even more thrilling than the shipwreck, though I keenly enjoyed both.'[12]

Eddy's heart had originally been set on service in China, but Mott persuaded him to work instead with the YMCA in India. He combined his official title of College Secretary of the YMCA in India with a further role as Travelling Secretary for the Student Volunteer Movement in India and Ceylon.[13] His report letters to the YMCA describing his early years in India from September 1896 are saturated with the

[8] Tissington Tatlow, *The Story of the Student Christian Movement of Great Britain and Ireland* (London, 1933), pp. 38–9. The article appeared in *The Student Volunteer* for January 1893.

[9] Eddy, *Eighty Adventurous Years*, p. 96; Nutt, *The Whole Gospel*, p. 23.

[10] Eddy, *Eighty Adventurous Years*, pp. 112–13, and *Religion and Social Justice* (New York, 1927), pp. 11–12.

[11] Nutt, *The Whole Gospel*, pp. 43, 46. Eddy took a further vow to forego all medicine in favour of total reliance on divine healing; for a year he even abandoned his spectacles in the assurance that God would correct his eyesight.

[12] Sherwood Eddy, *A Pilgrimage of Ideas: or the Re-Education of Sherwood Eddy* (London, 1935), p. 7.

[13] Nutt, *The Whole Gospel*, p. 31.

intense evangelical piety of the student movement of the 1890s. Yet his theological stance was never identical with what later became known as fundamentalism. At Yale he had imbibed the principles of modern biblical criticism from William Rainey Harper, whilst at Princeton he remained unconvinced by B. B. Warfield's lectures on biblical inerrancy.[14] To label Eddy a 'liberal' at this stage of his career would, however, be equally misleading. His first report letters described India as a 'land of night' awaiting the glory of Christ's coming kingdom and sunk in indescribable depths of idolatry, degradation, and sin.[15] One letter, on 'The Scourges of India', written in May 1897 in the aftermath of the Indian famine of 1896 and the ensuing bubonic plague epidemic, identified plague, cholera, leprosy, poverty, and famine as signs of divine judgement; they were 'eruptions of sin' disfiguring the complexion of the Indian body politic and indicative of a fatal moral disease in the nation's blood.[16] It was an astonishingly callous letter which in years to come must have caused this prophet of the social gospel intense embarrassment. These early letters leave little doubt that his original theological position was an exclusivist one, even if Eddy himself was subsequently reluctant to admit it. His subsequent claim that before he left Princeton he had abandoned belief in the eternal punishment of the 'heathen' is not easily squared with the language which permeates the report letters.[17] Hindus were 'perishing souls' who needed convincing from the evidence of the word of God of the falsity of their belief that all religions led to God; they exhibited the 'bleared and stupid minds' and 'hardened hearts of men who are *lost now*, and who need saving now from the spiritual death'.[18]

Eddy's early eschatology combined a confidence that through the witness and prayers of the Church, India would be won for God, with an expectation of the visible personal return of Christ. One report letter in 1897 ended with the words 'Till He come'; another urged his readers to 'keep looking for His return'.[19] Never a systematic

[14] Nutt, *The Whole Gospel*, pp. 13, 28.

[15] Yale Divinity School Library, Special Collections, MS Group 32, G. S. Eddy papers [hereafter Eddy papers], Box 3, Report Letters, especially No. 3 (March 1897).

[16] Eddy papers, Box 3, Report Letter No. 5 (May 1897). Eddy applied to India the judgements on spiritual apostasy of which God warned Israel in Deut. 28. 58–61.

[17] Eddy, *Eighty Adventurous Years*, p. 79; see also Nutt, *The Whole Gospel*, p. 28.

[18] Eddy Papers, Box 3, Report Letters Nos 14 (Sept. 1898), 20 (Dec. 1899) and 25 (Sept. 1901).

[19] Eddy Papers, Box 3, Report Letters Nos 4 (April 1897) and 7 (July 1897).

theological thinker, he made in his early letters no attempt to clarify the relationship between the *parousia* and the anticipated conversion of India. Much more prominent in the letters is the theme of the role of prayer in securing this objective. Although the students who constituted the primary target of YMCA evangelism were proving singularly resistant, what delayed the spiritual awakening of India was neither Hindu opposition nor the mystery of God's timing but simply 'the prayerless unbelief of His own followers'. In India Christ's modern disciples, like their New Testament predecessors, stood before 'devil-possessed heathenism' and found themselves unable to 'cast it out': 'This kind can come out by nothing save by prayer.'[20] Eddy was responsible for organizing a Day of Prayer for the awakening of India on 12 December 1897, which was observed by missionaries and churches throughout the country and to some extent beyond it. He predicted that 'the devil and his kingdom will stagger under the blows received that day in India till the end of time'.[21] For the devotees of the Morning Watch, prayer was not serene contemplation but a manly exercise in spiritual pugilism; it was activism transposed into a devotional key.

Beneath the surface of the intense evangelical fervour which Eddy faithfully transmitted to his YMCA supporters in the United States there was developing a crippling sense of acute failure. By November 1897, little more than a year after arriving in India, Eddy was on the verge of a nervous breakdown. In the midst of the crisis he took a step which he appears subsequently to have regretted. Shortly after his marriage in 1898 both Sherwood and Maud Eddy were convinced by a missionary from the Christian Brethren of the invalidity of their infant baptism, and were baptized as adult believers. The baptism evoked predictable criticism in Anglican and other circles and receives no mention in Eddy's autobiographies.[22] His problems of insomnia and the sense of evangelistic failure continued: 'my own particular work', he confessed in 1899, 'has been largely a failure.'[23] On medical advice he resumed his boyhood hobby of hunting, learnt on the American frontier, but his prey now ranged from bears to elephants and even

[20] Eddy Papers, Box 3, Report Letter No. 6 (June 1897). Eddy is alluding to Mark 9. 14–29. See also Letter No 2 (Jan. 1897).

[21] Eddy Papers, Box 3, Report Letter No. 10 (Dec. 1897).

[22] Nutt, *The Whole Gospel*, p. 44.

[23] Eddy Papers, Box 3, Report Letter No. 18 (July 1899).

tigers. Eddy's hunting expeditions, in contrast to many of those undertaken by the servants of the Raj, were small-scale affairs, often involving just him and an Indian hunter. Their rationale was ostensibly therapeutic, but they also afforded analogies with the mission enterprise which he used for years to come with telling effect: his ripping yarns of elephant-hunting nicely softened up student audiences in American campuses for the evangelistic punch-line: 'Fellows, the most thrilling hunting in the world is hunting men for Jesus Christ.'[24] The irony, hidden from the campus audiences, was that Eddy had taken up big-game hunting to release the intolerable emotional pressure created by the elusiveness of his human quarry.

Out of the disconcertingly wide gap between Eddy's expectations and Indian realities emerged two major and inter-related shifts in his mission principles. The first was a reorientation of effort from the attempt to convert the Hindu student elite directly towards the renewal in holiness and evangelistic zeal of the Indian Church. The new emphasis was first apparent in the first two months of 1899, when he accompanied the English Baptist and Keswick advocate, F. B. Meyer, on a tour of Indian cities out of a conviction that 'Christian India would have to be awakened before non-Christian India was ever evangelized.'[25] By 1902 Eddy was convinced that the key to spiritual advance in India lay with the two million Christians of South India: 'If these are moved India will be moved. If these are awakened India will be evangelized.' His hopes for the awakening of the Church rested in particular on the young Vedanayagam Samuel Azariah, the rising star of the Indian YMCA – 'one of the finest men I have ever known'.[26] From 1898 Azariah was Eddy's frequent companion in evangelistic itinerations throughout South India, and an abiding friendship developed between the two men. They were the prime movers behind the establishment of India's first two major indigenous mission agencies, the Indian Missionary Society of Tinnevelly in 1903 and the National Missionary Society in 1905.[27] Eddy was present at Azariah's

[24] Nutt, *The Whole Gospel*, p. 100. For an illuminating discussion of the connections of hunting with imperialism, muscular Christianity, and the American frontier spirit see John M. MacKenzie, *The Empire of Nature: Hunting, Conservation and British Imperialism* (Manchester, 1988), ch. 2.

[25] Eddy Papers, Box 3, Report Letter No. 16 (March 1899); see W. Y. Fullerton, *F. B. Meyer: A Biography* (London, nd), pp. 205–6.

[26] Eddy Papers, Box 3, Report Letter No. 28 (1902).

[27] See S. B. Harper, *In the Shadow of the Mahatma: Bishop V. S. Azariah and the Travails of Christianity in British India* (Grand Rapids, MI, and Richmond, 2000), pp. 73–90.

consecration in Calcutta as Bishop of Dornakal on the last Sunday of 1912, and at the subsequent baptism in the Ganges at Serampore, where the bishop baptized the first two converts of a successful evangelistic campaign conducted by Eddy and Mott in Calcutta in December 1912.[28] The poignant symbolism of both the consecration of the first Indian bishop and the baptism, conducted at the very spot where, on the last Sunday of 1800, William Carey had baptized his first Hindu convert, Krishna Pal, was not lost on Eddy: he discerned the dawn of a new era in Indian missions.[29]

Eddy had realized that intensity of zeal and fervour in prayer were not enough: behind his new commitment to indigenous mission agency lay an embryonic appreciation of issues of culture, society, and politics. The second shift in his strategic vision was never absolute, and was for a time obscured by the large attendances of an average of one thousand students a night recorded by Mott and Eddy in their evangelistic meetings in various Indian cities in late 1912, which rekindled Eddy's flickering hopes of a high-caste breakthrough.[30] The first signs, however, of this second reorientation were apparent as early as 1899. A month's tour in Jaffna that year convinced Eddy that a high-caste Christian community was in fact a decidedly mixed blessing, for it made almost impossible any evangelistic advance among the lower castes: Jaffna afforded 'a striking object lesson of the wisdom of Christ's method in beginning with the lowest first'.[31] Azariah's spiritual magnetism and power reinforced the point. Eddy accordingly resolved to learn Tamil to facilitate work with the rapidly expanding lower-caste Christian communities of South India. For two years from late 1900 he exploited his financial independence to grant himself virtual leave of absence from his YMCA work, and devoted his energies to learning Tamil, while serving as interim replacement for a Congregational missionary of the American Board at the Batlagunda station of its Madura mission.[32]

[28] C. H. Hopkins, *John R. Mott 1865–1955: A Biography* (Grand Rapids, MI, 1979), pp. 391–2.

[29] Eddy papers, Box 3, Report Letter No. 44 (15 Jan. 1913).

[30] Hopkins, *John R. Mott*, p. 391. Eddy had expressed the hope to E. C. Carter in January 1912 that his tour with Mott later that year might prove that the time had at last come 'to break through the ranks of caste and reap among high-caste students' (Yale Divinity School Library, Special Collections, MS Group 45, Mott Papers, Box 25, Eddy to Carter, 24 Jan. 1912).

[31] Eddy Papers, Box 3, Report Letter No. 19 (Oct. 1899).

[32] Eddy, *Eighty Adventurous Years*, pp. 41–2; Nutt, *The Whole Gospel*, pp. 51–4.

After this interlude, Eddy resumed his YMCA duties. From 1911 these were performed on a wider stage as a result of his promotion to the position of travelling secretary for Asia. He never abandoned his Indian student ministry, for which he was peculiarly gifted. In China, which Eddy first visited in 1907, and to which he returned with Mott in 1913 and repeatedly thereafter, he remained fully committed to a top-down evangelistic strategy aimed at the students and scholar-officials. Particularly after the Republican revolution of 1911–12, Eddy, like many other missionaries, interpreted the enthusiasm of these groups for Western ideas as an unprecedented opportunity for Christian evangelism. In India, by contrast, his strategic vision was no longer so clear. Whilst he had lost confidence in the sufficiency of student evangelism alone to promote the conversion of India, he reacted with dismay when in 1909 Azariah relinquished his work as secretary of the National Missionary Society to immerse himself in parish work among the poor villagers of Dornakal: Eddy believed Azariah was 'throwing his life away' in the service of a people so 'degraded' that no appreciable results could be expected.[33] Eddy's growing appreciation of the potential of work among outcastes was thus partial and gradual, and always qualified by a degree of racial scepticism about the capacity of uneducated Indians to manage their own affairs on Western democratic lines. His own Congregational tradition he believed to be unsuitable for the 'depressed and ignorant people' of India, who were used to government by *rajah* and *panchayat*. On these grounds Eddy favoured a constitutional form of episcopacy as the basis for negotiation towards church union in South India, of which he was an enthusiastic supporter.[34]

Eddy's first twenty years in Asia thus led him to reconceive his vision of the route whereby India would be won for Christ. Inevitably, there was also some moderation over the years of his originally extreme language about Hindus and their religious practices. By 1912 he was writing with greater sympathy of the search after religious truth indicated by the contemporary religious awakening in India, but

[33] Eddy, *Eighty Adventurous Years*, p. 54.

[34] G. S. Eddy, 'A national church for India', *The Harvest Field*, 31 (1911), pp. 213–19, cited in Brian Stanley, 'The reshaping of Christian tradition: western denominational identity in a non-western context', in R. N. Swanson, ed., *Unity and Diversity in the Church*, *SCH* 32 (1996), p. 411. As early as 1902 Eddy had commented on the inadequacy of Congregationalism to cope with the strains produced by mass movements in Travancore; see Eddy papers, Box 3, Report Letter No. 30 (30 Oct. 1902).

it was still described as a search doomed to disappointment without missionary intervention: 'Groping up the world's dark altar stairs to God, they need helping hands stretched down to grasp theirs in the darkness.'[35] Eddy's understanding of mission was still essentially one of a movement from West to East which consisted in an appeal to individual religious conversion. From 1916 onwards, that understanding was transformed by his personal experience of the First World War.

Initially, the onset of war appears to have made little impact on Eddy. In 1916, however, the YMCA appointed him associate secretary for foreign work (though he retained the title of secretary for Asia), and in July that year he sailed for Europe to work among allied troops in Britain and France.[36] Even before he neared the trenches, Eddy's personal and official correspondence began to sound what was for him a new note. A visit to Canterbury Cathedral in August 1916 led him to reflect on the tragic juxtaposition of the tombs of monks and saints and the regimental battle standards which adorned the nave above them. Holy men down the years had failed to Christianize the political, social, and industrial order, and Eddy realized 'how blind' he too had been to the great questions of social Christianity.[37] A tour of the army camps on Salisbury Plain aroused reflections on the massive scale of the human sacrifices currently being enacted in France, which, like their supposed predecessors centuries ago at Stonehenge, derived from a mistaken conception of God and a low conception of humanity.[38] His encounters with the troops in the camps evoked an ambiguous evaluation of human nature. On the one hand, Eddy became convinced that the deadliest foes which confronted the Allied armies were not German troops, but intemperance and impurity. Yet, on the other hand, he was driven by the evidence of human comradeship and bravery to a belief, 'not in the total depravity, but to a belief in the total goodness of these men in their deepest aspirations and desires'.[39]

In October 1916 Eddy returned to the United States for six months to raise funds for the YMCA. During this period, on 17 February 1917, his fourteen-year-old son, Arden, died of pneumonia. Eddy, and, to a

[35] Sherwood Eddy, *India Awakening* (New York, 1912), p. 53.

[36] Nutt, *The Whole Gospel*, pp. 116–18.

[37] Eddy Papers, Box 1, Eddy to his mother, 19 Aug. 1916; and to his wife, Maud, 21 Aug. 1916.

[38] Eddy papers, Box 1, Eddy to his mother, 30 Sept. 1916.

[39] Ibid.; also Eddy to Maud, 21 Aug. 1916; and Eddy, *A Pilgrimage of Ideas*, p. 181.

still greater extent, his wife, were deeply affected by this loss, which was one of the origins of what subsequently became a fascination with the nature of human existence after death.[40] Back in France, Eddy ministered in the base camps alongside figures such as D. S. Cairns, J. N. Farquhar, and A. G. Fraser. Eddy saw new relevance in the red triangle of the YMCA, symbolizing its commitment to meet equally the needs of body, mind, and spirit.[41] His evangelistic addresses to the troops followed a regular pattern. On the first night he would take the theme of 'The Greatest Battle of the War', namely, the moral battle against sin and temptation. On the second night he spoke on 'The Real Issues of the War – or What Are We Fighting For?' Eddy's answer was in terms of the building of a new world in which there would be no place for 'German materialism', 'Russian autocracy', 'Turkish cruelty', 'Balkan perfidy', nor, crucially, for the industrial oppression of Western society. On the third and final night of his series, his title was 'Over the Top and After: or Death and What Lies Beyond'. Eddy later commented that 'I knew nothing then about the subject of survival from a psychic standpoint, and I had no scientific evidence to offer the men, but heart-hungry before entering battle, they always crowded that third meeting.'[42] His talk on the final night regularly made use of the story of his son, himself a keen practitioner of the Morning Watch, and called for decisions for Christ using Arden's favourite hymn, 'Just as I am, young, strong, and free'. Eddy records that the story always made a deep impression.[43]

In 1918 Eddy published a book defending the entry by the United States into the war.[44] Within six years, however, he had moved to a committed pacifist position, as illustrated by his publication in 1924, jointly with his secretary, Kirby Page, of a book entitled *The Abolition of War*.[45] Eddy had come to see militarism as but one expression of the systemic evil of the supposedly Christian West: hitherto, by his own

40 For Maud's 'uncontrollable eagerness' to join Arden in the other world see Nutt, *The Whole Gospel*, p. 283.

41 Eddy Papers, Box 3, undated Report Letter [1917], 'Somewhere in France', and circular letter dated 31 July 1917; Sherwood Eddy, *With our Soldiers in France* (New York, 1917), pp. 101–3.

42 Sherwood Eddy, *You Will Survive Death* (Reigate, 1954), p. 9.

43 Eddy Papers, Box 1, Eddy to his mother, 3 Aug. 1917; Box 3, circular letter from Eddy dated 1 March 1917.

44 Sherwood Eddy, *The Right to Fight: The Moral Grounds of War* (New York, 1918).

45 Sherwood Eddy and Kirby Page, *The Abolition of War: The Case against War and Questions and Answers concerning War* (Garden City, NY, 1924).

admission, he had 'specialized in retail sins but knew little about the wholesale brand'; henceforth he was a champion of the social gospel.[46] Throughout the 1920s Eddy urged the Student Volunteer Movement to respond to the growing pressure from the post-war generation of students for the movement to espouse social Christianity. At the SVM quadrennial convention at Des Moines in January 1920, the first to be held after the war, Eddy abandoned his prepared address on the adequacy of the gospel for all humankind and spoke instead about the sin, both social and personal, which characterized the heathenism of North America.[47] At the Detroit convention at the close of 1927, Eddy famously repudiated the SVM Watchword as 'a Paul Revere's ride across the world'. No-one challenged him. One observer noted that, in the mind of the SVM leadership, the problem of missions had become the problem of world Christianization, a phrase which contained within it the full programme of the social gospel.[48] Reinhold Niebuhr's address at the 1927 convention, with its indictment of Western civilization as unchristian, convinced Eddy that the young Detroit pastor should be brought to New York to a more influential post. He persuaded the principal of Union Theological Seminary to appoint Niebuhr as associate professor of Christian ethics, and for two years Eddy was wholly responsible for paying Niebuhr's salary.[49] Eddy was by now an enthusiastic admirer of Ramsay MacDonald's Labour Party, believing it to represent the ideal political embodiment of Christian ethical principles. He was only slightly less enthusiastic about Soviet Russia, and organized regular study trips to the Soviet Union under the auspices of a group called the 'American Seminar'.[50]

Although the First World War was primarily responsible for converting Eddy to social Christianity, his continuing YMCA work also played its part. While remaining as YMCA travelling secretary for Asia throughout the 1920s, he spent some months of every year fund-raising among the business community in the United States. Such work Eddy found challenging, indeed 'as exciting as big-game hunting', but

[46] Eddy, *Eighty Adventurous Years*, pp. 117–19.

[47] Nathan D. Showalter, *The End of a Crusade: The Student Volunteer Movement for Foreign Missions and the Great War* (Lanham, MD, and London, 1998), pp. 88–9.

[48] 'Youth and missions', *The Christian Century*, 15, 2 (12 Jan. 1928), p. 40, cited in G. H. Anderson, 'American Protestants in pursuit of mission, 1886–1986', in F. J. Verstraelen, et al., eds, *Missiology: An Ecumenical Introduction* (Grand Rapids, MI, 1995), p. 394.

[49] Richard Wightman Fox, *Reinhold Niebuhr: A Biography* (New York: Pantheon Books, 1985), pp. 104–5, 262.

[50] Nutt, *The Whole Gospel*, pp. 202–17.

it also prompted critical reflection on the social system which made such wealth possible.[51] By 1927 he could write that 'Mammon is a much more potent idol than Kali or Siva.'[52] Some within the missionary movement understandably feared that Eddy and his fellow social gospel enthusiasts were sawing off the branch on which the entire overseas mission enterprise sat. Sherwood's own brother, Brewer, senior secretary of the American Board of Commissioners for Foreign Missions, expressed anxiety in 1925 about the impact of his brother's pronouncements on his own mission's funds, then already in a critical condition.[53] Within the American YMCA, whose finances were heavily dependent on support from the business community, opposition to Eddy as a 'Bolshevist' mounted, and in 1926 he survived an attempt to force him to resign only through the personal intervention of Mott.[54] He remained in YMCA service until his retirement in 1931.

In the minds of most of its leading advocates, the social gospel was conceived as a supplement to, and not a substitute for, the gospel of personal conversion. Eddy had abandoned belief in the Watchword but not in the missionary imperative itself. He took little notice of the Hocking report of 1932, *Re-Thinking Missions*, which appeared to reduce the aim of missions to the promotion of co-operation between the great religions in a common quest for truth.[55] He continued to conduct evangelistic campaigns in Asia until 1935, when a four-month campaign of twenty Chinese cities amassed a total of 2,476 decisions for Christ.[56] He never regarded Chinese communism with the same sympathy as he did Soviet communism, and, like many missionary leaders, pinned his hopes for the regeneration of China on Chiang Kai-shek, although becoming increasingly disillusioned with Chiang's failure to promote agrarian reform.[57] Even Eddy's enthusiasm for Soviet Russia gradually dimmed in the course of the 1930s, as he became more aware of the infringements of religious and civil liberty. Influenced by Reinhold Niebuhr, he eventually abandoned pacifism

[51] Eddy, *Eighty Adventurous Years*, pp. 112–13.

[52] Eddy, *Religion and Social Justice*, p. 185, cited in Nutt, *The Whole Gospel*, p. 185.

[53] Nutt, *The Whole Gospel*, pp. 191–2.

[54] Ibid., pp. 192–8.

[55] Ibid., p. 261; W. E. Hocking (ed.), *Re-Thinking Missions: A Laymen's Inquiry after One Hundred Years* (New York and London, 1932), pp. 44–59.

[56] Eddy, *Eighty Adventurous Years*, p. 77.

[57] Nutt, *The Whole Gospel*, pp. 223–4, 252–4, 309–10.

during the dark days of 1938. Haltingly, and in his own pragmatic fashion, he had come to share in some measure Niebuhr's profoundly theological repudiation of the liberal Protestant hope that the Kingdom of God would be inaugurated through the progress of Christian civilization; yet Eddy, despite his sustained support for Niebuhr, continued to think of himself as a liberal in theology.[58] His autobiography made clear that Eddy now adhered to a form of universalism. Yet he still insisted on the necessity to proclaim to all humanity the message of the love of God in Christ, and even claimed that 'to my last breath I shall make the same fervent appeal for missionaries "in this generation" that I made to the last generation'. Overseas missions, however, were now said to be 'not enough': 'the same love which the missionary takes to the uttermost parts of the earth must be the controlling power in the lives of men who profess Christianity at home'.[59]

The stages of Sherwood Eddy's religious pilgrimage were in many respects typical of trends in Anglo-American Protestant missions in the period from the 1890s to the 1940s. The broadening of his missionary message represented not an abandonment of the call to conversion, but rather an extension of that call from individuals to societies, and from the Orient to the Occident. The social gospel of liberal Protestantism was the first major endeavour to formulate a missiology for Western culture. Yet, like many other mission leaders between the wars, Eddy never quite succeeded in squaring his insistence that Western industrial society needed redemption with his continuing commitment to the propagation of Western ideals of progress and liberty to the rest of the world.

In one respect at least, however, Eddy's pilgrimage was unrepresentative of trends in the missionary movement as a whole. As early as 1925, the concern with the afterlife instilled by the First World War and by Arden's death in particular began to bear fruit in a serious endeavour by both Sherwood and Maud Eddy to investigate the scientific basis of spiritualist claims to communicate with the dead. After an initial visit to a medium in December 1925, their investigation appears not to have been sustained.[60] However, in 1937 their

[58] Ibid., pp. 292, 334; see Fox, *Reinhold Niebuhr*, pp. 136–7, 140.

[59] Eddy, *Eighty Adventurous Years*, pp. 80–1, 234–6. He continued to believe in hell only as a limited period of self-exclusion from the presence of God.

[60] Eddy, *You Will Survive Death*, pp. 145–8. For the explosion of interest in spiritualism in

interest in psychic phenomena was revived through a series of contacts with spiritualists arranged by a Quaker, Edward Cope Wood of Philadelphia, a long-standing friend of both Eddy and John Mott.[61] By 1938 Eddy was visiting mediums regularly, and making psychic contact with Arden and other deceased members of the family. One of his last publications was a book, *You Will Survive After Death*, expounding a spiritualist understanding of personal immortality.[62] These beliefs were, however, bolted on to his existing theological framework, and he never became a member of a spiritualist church. Eddy's spiritualism supplies evidence of the inadequacy of the label 'liberal' in his case. The intense and adventurous supernaturalism which had led him as a young evangelist to hunt for the souls of Hindus with such fervour had in his old age found an outlet in a hunt for souls beyond the grave. 'For me', wrote Eddy at the conclusion of *Eighty Adventurous Years*, 'this study of survival has been a great adventure.'[63] At one point in the 1950s, Eddy asked his spirit contact, 'Father Tobe', whether humans would be permitted to destroy the planet through atomic weapons. Father Tobe had replied that, though they would not be so permitted, even if such destruction of humanity were to take place, it would not matter, since 'from our point of view, there is no death', only a 'swift and relatively painless transition to a better environment'.[64] Although Eddy subsequently records that he did not agree with every tenet of Father Tobe's 'theology', the comment of Eddy's recent biographer that he had apparently substituted a concept of the immortality of the soul for the Christian understanding of resurrection seems apposite.[65] Perhaps there is, after all, some continuity with the young India missionary who could describe plague and cholera as the judgements of God. For all his enthusiasm for social Christianity, the question remains whether

the aftermath of the war see Ruth Brandon, *The Spiritualists: The Passion for the Occult in the Nineteenth and Twentieth Centuries* (London, 1983), pp. 220–2.

[61] Eddy, *You Will Survive Death*, p. 7; Mott Papers, Box 25, Mott to Eddy, 24 Sept. 1940, and Eddy to Mott, 26 Sept. 1940.

[62] Sherwood Eddy, *You Will Survive After Death* (New York, 1950). The book was published in Britain as *You Will Survive Death* (Reigate, 1954). I have used the British edition.

[63] Eddy, *Eighty Adventurous Years*, p. 224.

[64] Eddy, *You Will Survive Death*, pp. 137–8.

[65] Ibid., p. 127; Nutt, *The Whole Gospel*, pp. 333–4. 'Father Tobe' was the 'control' of the medium, E. A. Macbeth, and, as Tobias McCarthy, had been an Irish monk in the nineteenth century.

Sherwood Eddy ever learnt to take with proper seriousness the physicality implicit in the Christian doctrines of creation, incarnation, crucifixion, and resurrection.

St Edmund's College, Cambridge

THE GOVERNOR A MISSIONARY? DUTCH COLONIAL RULE AND CHRISTIANIZATION DURING IDENBURG'S TERM OF OFFICE AS GOVERNOR OF INDONESIA (1909–16)

by PIETER N. HOLTROP

INTRODUCTION

'AS a result of forced Christianization, the motherland threatens to alienate the indigenous population of our colonies from herself.' With this slogan a combination of left-wing political parties entered the elections for the Dutch Parliament in June 1913.[1] This combination won the elections and in the end it was the liberal Cort van der Linden who was commissioned to form a government. The then governor-general of what was called the Dutch East Indies, the Christian statesman A. W. F. Idenburg (1861–1935),[2] consequently considered relinquishing his post, now that a government would be formed of a political colour different from his own. On the advice of the leader of his party, the Dutch politician, journalist, and church leader Abraham Kuyper, however, he decided that his decision to stay or to resign would depend on the possibilities of co-operation with the new minister of colonial affairs. But he had no illusions about the opinion of the European press in Indonesia. 'Against me,' he wrote in a letter to the outgoing minister of colonial affairs, J. H. de Waal Malefijt (1852–1931), a fellow party member, 'a devilish howling has burst out in some of the papers. They all agree that I must go.'[3]

That was, true enough, the opinion of the vast majority of the

[1] In *Parlement en Kiezer, 1913–1914* (The Hague, 1913), p. 49.

[2] In writing this paper I have made use of the rich family archives of A. W. F. Idenburg, which are kept in Het Historisch Documentatiecentrum voor het Nederlands Protestantisme (1800–heden) of the Free University of Amsterdam. I would like to thank Prof. Dr J. de Bruijn for the permission to consult these archives. I also used C. J. Middelberg-Idenburg, *A. W. F. Idenburg* (The Hague, 1935); F. L. Rutgers, 'Idenburg en de Sarekat Islam in 1913', thesis, Free University of Amsterdam (1939); B. J. Brouwer, *De houding van Idenburg en Colijn tegenover de Indonesische Beweging* (Kampen, 1958); J. de Bruijn and G. Puchinger, eds, *Briefwisseling Kuyper-Idenburg* (Franeker, 1985) [hereafter *Correspondence*]. I intend to publish a more elaborate study on 'Missions and the Government in the Dutch East Indies'.

[3] 7 July 1913, in *Correspondence*, p. 377, n.2.

European press in Indonesia. The authoritative paper *De Locomotief* wrote on 28 June,

> Mr. Idenburg rules as a Christian statesman here, – he would not deny it himself –, in the service of a Christian government, of which he himself was the minister of colonial affairs. . . . Idenburg should go, because the electorate's verdict on the clerical cabinet is also a verdict on the Christian colonial government policies that were inspired by this cabinet.

A similar judgement was passed by the newspaper *Soerabaiaasch Handelsblad*, which had been a declared opponent of Idenburg's views, policies, and actions from the beginning of his term of office. 'We have a governor-general here whose thinking is too much influenced by Kuyper, who has too many apostolic aspirations.'[4]

What did this governor-general do during his seven-year term of office (from 1909 till 1916) for the European press in Indonesia to attack him so fiercely? The answer is: 'Forced Christianization', and this allegation will be the subject of this paper. We will try to answer the question whom or what this accusation was really aimed at, and if or to what degree this was a just accusation. Before we can answer this last question it is necessary to say something about Idenburg, about the political movement he belonged to, about the leading ideas of the Dutch colonial policies in those days, and about Idenburg's policies as governor-general.

A. W. F. IDENBURG

Alexander Willem Frederik Idenburg was born as the son of a physician in an orthodox Protestant family in Rotterdam. There he developed his piety, that of the Protestant nineteenth-century Revival. Politically, ecclesiastically, and culturally, he was influenced by the (militant) ideals of the great nineteenth-century theologian and statesman Abraham Kuyper (1839–1920), founder of an ecclesiastical denomination (*Reformed Churches in the Netherlands*), leader of a Christian political party (*Anti-Revolutionary Party*), chief editor of a daily (*De Standaard*), founder of a university (*Free University* in Amsterdam), and prime minister.

[4] 21 June 1913, quoted in *Correspondence*, p. 386, n.2.

From 1882 till 1900 Idenburg served with the army in Indonesia. He was stationed in various places on Java – and even in Aceh for some time – and finally he was appointed to the Department of War in Batavia. Most remarkable were his orthodoxy, his involvement in the orthodox Christian Reformed Church in Batavia, and his principled attitude to life. He refused to participate in some of the ceremonies in military circles. During a furlough in 1896 Idenburg personally met with Abraham Kuyper, whose journalistic work had made a deep impression on him. After some deliberations Idenburg was elected a Member of Parliament in 1901, as a representative of Abraham Kuyper's Anti-Revolutionary Party. From 1901 rightwing parties, including Kuyper's party, gained a majority in parliament; Kuyper became prime minister. From that moment on Idenburg's career rocketed. He was asked to be minister of colonial affairs in 1902, a calling Idenburg did not dare to decline. After the fall of Kuyper's rightwing cabinet in 1905, Idenburg became governor of Holland's other colony, Surinam. From 1908 onwards Idenburg again served as minister of colonial affairs, a position he exchanged for the office of 'viceroy of the Indies' in 1909. After his retirement as governor-general, Idenburg held the office of minister of colonial affairs for the third time, 1918–19. From 1920 till 1924 he was minister of state and a member of the Senate, and in 1924 he became a member of the Privy Council and Queen Wilhelmina's personal advisor. He died in 1935.

ETHICAL POLICY

Idenburg's political views gain relief against the background of the political views of his party, the Anti-Revolutionary Party, on Holland's colonial policies at the beginning of this century. These were called the 'ethical policy', and these views were guided by the idea of the moral obligation of the motherland toward its colonies.[5] On this, the Anti-Revolutionary Party stood in the tradition of a number of great nineteenth-century Christian statesmen,[6] who were of the opinion not only that the government was not allowed to prevent missions, but even that the government had the duty to *promote* missions. Christianization, they said, was the necessary condition for spiritual and cultural

[5] Cf. Brouwer, *De houding van Idenburg*, pp. 2–4; C. Fasseur, *Wilhelmina. De jonge koningin* (Amsterdam, 1998), pp. 456–9.

[6] Such as Elout van Soeterwoude, Groen van Prinsterer, and Keuchenius.

development. One of those famous Christian statesmen, Groen van Prinsterer, stated that it should not be civilization first and Christianity afterwards, but Christianization first. And one of Idenburg's predecessors as a minister of colonial affairs, the Christian statesman Keuchenius, became famous for his blunt criticism of what he called 'the Christ-barring service of Mammon' of the conservatives.

It was, however, Abraham Kuyper who placed the Anti-Revolutionaries in sharp contrast with the conservatives on the one hand and the liberals on the other. As early as 1879 he wrote a political manifesto for his party, which has become famous in spite of its unimaginative name, *Our Programme*. During many decades this programme pointed the way for the Anti-Revolutionary Party. Article 18 is quite clear about the direction in which the party wanted to steer colonial policies: 'As for colonial matters, it holds that the tendency of our policies to selfishly exploit the colonies for the benefit of the state or private persons should give way to policies of moral obligation.'[7]

These words sounded once again two decades later, but now in the broader context of the so-called 'ethical policy', that is, the policy which gave priority to the interests and the economic and cultural elevation of the indigenous population. The 'ethical policy', the policy of 'moral obligation', derives its contents to a high degree from Abraham Kuyper's ideas as they had appeared in *Our Programme*, but also from the ideas of the lawyer and politician C. Th. van Deventer (1857–1915), who had published his famous article, 'Our Debt of Honour', in the magazine *De Gids* in 1899. This policy, which flourished during the first quarter of the twentieth century, may be regarded as the other side of the imperialism which determined thought and action in The Hague and in Buitenzorg. In the Indonesian archipelago around the turn of the century it led to the large-scale actions of 'pacification', which were meant to bring the 'outer provinces' directly under Dutch authority. Subjugation was followed by Dutch governance; those who governed at that time were aware of the 'white man's burden'. In the areas which had come under Dutch governance, taxes were levied, but also roads were constructed, schools were founded, and hospitals were built.

[7] A. Kuyper, *Ons Program* (Hilversum and Pretoria, 1907), p. 5.

MORAL CALLING

But Kuyper and the politicians of his party had their own interpretation of this notion of 'moral obligation'. 'If', Kuyper wrote as early as 1878, 'the Empire has to fulfil the duties of a guardian towards its possessions overseas, and if at the top of this list of duties we find the obligation "to *morally educate* the foster-child," then a colonial programme of the Anti-Revolutionaries in which the christianization of the Indies is not the point of departure, is unthinkable.'[8] Even though Kuyper was conscious of the fact that the government itself was not called to the work of Christianization, he had no doubt that it had to do everything in its power to clear the way for the efforts of missionary organizations.

So, when in 1901 Kuyper became the prime minister, it is not surprising that in the Speech from the Throne of 1901 he connected the idea of the Netherlands as a 'Christian Power' to its 'moral calling' towards Indonesia.

Idenburg too regarded the Christianization of the Indies as the starting-point, more precisely as the *distinctive contents* of the Anti-Revolutionary colonial programme. He said as much in his maiden speech in Parliament in 1901, and repeated it in 1928, in his contribution to a commemorative volume of the Anti-Revolutionary Party.[9] In that article he showed that he was conscious of the culture-clash occurring in Indonesia. He therefore pointed to the necessity of giving a religious foundation to education in Indonesia. The only possibility for the various cultures and races in Indonesia really to come together – and he still believed in this possibility of 'association' – was, in his opinion, for the West to come to the East not 'religionless', but by showing the East 'that the West does have a soul'. And this soul was, to Idenburg, Christianity. What Christianity had achieved in the first centuries of our era could still be accomplished nowadays;[10] he wrote:

> It can give to the cultural development in the Indies the roots that support our culture, from which our culture is still receiving its

[8] *Ons Programme*, p. 338 (par. 258).

[9] A. W. F. Idenburg, 'Ons beginsel voor koloniale politiek', in *Schrift en Historie. Gedenkboek bij het vijftig-jarig bestaan der georganiseerde antirevolutionaire partij 1878–1928* (Kampen, 1928), pp. 203–22.

[10] Ibid., p. 216.

> nutritious saps. The danger of contact with our 'modern culture' is that cultural adaptation is merely external; that technology and science, law and methods are adopted, but that there is no soul in it; a split personality is the result. The danger is that one obtains a plant which has been cut loose from its roots and is therefore destined to wither. For such is a culture without religion.

Idenburg was not naive. He acknowledged the opinion of the influential Dutch expert on Islam, Chr. Snouck Hurgronje (1857–1936), who, though he had a high regard for the significance of Christianity, saw little future for it in 'countries on which the breath of Islam has descended'. Even so, Idenburg refused to call it utopian to expect Christianity to take possession of minds in Indonesia and to gain ground in areas controlled by Islam. In his speech in parliament in 1902 he responded to the pessimism of the socialist Member of Parliament H. H. van Kol (1852–1925). He conceded that the Christianization of Indonesia would not be easy, but said that missions, not the government, could yet attempt to 'transform the spirit of the people in such a way that at the societal level the principles of Christianity would be accepted as the foundations of the people's lives.'[11]

IDENBURG'S POLICIES

Fasseur called Idenburg 'the incarnation of the Christian version of the ethical colonial policy'[12] and it is hardly possible to think of a better characterization. But if so, what part of Idenburg's policies caused such a rage in the European press during his rule as a governor-general in Indonesia? One can point to three issues: Idenburg's circulars about Sunday rest of 1910, his regulations concerning private (i.e. Christian) schools, and his attitude and (moderate) actions towards the *Sarekat Islam* (Muslim League).

Sunday rest

In August 1910 Idenburg sent a circular letter to the provincial authorities. In it he expressed his wish that civil servants should not be officially involved in public festivities on Sundays. He asked them to

[11] *Handelingen Tweede Kamer* (1902–3), p. 106.
[12] Fasseur, *Wilhelmina*, p. 460.

see to it that no public festivities would be held during the times of church services on Sundays, or at least that those festivities would not be of an official character. At the end of the same month Idenburg sent another circular letter, in which he asked them to discourage the Sunday markets. This second circular in particular aroused great indignation on the part of the European press in Indonesia. The *Javabode* (1 September 1910) wrote that 'because of his peculiar religious views – which, of course, are all to be respected – the Governor mixes matters of religion with purely economic matters.' 'They rose in rage', Idenburg wrote to Kuyper on 9 October, 'not so much against what I have written, but more against what they thought I had written or would write.' And to his superior, the minister of colonial affairs, Idenburg wrote, 'It is as if all hell has broken loose.' And in a later letter,

> I have seen a fair share of the world, but I had never thought that the enmity against positive Christianity – in fact, it wasn't even positive Christianity – would be so great and bitter among so-called Christians. It is really true that the so-called European press, – that is the Indies press which is edited by Europeans and Indo-Europeans, – has roused the indigenous press and irritated the indigenous population *much more* than was necessary taking into consideration the standpoint of the population itself.[13]

He confided to another leader of a Christian party in the Netherlands (A. F. de Savornin Lohman, 1837–1924) that it was by no means his intention to adopt legislation concerning Sunday. Such laws would certainly not find support in the conscience of the population, he wrote. He added that it had become clear to him that in several places the Sunday markets had been instituted by European officials – not in order to protect Indonesian customs, but with the aim of entertaining Europeans on Sunday mornings. The issue was even discussed in the Dutch parliament, but the minister protected the governor and the matter ended there – at least for the time being.

Private schools

Idenburg's education policies evoked even more vigorous opposition than his circulars on Sunday rest. Because of the continuing expansion of the colonial territories and the educational orientation of the ethical

[13] Idenburg to De Waal Malefijt, 9 November 1910. Cf. *Correspondence*, pp. 216–19.

colonial policy, the authorities in the Indies faced at the turn of the century the problem of how to cope with the increasing demand for education. The organizational innovations which found expression in the founding of village schools besides the state schools were strongly encouraged by Idenburg. His policies were aimed at supporting and subsidizing private initiative in the area of education, especially that of missions. He wrote to Kuyper on 22 February 1912,

> I heartily hope that in the Netherlands enthusiasm for Christian education in the Indies will flare up and continue to burn intensely. I must repeat again and again that until now very little has been done in this area in the Netherlands, and the task at hand is enormous. Not just for the Muslim world, but also for the pagan world. In the fallow lands we want to try out the policy of having *only* Christian education, with almost full reimbursement of expenses (on Sumba, among other places).

This policy of conscious encouragement of missionary initiatives, however, provoked heavy opposition, not just in Indonesia, but also in the Netherlands. At the end of 1911 a war broke out in the Dutch parliament. Referring to the fierce battle that was waged in the Netherlands on the issue of state versus private, that is Christian, schools, Fasseur rightly spoke of the 'Indies battle on the schools', thus comparing it with the endless battle in the Netherlands on private (that is, Christian) schools. In his speech of 20 November 1911, when the Indies budget was discussed, Kuyper urged his fellow party member, the minister of colonial affairs, to apply the Anti-Revolutionary principle, 'private education is the rule, state education the exception', in Indonesia too, and to give priority to private schools over state schools. Subsidies to private schools, including missionary schools, should be raised, Kuyper said.[14] The minister's response was quite cautious. He pointed out that in Java, Christianity had very few adherents, and that the Muslim population lacked the organization to found its own schools. In other words, education could not be left to private initiative there. Further, he indicated that in subsidizing missionary schools the government should avoid appearing to force Christianization backed by the state. The minister deemed Christianization desirable for political reasons (if only to defeat Islam), but the government could not promote it directly, he said.

[14] Cf. *Correspondence*, pp. 267–74.

Kuyper then launched a frontal attack on his fellow party member, who, astonished by Kuyper's discourtesy, informed Idenburg that he thought there was something wrong with Mr Kuyper's mind. We need not go into the details of this bitter struggle now. Suffice it to say that the discord among the rightwing, Christian party ranks was welcomed by the opposition. The lawyer, Th. H. de Meester (1851–1919), chief editor of *Het Vaderland* and Member of Parliament for the left-wing opposition, in line with van Deventer, raised serious objections to the subsidization of missionary education. 'The continuous founding and subsidization of missionary schools', de Meester said, 'gives rise to unrest and hidden resentment. . . . Considering the plans to start missionary work in Solo in the near future, there is much reason to fear that dangerous fuel is being accumulated in these previously tolerant principalities.'[15]

Idenburg was most unhappy about the actions of his fellow party members in parliament. In a letter to the minister of colonial affairs he pointed out that since the speeches of his fellow party members in parliament, and also due to the agitation in the European press in Indonesia, a spirit of resistance was manifesting itself in Indonesia, especially in the highest strata of the indigenous world, against Christianity and missions in particular. Idenburg was much troubled by this, and even wondered whether it were better to resign from office.[16]

> These things too weigh me down, and they make me wonder whether it would be better for me to leave. You could then send somebody who is moderately indifferent, – who would not bring a certain Christian reputation along, – and probably things would quieten down here as a result. . . . Would you, please, consider this seriously and honestly tell me your opinion. There is no place for personal sensitivities here. We serve our country and our Queen and, first of all, our heavenly King – and not ourselves. It may well be that the Indies cannot be ruled Christianly, because the vast majority of the natives are Mahometans and because the vast majority of the white people are pagans. One is confronted by a public opinion which is alien to our principles. . . . As long as everything was quiet all went well, with the missions too, – because of the gentle character of the people. But now that this

[15] *Handelingen Tweede Kamer*, 25 November 1912.
[16] In a letter to De Waal Malefijt, 29 March 1912.

> rest is disturbed, all I do and say is met with suspicion, this difference becomes quite obvious, and I wonder whether I had not better leave.

Sarekat Islam

A third issue which roused the feelings of particularly the Europeans in Indonesia was the rise of the nationalist movement, of which the 'Indische Partij' (Indies Party) of E. F. E. Douwes Dekker (1879–1950) and Sarekat Islam were indicative, the latter in its own special way. The focal point of the discussion was whether the governor-general should officially grant Sarekat Islam the right to act in public.[17] Sarekat Islam was an Islamic League which aimed at strengthening the economic position of the indigenous, especially the Muslim, population. Idenburg did not give in to the pressure of the European and Indo-European entrepreneurs to use violence. By manoeuvring cautiously he could assuage feelings. He was convinced that this movement in Indonesia was not anti-Dutch as the one in British India was anti-British (although the two movements can be compared in detail).[18]

In the Indies press, Idenburg's policies of Christianization were blamed for the rise of the nationalist movement and of Sarekat Islam in particular. In a letter to the Editor in the *Nieuwe Rotterdamse Courant* of 25 June 1913, Idenburg was blamed for his attitude, because of which 'hundreds of our tribe live in danger of death'. Although Idenburg was somewhat worried about the usually tactless attitude of the missions towards Muslims, he rejected this idea. He wrote to his superior in The Hague that officially there was no reason for him to suspect the League, since it behaved 'properly', 'loyally', and 'not in a revolutionary way'.[19] 'And yet', he added,

> I cannot say that I fully trust it. Partly because I don't really understand it. It is so new, so extraordinary, it is such a rapid organizing of the indigenous population, penetrating everywhere, that one wonders: whence and whereto? It is not exclusively a movement against the Chinese, it is not an organization directed against missions, but then, what is it? Undoubtedly, the pert behaviour of the Chinese and the fact that they received more

[17] See the discussion on this issue in Rutgers, *Idenburg en de Sarekat Islam in 1913*.

[18] Idenburg pointed at the similarity in his letter to Kuyper, 1 June 1913. Cf. Percival Spear, *India. A Modern History* (Michigan, 1961), pp. 318f.

[19] To De Waal Malefijt, 19 March 1913.

> freedom of movement have been conducive to the Sarekat Islam's foundation and its expansion. The alleged attempt of the state to Christianize the population has also been used as a means to get the people organized. . . . But if the deepest *cause* is not to be found in an anti-Chinese spirit or in an anti-Christian mission-spirit, if these are but accompanying factors, what then is the cause? It cannot be denied that during the last few years a spirit of awakening, of becoming conscious of oneself, has been moving through the East.

For Idenburg and for the defence of his policies concerning Sarekat Islam it was of great importance that a declaration was issued from unexpected quarters. The chief editor of *Oetoesan Hindia*, Tjokroaminoto, and two other leaders of Sarekat Islam in Surabaya, Tjokrosudarno and Hadiwidjojo, declared in a notarial act of 8 July 1913 that the movement's origins did not lie in anti-missionary feelings. The leaders stated that they were familiar with the history of Sarekat Islam's genesis. Explicitly they asserted

> that the genesis of the association 'Sarekat Islam' has nothing to do with what is repeatedly alleged in the Indies dailies, as if there would be any pressure from the government on Mahometans to cross over to the Christian religion;
> that neither have they detected in their surroundings that the attempts just mentioned (if there were such attempts) have caused any vexation among the natives;
> that the natives are not hindered in the execution of their Mahometan religious duties . . ., but that it may be accepted for sure and certain that the association 'Sarekat Islam' has not been founded as a bulwark against the Christian religion, or against any other religion whatsoever.[20]

IDENBURG'S OWN ASSESSMENT OF HIS POLICIES

There is no doubt that the Indies press was negative about Idenburg's policies. But how did Idenburg himself assess them? Or, to be more precise: how did he assess his relationship with the missions and his contribution as a governor-general to missionary work? Idenburg

[20] Text in Rutgers, *Sarekat Islam*, p. 41.

spoke about this on several occasions, both in his correspondence and in his autobiography.

In his autobiography he wrote that he was fully convinced that he had done the right thing in promoting missions, because he reckoned it to be in the spiritual interest of the population. 'To me', he wrote,[21]

> the interest of the population is closely linked with the expansion of Christianity. Therefore, I have promoted it as much as I could, but, as far as I know, without ever favouring or harming anybody because of his religious conviction. In my way of life, – going to church, prayer at meals, visits to missionary schools and hospitals, – I showed my appreciation of missionary work. And I flatter myself with the view that in those years . . . some influence in this matter was indeed exerted on public opinion.

He then pointed to the Sunday circulars and concluded, 'It is a fact that despite the opposition, not from the indigenous but from the European population, the idea of Sunday rest in businesses, in the country's service and on plantations has not been silenced.'

He was especially proud of the fact that through his actions missions had gained admission to the principality of Solo, which until then had been hermetically sealed against missions.

> And it is with gratitude that I remember having gained access to Solo for missions. Successive residents had continually opposed this opening up (in contrast with those of Djokja), making use of the Susuhunan, who, being a Mahometan prince, could not be expected to open up his land for Christian missions. When shortly after I had become governor I raised this matter and received the same response, I said that I could understand this (so-called) standpoint of the Susuhunan; that for that reason it was my wish that the opinion of the Susuhunan in this matter would no longer be asked, but that he would be informed of my decision that Christian missions would be admitted to Surakarta, just as they had been in Djokja and in the areas directly under the government's control, and that I expected him not to place any hindrance in their way. I also, somewhat emphatically, notified the resident of this, from whom I expected more hindrances than from the Sunan. The resident listened to reason and soon resigned.

[21] *Autobiografie* (ms. in Idenburg family archives), pp. 51c–52a, also quoted in *Correspondence*, pp. 52f.

At the end of his term of office (which was extended because of the war) he was less content about his contribution to the cause of Christianity in Indonesia. He wrote to his wife[22] that the last five years had produced little fruit, and, in a spirit of pietistic introspection he added,

> Has, then, God abandoned me? I certainly have not deserved that He would make me into a blessing or into an influence for the good. But will He allow His name to be slandered because of me? That they will rightly say, 'This Christian governor-general was no good, he did not move things forward.' The brothers (from the ARP) are discontented with me – at least, that is what I suspect – because I have not served their cause.

And in a later letter (13 February 1916) he wrote to his wife, full of self-reproach, that he felt he had denied the Lord:

> I have made myself believe that one should not cast pearls before swine, and that this holds in particular when one is faced with a Mahometan population whose religious zeal is roused so easily by the inimical European press, – but have I not made myself believe this for convenience's sake? I have told myself that a public office in a country with a mixed population is different from the office of a minister of the Gospel – but is such an idea not in fact a blindfold hindering me from seeing my real duty?

ATTACKS BY THE PRESS

Meanwhile, there was no doubt in Idenburg's mind about the reasons for the vicious attacks in the press. He wrote to Kuyper shortly after the elections of 1913 that the reason for the general aversion was 'his being a Christian' and (as the press called it) his 'sick ethics'. He was convinced that the latter was the real reason for the opposition. 'I have always kept in remembrance', he wrote to Kuyper,[23]

> that the Government's Regulations prescribe me in Article 55, 'One of the most important duties of the Governor-General is to protect the indigenous population against the arbitrariness of whomsoever.' That is why I have come into conflict with

[22] 9 May 1915.
[23] 4 July 1913.

conservative views and tendencies, with financial interests and personal sensitivities. They have clearly stated that they will pursue the economic elevation of the native, that they want to raise his intellectual and material position – but as soon as only a touch of this starts to happen they howl, 'Not in this way! For then the native's meekness is reduced and I will have to pay more.'

Of course, they don't *say* it in this way; they only whisper it, and they *say*: the population 'sinks back into savagery'. That which they mean is a consequence of the fact that the native starts to think about himself and about his environment. It is the beginning of his 'awakening'. And this does not need to be a 'sinking back into savagery' (and so far it *is not*; I challenge anyone to prove me wrong in this), but it is the end of the 'taillable et corvéable à merci'.[24] We should *rejoice* about this, even if it causes us some trouble; this is what we wanted, – at least, we said so, – and we have promoted it by our education. And there would be only cause for rejoicing if at the same time Christianity could penetrate more freely and deeply. But the liberals and especially the press here have made sure that it cannot.

WAS THE GOVERNOR A MISSIONARY?

Implicitly in this quotation we find the answer to the question at the beginning of this paper: was the governor a missionary? The answer must be that he was, in the sense that he was passionate about the ethical ideals of his time and that these ideals led him to progressive policies. Someone has rightly called him and his successor, J. P. graaf van Limburg Stirum (1916–21), 'the two most eminent and progressively thinking governors-general to have ruled the Indies'.[25] In Idenburg's case these ideals were rooted in his Christian faith and moulded by the Anti-Revolutionary colonial programme. More than his predecessors Idenburg was aware of the fact that the *common* good was served by the activities of the missions and by private education. He promoted these activities and utilized them as part of an overall plan, so that missions could work side by side with the government in fulfilling Holland's duty towards the population of the Indies.

[24] 'Obliged to all sorts of forced labour and taxes.'

[25] M. C. Jongeling, *Het zendingsconsulaat in Nederlands-Indië 1906–1942* (Arnhem, 1966), p. 292.

But Idenburg was not a missionary in the sense that he used his office for ecclesiastical activities. He repeatedly stated that to him there was a clear distinction between church and missions on the one hand, and the state on the other hand.

Kampen Theological University

RE-READING MISSIONARY PUBLICATIONS: THE CASE OF EUROPEAN AND MALAGASY MARTYROLOGIES, 1837–1937

by RACHEL A. RAKOTONIRINA

IN 1835 the missionaries of the London Missionary Society (LMS) were ordered by the Merina government in Antananarivo to leave Madagascar, only twenty-seven years after their mission had been established. In 1837 the first Malagasy Christian was killed because of her faith. The era of persecution against the internationally isolated Malagasy Christian community began in 1835 and continued sporadically until 1861 with the death of Queen Ranavalona I, whose reign had seen the introduction of anti-Christian legislation. Estimates of the number of Christians who died as a result of refusing to denounce their faith vary between 50 and 200. The numbers who died indirectly due to suffering imprisonment, a poison ordeal, or exile are estimated at between 1,500 and 3,000.[1] However the church which emerged from the era of suppression was said to have been numerically between four and ten times stronger than in 1835, with between three and twelve thousand members and adherents.[2] European missions returned in 1862. From the beginning, the martyr story proved to be a popular subject for missionary publications.

Eric Sharpe, writing in 1989 in *the International Bulletin of Missionary Research*, comments: 'The question "What happened [in mission history]?" has been asked and answered often enough; what would seem hardly to have been asked at all is, "Why has the missionary record been written up in the way it has, and in response to what impulses and constraints?"'[3] He goes on to suggest that mission

[1] S. Ellis, 'The Malagasy Background II: The Nineteenth Century', in F. Fuglestad and J. Simensen, eds, *Norwegian Missions in African History. Vol. Two: Madagascar* (Oslo, 1986), p. 31; G. Campbell, 'The Role of the London Missionary Society in the Rise of the Merina Empire, 1810–1861. A Contribution to the Economic History of Madagascar' (University of Wales Ph.D. thesis, 1985), p. 350; F. Raison-Jourde, *Bible et Pouvoir à Madagascar au XIXe Siècle: Invention d'une Identité Chrétienne et Construction de l'État* (Paris, 1991), p. 288.

[2] M. Rasoamiaramanana, 'Le rejet du christianisme au sein du royaume de Madagascar (1835–1861)', in B. Hubsch, ed., *Madagascar et le Christianisme* (Antananarivo, 1993), p. 229; Raison-Jourdel *Bible et Pouvoir à Madagascar*, p. 167.

[3] Eric Sharpe, 'Reflections on missionary historiography', *IBMR* April (1989), p. 76.

literature be interrogated as to how it produced and sustained images of mission for Christians.[4] In his 1996 overview of church historiography on Southern Africa, Norman Etherington remarks that 'Missionary Christianity . . . supplies dozens of discourses to deconstruct. With a couple of exceptions, the study of images and representations has . . . been hardly touched.'[5]

There has been insufficient analysis of how popular mission literature has represented mission history.[6] Nineteenth-century missionary societies were among the most high-profile pressure groups in British life.[7] They produced and circulated vast amounts of written material.[8] The nature of the publications to which missionary societies exposed the British public, the images of Africans, Pacific Islanders, Indians, and others that they circulated, demand critical study.

This paper analyses the representational strategies of missionaries and Christians in Madagascar in relation to the highly contested literature of martyrology. The source materials are accounts of the Malagasy persecutions which were produced over the pre-colonial and colonial period of 1837–1937. They consist of letters from Christians during the era of persecution, published books and journal articles by European missionaries produced in English and French between 1837 and 1937, and published books and journal and newspaper articles by Malagasy Christians written between 1900 and 1937 in Malagasy. A selection of these martyrological texts are analysed as a discourse and their interrelation in creating and representing a tradition, history, and identity, assessed.[9]

The martyrologies on the Malagasy martyrs have five distinct characteristics which are, on the whole, common to all. The first is the prominent and revealing introductory sections which discuss the Malagasy people and their cultural and religious practices. The second

[4] John Peel has commented on the need for a form of source criticism of published mission materials: J. D. Y. Peel, 'Problems and opportunities in an anthropologist's use of a missionary archive', in R. A. Bickers and R. Seton, eds, *Missionary Encounters. Sources and Issues* (Surrey, 1996), p. 70.

[5] Norman Etherington, 'Recent trends in the historiography of Christianity in Southern Africa', *Journal of Southern African Studies*, 22, 2 (June, 1996), p. 218.

[6] Andrew N. Porter, *European Imperialism, 1860–1914* (London, 1994), p. 22.

[7] Susan E. Thorne, 'Protestant ethics and the spirit of imperialism: British Congregationalists and the L.M.S. 1795–1925' (Michigan Ph.D. thesis, 1990), pp. 85, 87–9, 93–100.

[8] Porter, *European Imperialism*, p. 22; J. Comaroff and J. Comaroff, *Of Revelation and Revolution: Christianity, Colonialism and Consciousness in South Africa* (Chicago, 1991), p. 37.

[9] For a detailed analysis of all texts see Rachel A. Rakotonirina, 'Representations of Martyrdom. The Case of Madagascar, 1837–1937' (Birmingham Ph.D. thesis, 1998).

is the representation of the Malagasy Church before and during the persecutions. The third is the image produced of the martyrdom and suffering of Malagasy Christians. The fourth is the description of the Malagasy governing authorities during the era of persecutions. The last is the representation of European Protestant missions. Analysis of these five categories is enhanced when the representations they give rise to are assessed in the light of postcolonialism.

Postcolonialism is a useful methodology for the study of martyr-ological and mission discourses on Madagascar. According to Laura E. Donaldson, 'postcolonialism specifically addresses the historical, textual, discursive and epistemological legacies of colonialism.'[10] Even though the case of Madagascar in particular, and the history of missions generally, suggest that the link between missions and colonialism is debatable, there is much of relevance in postcolonial methods for mission historians. The concentration on literature and discourse and on how power, colonial or otherwise, is captured, wielded, maintained, and resisted in cultural forms provides for new fields of research in mission history.

One premise of a postcolonial approach is that historical documents and histories, as much as other literary genres, are not concerned with the disinterested production of facts, but rather with the interested construction of representations through which power is expressed, reflected, and exercised.[11] Such an approach is concerned to identify the way in which Europe subordinated and objectified in literature those non-Europeans it encountered in its imperial expansion. Edward Said has shown how the colonial subject, or 'Other', is determined by European writers, travellers, and historians, with the prejudices, biases, preoccupations, and ulterior motives of these image-makers intricately entangled in the pictures they produce.[12] A postcolonial approach also focuses on the way in which indigenous histories were appropriated as part of colonial history.

Even though the European discourse on the Malagasy martyrs cannot be easily linked to a dominant European settlement or presence which was colonial, it had aspirations to be dominant or hegemonic, in this instance, in the way it defined and controlled 'correct' historical

[10] Laura E. Donaldson, 'Introduction', *SEMEIA* (1996), p. 1.

[11] Cf. Gayatri C. Spivak, 'The Rani of Sirmur', in Francis Barker *et al.*, eds, *Europe and Its Others*, 2 vols (Colchester, 1984), 1, p. 134.

[12] Edward Said, *Orientialism* (2nd edn Harmondsworth, 1985); idem, *Culture and Imperialism* (2nd edn London, 1994), p. 59.

and theological interpretations of the martyr story. It also pursued issues of power through the discourse, and sought to appropriate the story as a part of mission history.

The image of Malagasy Christianity and its martyr history was predominantly produced and defined, controlled, and distributed by Europeans for other Europeans. At a practical level, European missions dominated the production of the martyrological discourse throughout the first hundred years. It was published largely outside Madagascar, mostly in English and without Malagasy translations.[13] The martyr story was further controlled and mediated by Europe because, although there was a thriving literature in the Malagasy language produced by mission presses in Madagascar, nothing in Malagasy on the martyrs was produced on mission presses before 1881.[14] This was partly due to the government-led silence on the persecutions after 1862 which was acquiesced in by the missionaries. The silence was an attempt to avoid provoking the displeasure of former officers of Queen Ranavalona I's government with reminders of their involvement in the persecutions.[15] However even after 1881 when the ban was lifted, very little was written by missionaries on the martyrs in Malagasy.

Despite being little used in Madagascar, the martyr story was widely promoted in Britain and other mission fields. Europeans appropriated the story and used it to promote the efficacy of Christianity generally and Nonconformity and missions in particular to a sceptical and critical public at home, and in order to persuade Christian converts in other fields.[16]

[13] Raison-Jourde, *Bible et pouvoir à Madagascar*, p. 603.

[14] W. E. Cousins, *A Brief Review of the LMS Mission in Madagascar from 1861 to 1870* (Antananarivo, 1871), pp. 34–7; cf. Raison-Jourde, *Bible et pouvoir à Madagascar*, p. 625. B. Briggs, *Ten Years' Review of Mission Work in Madagascar 1870–1880* (Antananarivo, 1880), pp. 248–56, which details all the publications of the LMS press between 1870 and 1880. There is no reference to publications relating the events of the persecutions. Similarly in the *Antananarivo Annual* 1874–1900 no reference is made in the Literary Notes to publications on the persecutions in any language.

[15] Raison-Jourde, *Bible et pouvoir à Madagascar*, pp. 604, 625, 768; H. A. Ravelojaona, *Les Commémorations protestantes (1895–1987). Un enjeu politique et social dans la vie des hauts-plateaux malgaches* (Paris VII, Mémoire de Maîtrise, 1988), p. 26; Marc Spindler, 'L'Histoire des martyrs malgaches vue d'Indonésie', in S. Evers and M. Spindler, eds, *Cultures of Madagascar. Ebb and Flow of Influences* (Leiden, 1995), p. 195.

[16] The martyr story led several Christians in Britain to missionary service: see W. White, *Friends in Madagascar* (London, 1967), p. 3; A. J. and G. Crossfield, *A Man in Shining Armour: The Story of the Life of William Wilson. Missionary in Madagascar* (London, nd). Christian converts in Siberia, Indonesia, China, and Zaire knew of the Malagasy martyr story: London, School of Oriental and African Studies (SOAS), CWM, Incoming Letters, Box 7, Folder 9,

The martyrological discourse, in the possession of Europe, developed five normative interpretative positions by the late nineteenth century. The first of these was the construction of derogatory and patronizing images of timeless, ignorant, immoral Malagasy culture and religion. By the 1870s the assessment of the Malagasy was overwhelmingly pessimistic. William Ellis in 1870 writes for example: 'In many of their communications . . . truth was accidental. Deception . . . was . . . at times rewarded as a virtue.'[17] Mirroring Ellis, A. T. Pierson in 1891 claimed that the Malagasy 'people were a nation of thieves [and] liars', cruel and without 'virtue'.[18]

The second normative interpretation was the denial of an independent and Malagasy Church, combined with a limited discussion of its response to persecution. It is common for texts after 1861 to ignore the existence of a Church and instead only refer to 'converts'. Many texts, particularly those of the early twentieth century, overlook Malagasy Christian initiatives in organizing prayer meetings, preaching, and establishing churches. These weak and partial European representations of the independent Church of the persecutions are perhaps a reflection of late-nineteenth-century missionary attitudes which were unable to contemplate the ending of mission control.

The third dominant trend was the creation of idealized and European-styled martyrs. Rasalama is discussed as the most significant martyr, and little information about the other Christians who suffered the same fate is provided. Even so, the detail that Rasalama had been among the first Malagasy to be baptized in 1831 disappears from the discourse after 1861. This obscured image is perpetuated by authors who frequently dwell only on the horrific manner of the martyrs' deaths and by so doing fail to relate the martyrs' witness and willingness to sacrifice their lives for Christ. There is virtually no reference to named martyrs or their lives as committed Christians.

The fourth influential approach involved the construction of a demonic, despotic and irrational government, presented as the inevitable result of its being Malagasy. The description used by

Jacket B 1841, 10 July Swan Wm. Leith to LMS and B.7, F. 10, J. B 1841 23 Nov. Swan Wm. Leith to LMS which record Siberian Christians asking to correspond with the escaped Christians in England. James T. Hardyman, 'Malagasy refugees to Britain 1838–1841', *Omaly sy Anio*, 5–6 (1977), p. 165; Spindler, 'L'Histoire des martyrs malgaches vue d'Indonésie', pp. 193–206. Personal communications with Dr George Hood and Prof. Werner Ustorf.

[17] W. M. Ellis, *The Martyr Church* (London, 1870), p. 23.

[18] A. T. Pierson, *The Miracles of Missions or The Modern Marvels in the History of Missionary Enterprise* (London, 1891), pp. 163–4.

Prout in 1863 is typical of the tone and form of attack. He claims that Queen Ranavalona I was 'a bold, bad, woman, with strong purpose and no principle', who acted out of 'blind fury [and] mad infatuation'.[19] The complexities and ambiguities of the era are ignored. The leniency of the authorities, the assistance they gave the missions, and the oppression which affected other people more severely than it did Christians are all overlooked in an effort to present the authorities, particularly Queen Ranavalona I, as determined enemies of Christianity.

The fifth pervasive image was the portrayal of foreign missions as indispensable to the survival of Christianity during the persecutions, despite their absence. Ryan in 1863 claims that 'the true character of Christian Missions' is illustrated by the story of the martyr Church, despite the absence of missions in Madagascar during the persecutions.[20] The majority of texts give excessive and undue praise to the role of the first mission in preparing the Church for persecution. This is combined with the assertion of exclusive European mission claims to truth, knowledge, civilization, and the means of moral and material improvement.

This five-part interpretation became increasingly common from about 1870. By the 1880s this was the dominant interpretation in circulation. The images that characterized this European discourse created an interpretation which privileged European cultural and political norms as well as European missions, whilst undervaluing Malagasy Christian expression and commitment.

European dominance over interpretation is also reflected in the Malagasy discourse of 1900–37. Malagasy authors used European texts and some accepted European interpretations. For example Rajosefa Rakotovao dismisses the era before the arrival of Christianity as a time of 'night . . . when people were lower than the low'.[21] Ravelojaona criticizes the pre-Christian Malagasy for living immoral and ignorant lives in 'darkness and baseness'.[22] Some authors portray the missionaries as benevolent parents or shepherds. The proximity of the European and Malagasy discourses was compounded by the fact that

[19] E. Prout, *Madagascar: Its Mission and Its Martyrs* (London, 1863), pp. 11, 25.

[20] V. W. Ryan, *The Gospel in Madagascar* (London, 1863), p. 227.

[21] Rajosefa Rakotovao, 'Ny Martiora', *Gazety Teny Soa* (April-June, 1938), pp. 10–11.

[22] H. A. Ravelojaona, 'Teny fisavan-dalana nalahatry ny mpitaridraharaha', *Gazety Fiainana* (August, 1937), p. 230.

the Malagasy discourse was produced on mission presses, and subject to French and mission approval.[23]

However the positions of textual dominance outlined above were not arrived at immediately, nor smoothly. There were European exceptions and Malagasy resistance to the dominant interpretations. These strands together serve to challenge the dominance of mission discourse, and expose its fragmentary and ambivalent nature.

The changing nature of the discourse suggests that it is not as homogeneous as it first appears. It is important to identify 'epistemological breaks'.[24] Thus the evolution of the martyr discourse needs to be appreciated as much as its positions of dominance. The earliest examples of the discourse, in general, contradict the later interpretations which positioned themselves as definitive. With only a very few exceptions the early European discourse, before 1861, produced non-critical descriptions of the Malagasy. It was prepared to present images of an active and independent Malagasy Church before and during the persecutions. For example, Freeman and Johns in 1840 report that weekday prayers were held by Malagasy Christians before 1835: 'these meetings are convened and conducted by natives themselves . . . they consider themselves as acting on their own convictions . . . and from a consideration of [an] obligation to spread around their respective neighbourhoods the knowledge of the true God.'[25] Ellis in 1858 writes of the persecuted church: 'the Martyr Church of Madagascar . . . has been built by its own members, guided . . . by God's Spirit, upon the foundation of the few solid and imperishable principles set forth in the teaching of the New Testament.'[26] The early European discourse also produced simple and plain accounts of martyrdom, treating martyrs with exactly the same respect as other Malagasy Christians, and kept

[23] Bonar A. Gow, *Madagascar and the Protestant Impact. The Work of the British Missions, 1818–1895* (London, 1979), p. 138; L. Rabearimanana, *La Presse d'opinion à Madagascar de 1947 à 1956. Contribution à l'histoire du nationalisme malgache du lendemain de l'insurrection à la veille de la Loi-Cadre* (Tananarive, 1980), p. 43; J. Randriamanantena, 'Un lieu de rencontre entre l'Europe et Madagascar dans la deuxième-moitié du XIXe siècle: La revue *Teny Soa* (Bonnes Paroles)', *Revue française d'histoire d'outre-mer*, LXXIII, No. 270 (1986), p. 30; F. Koerner, *Madagascar colonisation française et nationalisme malgache XXe siècle* (Paris, 1994), p. 115.

[24] Cf. D. Porter, '*Orientalism* and its problems', in P. Williams and L. Chrisman, eds, *Colonial Discourse and Post-Colonial Theory. A Reader* (New York, 1994), pp. 152, 160; Peter Hulme, *Colonial Encounters. Europe and the Native Caribbean 1492–1797* (London and New York, 1986), p. 12.

[25] J. J. Freeman and D. Johns, *A Narrative of the Persecution of the Christians in Madagascar* (London, 1840), p. 77.

[26] W. M. Ellis, *Three Visits to Madagascar* (London, 1853), p. 158.

discussion of the Malagasy authorities moderate in tone. It also minimized the discussion of foreign missions before and during the persecutions.

The representational strategies of dominant discourse are not automatically conceded to by all who participate in their construction. Bart Moore-Gilbert asserts that the possibility of 'variation and struggle within [the] imperial discourse' challenges the assumed authority of colonial discourses.[27] Indeed long-term missionaries to Madagascar tended to take a distinctive approach to constructing martyrologies, allowing Malagasy insights to influence their representations. Some of these authors provided non-critical detailed descriptions of Malagasy society and culture, and some took seriously Malagasy religious understanding. Sibree and Cousins's argument as early as 1870 that an understanding of a high God existed in Malagasy belief systems, whilst clearly opportunistic in its search for an indigenous hook on which to attach Christianity, was a significant attempt to take seriously the Malagasy foundations upon which Christianity stood. They did not subscribe to the dominant discourse's creation of a *tabula rasa* upon which Christianity could be effortlessly inscribed. William Ellis and T. T. Matthews, in 1870 and 1881 respectively, are ready to portray the Malagasy Church as a well-organized community with significant numbers of able pastors and leaders during the persecutions. Ellis, for example, writes in praise of the pastor Andriambelo: 'I was deeply impressed with his varied intelligence, great activity, and unremitting endeavours to strengthen the faith of his brethren . . . sincerity and earnest devotedness to Christ appeared to be the distinguishing features of his character.'[28]

However none of the authors provide a straightforward challenge to the dominant discourse. Whilst in some ways they expose the contradictions of the discourse, they do so while supporting and confirming, in other ways, the discourse's dominant interpretations. So, for example, Ellis's 1870 denunciation of Malagasy customs and beliefs firmly places him within, if not leading, the mission hegemonic discourse, and Sibree and Cousins are conspicuous in not seeking to portray the independent working of the Malagasy Church of the persecutions. Yet the presence of fissures from the dominant discourse

[27] Bart Moore-Gilbert, *Writing India, 1757–1990. The Literature of British India* (Manchester and New York, 1996), pp. 19, 25.

[28] W. M. Ellis, *The Martyr Church*, pp. 186–7.

in all of these authors' works, even if they are made to seem insignificant next to other examples of conformity to the ascribed norms of representation, is nonetheless important. It signals the contradictions of the mission martyrological narrative that claims unity and absoluteness, only to be faced with authors who write against the dominant discourse while writing out of it.

The ambivalent position of the 'Other' as Europeanized while indigenous meant that he or she was able to disrupt dominant knowledges with alternative ways of seeing. Homi Bhabha argues that by appropriating the colonizer's language, discourse signs, and strategies of power, the indigenous elite engaged itself in a form of resistance to dominant discourses.[29]

Malagasy writings about the Christians of the persecutions are distinguished from missionary versions by their attention to detail and their use of new information. In all of their discussions the people involved are named and the roles they played defined. The emphasis of Malagasy authors is on showing the Malagasy Christians as organized, with extensive leadership structures, established systems of worship, and effective support networks. Above all the authors seek to position the members of the persecuted Church in ancestral lineages recognizable and relevant to their readers.

Malagasy authors mostly reject the need for preambles that classify the Malagasy, they avoid apportioning blame to Queen Ranavalona I, and do not indulge in critical descriptions of the authorities. They also do not mythologize the role of European missions. Their descriptions of the Malagasy Christians include new details about leaders and church activities. For example Andrianaivoravelona discusses the pastors Andrianaivoravelona and Andriambelo, revealing that they were baptized at the height of the persecutions in 1857 and 1849 respectively by other Malagasy Christians and thereafter preached across Imerina, Betsileo and Vonizongo.[30] Malagasy authors tend to provide more detailed portraits of martyrs as committed Christians. The work of Rabary in particular reveals that many of the martyrs were distinguished and experienced ministers and evangelists in the long-established and thriving church in Vonizongo.[31]

The use of oral accounts provide images which extend or even

[29] Homi K. Bhabha, *The Location of Culture* (London and New York, 1994), pp. 85–92.

[30] J. Andrianaivoravelona, 'Tapa-porohana susa tsy may', *Mpanolo-tsaina* (July, 1937), pp. 143–50.

[31] Rabary, *Ny Maritioran Ivonizongo* (Tananarive, 1933).

challenge missionary representations. Such representations serve to underline the Malagasy heritage of the Church from its very beginnings and would have enabled the readers to look to both Malagasy and missionary founding figures.

The Malagasy discourse was not radical in as much as it did not make calls for church autonomy on the basis of the martyr experience, nor did it go so far as to turn the persecuting Queen Ranavalona I into a patriot who defended Madagascar against European imperial threats. However it is not to be expected that the early twentieth-century Christian elite would produce martyrologies radically different from those of their missionary teachers. Instead one must expect to uncover, as Spivak puts it, a 'repetition of as well as a rupture from' the European discourse.[32]

The Malagasy writers call into question the united, absolute, and hegemonic claims of the European discourse by their unique interpretation and methods. They appreciate missionary contributions, being unwilling to reject entirely an influence which has helped shape them as Christians. However the authors remain between the Malagasy culture they grew from and the European world they grew into, and they never belong entirely safely to either. They question the dominant discourse's authority to speak in a world that is not European. In this way those who are products of the discourse disavow and disown it, intentionally or not, by their difference.

The European and Malagasy authors, by naming and renaming the Malagasy martyrs, lay claim to their power as legitimizing symbols of authority.[33] The discourse achieves, maintains, and exercises power. Mission power was maintained through the use of martyrologies to raise funds with which to increase the size, means, and ultimately, power of missions in Madagascar. Power was also gained by controlling knowledge about the martyrs. The missionary willingness to participate in a government silence on the martyrs within Madagascar until 1881 can be read as an attempt to remove the potential of the story of the martyr Church to compete with the missionaries as spiritual inspirations and symbols of authority.

The Malagasy discourse also pursues its own expressions of and aspirations to power. The identification of the martyrs as Christian

[32] G. C. Spivak, 'Subaltern Studies: Deconstructing historiography', in R. Guha, ed., *Subaltern Studies IV* (Delhi, 1990), p. 338.

[33] S. Z. Klausner, 'Martyrdom', in M. Eliade, ed., *The Encyclopaedia of Religion* (New York, 1987), p. 231.

ancestors was a profound cultural celebration. The reappropriation of the martyr story was part of, and contributed to, a wider process in which Malagasy intellectuals rediscovered their past in order to raise their self-esteem in the face of colonial negations of Malagasy history. For example Rajosefa Rakotovao asserts, 'Madagascar was nude before and the martyrs put clothes on it to prevent its shame, that is the right which sparkles like a diamond, a right more precious than gold and sapphire, a right to make the Malagasy equal with great nations.'[34] The nationalist movement grew out of an appreciation of the worth of Malagasy culture and history, with the martyr story at its heart.

The Malagasy discourse also pursued a particular power agenda. The martyrology acts to powerfully reiterate Merina, noble, and Antananarivo claims to the martyr inheritance and is silent about non-Merina participation in the martyr Church. Malagasy accounts of the persecutions, written by Merina elite pastors, concentrate their attention on the events and personalities of the central highlands, discussing only the Merina. Similarly Christians who were of free or slave castes in Imerina are absent from Malagasy martyrologies. The power and position of elite authors like Rabary was thus legitimized and reinforced. This use of silence is a feature of both European and Malagasy contributions to the discourse on the martyrs. Reading such silences exposes the unspeakable and unspoken, and traces the anxieties of power which rely on silence to maintain their dominance.[35]

A further silencing process is evident in the way in which the martyr story is absent from virtually all European missionary discussions, unless channelled into a specific published text. The remark of a missionary in 1920 at an inter-missionary conference in Antananarivo discussing the future autonomy of the Malagasy Church is typical of the collective European missionary amnesia on the martyrs: '[The Malagasy Christians] out of their own spiritual experience, have little or nothing to give.'[36] The missionary was able to declare this despite it being accepted in some publications distributed outside Madagascar that the Church which survived persecution was not only numerically strong but also spiritually mature. No other delegate in 1920 made reference to the martyr history in the debate.

[34] Rajosefa Rakotovao, 'Ny Martiora' (April–June, 1938), p. 16.

[35] Cf. S. L. Graham, 'Intertextual trekking: Visiting the iniquity of the fathers upon "The Next Generation"', *SEMEIA*, 69/70 (1995), p. 210.

[36] John Sims, *Report of the Second Inter-Missionary Conference November 8–17, 1920* (Antananarivo, nd), p. 34.

Similarly in 1935 a Congregational Sunday School text on the martyrs proclaimed:

> Of the saints of the persecution and the heroes remembered . . . it remains still to be said 'that they without us should not be made perfect'. . . . In practice it has been found that the Malagasy are not yet able . . . to evangelise new areas without missionary direction. Their national characteristic is to tire of a protracted task before it is complete, and to grow slack if left without European supervision and stimulus.[37]

This opinion was produced contemporaneously, on the same mission press as Sunday School texts glorying in the triumph of the Malagasy martyrs and their relevance for Western Christians. There seems to be a mismatch between these texts. The thinking of Western missionaries, discussing the future of the missionary church, and the message of Western mission accounts of the martyrs are not allowed to influence each other. Those considering the Church's future are silent on, and apparently blind to and unmoved by, the martyr story and its example of successful, strong, and independent Malagasy Christianity. On reading missionary reports and correspondence, from the commencement of the second LMS Madagascar mission in 1862 until 1937, the lasting impression is that the martyrs did not exist. There is little or no reference by missionaries to the martyr inheritance and absolutely no reflection on the formative importance of the martyr experience for the Christians with whom the missionaries worked. This is as true of material written two to three years after the events of the persecutions as it is for correspondence produced seventy-five years later during the run-up to the 1937 centenary of the death of the first martyr.[38]

Those using the propaganda opportunity of the martyr story as Christian exemplar and means of fund-raising are equally blind to and silent on the propaganda potential of the victorious, independent Malagasy Church of the past as a key to the establishment of an independent Malagasy Church. Silences, as much as the events and theories enunciated, thus serve to define the nature and boundaries of the martyr discourse, both European and Malagasy. Controlling images of the Church of the past and its martyr experience, it would appear,

[37] Anon., *Examination Edition Supplement to 'The Martyr Church and its Book'* (London, 1935), pp. 28, 25.

[38] R. A. Rakotonirina, 'Representations of Martyrdom', pp. 249–54.

was an important part of controlling the Malagasy Church of the future.

In response to recent calls for the jettisoning of Eurocentric methods of writing non-Western church history, and acknowledging the contribution of postcolonialism, I argue the need for church historians to interrogate mission and church discourses, published and also archival, in order to expose the complicity of power, knowledge, and representations. My research acknowledges that mission discourse between Europe and its 'Others' is shaped by particular perspectives and assumptions arising out of, often perpetuating, and sometimes resisting, an exploitative power relation. Historians should also take account of their own role in this process.

WOMEN IN THE IRISH PROTESTANT FOREIGN MISSIONS c. 1873–1914: REPRESENTATIONS AND MOTIVATIONS

by MYRTLE HILL

THE importance of women's contribution to foreign missionary work has now been well established, with a range of studies, particularly from Canada, America, and Britain, exploring the topic from both religious and feminist perspectives.[1] The role of Irishwomen, however, has neither been researched in any depth nor recorded outside denominational histories in which they are discussed, if at all, only marginally, and only in relation to their supportive contribution to the wider mission of the Church. The motivations, aspirations, experiences, and achievements of the hundreds of women who left Ireland to do God's work in India, China, Africa, or Egypt are yet to be explored. My intention in this paper is to discuss their work and the ways in which they have been represented in the context of socio-economic developments in late nineteenth- and early twentieth-century Ireland, to determine how the interaction of class, gender, and religion helped shape their missionary endeavours.

Social, religious, and feminist histories of Ireland in this period have all stressed that, despite the introduction of some modernizing features, this is a society in which religious influences remained particularly strong, and it does seem that secularization was a trend resisted more successfully than in most other parts of Britain.[2] Moreover, as Catholic and Protestant relations came to dominate the political agenda, religion at grass-roots level assumed popular and vibrant characteristics, to which women were particularly responsive. As a result of the devotional revolution within Catholicism, for example, the number of nuns in Ireland rose from fifteen hundred in 1851 to over eight thousand in 1901. While a similar pattern was

[1] See, for example, Rosemary R. Gagan, *A Sensitive Independence: Canadian Methodist Women Missionaries in Canada and the Orient, 1881–1925* (Montreal and London, 1992); Jane Hunter, *The Gospel of Gentility: American Women Missionaries in Turn-of-the-Century China* (New Haven, CT, 1984); Pat Barr, *To China with Love* (London, 1972).

[2] J. Lee, *The Modernisation of Irish Society 1848–1918* (Dublin, 1973); Maria Luddy, *Women and Philanthropy in Nineteenth-Century Ireland* (Cambridge, 1995).

seen throughout Europe generally, this five-and-a-half-fold increase is particularly noteworthy.[3] Similarly, the religious revival which swept through the northeast of the country in the summer of 1859 was noted for the disproportionate participation of women.[4] Ireland itself was also a field of missionary endeavour, with attempts to convert the Catholic peasantry a major concern of both English and Irish Protestants. By the second half of the century most Protestant denominations operated domestic missions which targeted the 'superstition and ignorance' of the majority population.[5] Women were again active sponsors and supporters of these campaigns, and one recent commentator has suggested that in their involvement in foreign missionary work they were merely 'bringing to foreign parts that religious message which their fund-raisers and supporters already saw in action though on a different scale in Ireland'.[6]

Irishwomen had of course accompanied their missionary husbands from the beginning of the foreign mission campaigns in the early nineteenth century, and, despite the lack of recognition or remuneration accorded to that work by the churches, made a significant and distinctive contribution to overseas developments. A small number of individuals also ventured into this field, forging a place for themselves independently of the established missionary societies; Mary Whateley, daughter of the Archbishop of Dublin, for example, founded a school for girls in Damascus in 1860.[7] In the last quarter of the century, however, women came to be seen as an important, indeed essential, tool in the crusade to convert heathen lands, and the major denominations developed new institutional structures to facilitate and encourage their participation.[8] In the course of the 1860s and 70s, Anglicans and Methodists established Hibernian female auxiliaries to

[3] Tony Fahey, 'Nuns in the Catholic church in Ireland in the nineteenth century' in Mary Cullen, ed., *Girls Don't Do Honours: Irish Women in Education in the 19th and 20th Centuries* (Dublin, 1987), pp. 7–30; Bonnie G. Smith, *Changing Lives: Women in European History since 1700* (London, 1989), p. 211.

[4] Myrtle Hill, 'Assessing the awakening: the 1859 revival in Ulster', in Ingmar Brohed, ed., *Church and People in Britain and Scandinavia* (Lund University Press, 1996), pp. 197–213, esp. p. 199; Janice Holmes, 'The world turned upside down: women in the Ulster revival of 1859' in Janice Holmes and Diane Urquhart, eds., *Coming into the Light: The Work, Politics and Religion of Women in Ulster 1840–1940* (Belfast, 1995), pp. 125–53.

[5] David Hempton and Myrtle Hill, *Evangelical Protestantism in Ulster Society 1740–1890* (London, 1992); Desmond Bowen, *The Protestant Crusade in Ireland 1800–1870* (Dublin, 1978).

[6] Luddy, *Women and Philanthropy*, p. 63.

[7] Mrs E. R. Pitman, *Missionary Heroines in Eastern Lands* (London, nd), pp. 129–60.

[8] David Savage, 'Missionaries and the development of a colonial idology of female education in India', *Gender & History*, 9, no. 2 (August 1997), pp. 201–21.

parent societies based in Britain, while the Dublin University Mission and the Mission to Fukien, which were both Anglican, also included women in their work.[9] The main focus of this paper will be the Female Association for Promoting Christianity among the Women of the East, (hereafter the Female Association) formed by the Presbyterian Church in Ireland in 1873, and, with extensive missionary archives yet to be explored, what follows should be regarded as work in progress.[10] Women do not appear to have been sent by Irish Baptists or Brethren in this period, but Presbyterian and Anglicans, between them, sent around two hundred women missionaries abroad before 1914.[11] India and China were the most usual destinations, though Presbyterian women also served in Damascus, and Anglicans in Africa, Burma, Egypt, Persia, Palestine, Ceylon, and Japan. Reports from female missionaries frequently drew attention to the significant contribution to their work made by missionary wives, who probably accounted for at least another two hundred individuals.[12] With around two hundred and sixty male missionaries from the same two denominations operating in the same period, the proportional significance of Irishwomen's contribution to this type of evangelistic work is clear; indeed in some areas, women missionaries outnumbered their male counterparts.[13]

The recruitment of women to the missionary cause was an acknowledgement of the need to infiltrate the private sphere of the home and to influence the mothers whose role in the moral regeneration of the country was recognised as critical,[14] and four main areas of endeavour were thus marked out for female labours – orphanages, the domestic or zenana mission, schools, and medical work. However, both their lack of ordination and the ideology of separate spheres for the sexes ensured that their relationship with their male counterparts stressed the differences rather than the equality of

[9] F. E. Bland, *How the Church Missionary Society came to Ireland* (Dublin, 1935); N. W. Taggart, *The Irish in World Methodism* (London, 1986).

[10] The printed reports of this association are held in Church House, Belfast. See also Jack Thompson, ed., *Into All the World: A History of The Overseas Work of Presbyterian Church in Ireland* (Belfast, 1990).

[11] Thomas McDonald, 'The Church overseas', in Michael Hurley, ed., *Irish Anglicanism, 1869–1969* (Dublin, 1970), pp. 93–100.

[12] See for example, *Annual Report of the Female Association for Promoting Christianity among the Women of the East* [hereafter Report of the Female Association] (1895).

[13] Jack Hodgins, *Sister Island: A History of the Church Missionary Society in Ireland 1814–1994* (Belfast, 1994), p. 127.

[14] Savage, 'Missionaries', p. 211.

the sexes. For example, while it was frequently acknowledged that women's work in these areas was critical to the success of the missionary enterprise, male religious leaders preserved traditional gender differences by stressing that women's aptitude for missionary work was based on what were perceived as the major defining features of femininity:[15] 'Submission, love, tenderness, self-sacrifice, devotement, sympathy, are characteristic features of the piety of women, and when joined with gifts, knowledge, and grace, they make a model missionary.'[16] The more 'negative' characteristics of femininity offered by the dominant ideology of the period could also be drawn upon to justify the subservience of women to male control in the mission field. Thus, one missionary report warned that while women were essential to the work,

> at the same time there is no doubt that the circumstances and experiences of missionary life tell more severely upon women than upon men. Women are constitutionally – though there are striking exceptions – more emotional and less controlled, more anxious-minded, more easily 'worried', more given to over tax their strength.[17]

Male superiority was visibly demonstrated at the Annual General Meetings of the Presbyterian Church when the annual reports of female missionaries were presented by the resident male missionary with, from 1888, separate conferences ensuring that men were not on these important occasions overwhelmed by the numerical strength of women.

The type of discourse generated by these attitudes is as much a barrier to historical interpretation as are the stereotypical images of female missionaries as figures of romance and adventure presented by congregational and family biographies as well as in religious literature more generally. These representations by others are frequently reinforced by women's own writings about their missionary experiences. Usually intended for a particular type of audience, they aimed to encourage and inspire, and are thus reflections of faith rather than

[15] Wendy Holloway, 'Gender difference and the production of subjectivity', in Helen Crowley and Susan Himmelweit, eds, *Knowing Women: Feminism and Knowledge* (Cambridge, 1992), pp. 40–74.

[16] *Report of the Female Association* (1876).

[17] *World Missionary Conference, 1910: V Preparation of Missionaries* (London, 1910), p. 149.

[18] *Report of the Female Association* (1892).

expressions of individualism. They also reveal the extent to which women missionaries had themselves internalized religious discourses of humility and passivity: 'We are born to serve the world' was the rallying cry offered by one female Irish Presbyterian missionary.

Much of this rhetoric, however, is at odds with the strength of character, assertiveness, and courage which were also necessary attributes for missionary work, and which led many women into actions which significantly expanded traditional notions of what constituted appropriate female behaviour. That extensive travel, difficult cultural adjustments, intellectual training, and a satisfying career, independent of husband or family, could be grafted on to the traditional model of femininity without fundamentally altering the dominant ideological concept of womanhood, reflects the importance of language, imagery, and symbolism in perpetuating conventional gender roles. Thus, while there is a wealth of archival material, the reams of official reports, letters, and memoirs reflect a range of assumptions and expectations which may not tell the whole story of the subtle shifts of status and power made possible by the female missionary enterprise. An appreciation of the complexity of multiple motivations and responses to the new opportunities requires an understanding of the wider context of such sources.

The vast majority of Irish female missionaries were single and in the twenty-five to forty-five age group, though there were occasions when exceptions were made – perhaps for pragmatic reasons. Mrs Jacobs, for example, was accepted by the Presbyterian Female Association after her husband's death. The only widow in their ranks in this period, she did have relevant qualifications; she was the daughter of a missionary and had been for some years the Foreign Corresponding Secretary of the mission. Perhaps more importantly, however, she was also able and willing to pay her own travel and work costs.[18] Dr Elizabeth Beatty at fifty years old was also considered a very doubtful candidate, but objections to her age disappeared when a member of her family offered to pay her salary.[19] Indeed, it appears that the majority of recruits in this period were middle class, the daughters of ministers, doctors, and business men, who were in several cases able to train and travel without cost to the mission, and to work without salary.

The 'devotional domesticity' of middle-class Victorian family life

[19] *Report of the Female Association* (1906).

[20] Various issues of *Women's Work*.

seems to have been an important factor in inculcating the sense of duty, mission, and purpose which characterized the missionary candidate. Many missionary women had entered into evangelical and charitable work at a local level, and at an early age, before venturing into foreign parts. Dr Margaret McNeill, for example, had become a Sunday School teacher at the age of thirteen, Dr Mary McGeorge, daughter of a J.P., had also established an evening Sunday School and regularly visited the sick in her area, and others took part in evangelistic work amongst Belfast mill-girls. Many, like Susan Brown, the first women sent to India by the Presbyterian Female Association, drew inspiration from, and followed the example of, missionary fathers, brothers, or other family members. Daughters of the manse also appear to have been proportionately significant.[20]

During the latter half of the nineteenth century, when 'the church absorbed women's physical and intellectual energy in a way no other institution did',[21] class and gender interacted in a plethora of vibrant female networks. Wealthy congregations such as that of Fisherwick Presbyterian Church in the prosperous Malone Road area of Belfast, for example, contributed a large portion of its annual income to the Female Association, paying for the training of medical missionaries and sponsoring mission schools. Indeed, of the eighteen female missionaries sent to China by this mission, one third were from the Fisherwick congregation, and all but one of these were connected to two of its most active and influential families – their mothers avid fund-raisers on their behalf.[22] Research on the financial, business, and marketing arrangements of the Female Association has also highlighted the extent of this contribution, with middle-class women acting as unpaid managers, collectors, editors of the journal, and so forth.[23] Their enthusiasm at the home base made possible the work in foreign fields, and also had the effect of 'fostering a special relationship between church and mission'.[24]

[21] Smith, *Changing Lives*, p. 211.

[22] I am grateful to Gillian McClelland for helpful discussion on this topic, which draws on her forthcoming thesis on Fisherwick Working Women's Association.

[23] A paper entitled 'Women's work: Irish Presbyterian women missionaries, 1874–1914' is shortly to be published by University College, Dublin.

[24] William Palmer Addley, 'A study of the birth and development of the overseas mission of the Presbyterian Church in Ireland up to 1910' (Queen's University of Belfast Ph.D. thesis, 1994), p. 247. The Presbyterian Church reported in 1877 that the auxiliaries of the Female Association contributed two or three times as much as the congregations they

Many of the female missionaries could also trace their desire for a religious vocation to their secular educational experience. Largely a result of the progress made by nineteenth-century liberal feminists, education for middle-class girls in Ireland had been revolutionized in the 1860s, with the founding of several progressive new colleges. Mary Daly points out that, while the expansion of women's education was a European-wide trend in the second half of the nineteenth century, the proportion of women reaching second- or third-level education relative to men was extremely high in Ireland,[25] and it would seem that a high proportion of women missionaries were beneficiaries of such a trend. Many, for example, were past pupils of Victoria College in Belfast or Alexandra College, Dublin, the two most prestigious girls' schools in Ireland. Both schools not only provided their pupils with a sound academic education, but also instilled in them a set of values and a moral code which befitted them well for work of a religious nature. The girls at Victoria College, for example, were hand-picked by the principal, Mrs Margaret Byers. Herself a missionary widow, she offered a fifty per cent reduction in school fees for daughters of teachers and missionaries.[26] Alexandra College – whose first principal left her post to take up missionary work – also offered reductions for daughters of Church of Ireland ministers.[27] Andrea Brozyna has demonstrated the ways in which the literature and ethos of these establishments inculcated in their young female students the dominant versions of appropriate behaviour, in particular, a deep sense of their own privileges and their consequent responsibility to others.[28] Links with foreign missionary work were also made more directly: the girls of Alexandra College supported a native child (whom they named Alexandra) in the Church of Ireland Mission school near Zanzibar, formed a Missionary Association in 1889, and developed close links with the Dublin University Mission to Fukien in China and with the mission at Chota Nagpur in India.[29] Victoria College achieved a

represented gave to the (male-dominated) foreign mission, collections alone amounting to almost £125,000 between 1874 and 1911: *Report of the Female Association* (1877).

[25] Mary Daly, *Women and Work in Ireland* (Dublin, 1997).

[26] Alison Jordan, *Margaret Byers: Pioneer of Women's Education and Founder of Victoria College, Belfast* (Belfast, nd).

[27] Anne V. O'Connor and Susan M. Parkes, *Gladly Learn and Gladly Teach: A History of Alexandra College and School, Dublin, 1866–1966* (Dublin, 1996).

[28] Andrea Brozyna, *Love, Labour and Prayer: Female Piety in Ulster Religious Literature, 1850–1914* (Belfast and Montreal, 1999).

[29] O'Connor and Parkes, *Gladly Learn and Gladly Teach*, pp. 36–7.

particularly high record in this area – by 1903, twenty-two old Victorians were in the mission field, three founded a girls school in Damascus, and many others were wives of missionaries.[30] Missionary sales and frequent visits by missionaries on furlough reinforced the students' sense of involvement in the campaign to improve the lot of their 'dark sisters'. The stark contrasts which were frequently drawn between the heathen and the civilized worlds helped to reinforce the equation between 'feminization' and 'civilization' pointed out in missionary literature. Family, school, and church life thus combined to intensify the 'messages' of middle-class evangelical Christianity with its stress on moral behaviour and social justice.

That many middle-class Irish parents were prepared to pay the fees to keep their daughters at school and to equip them for a career was to some extent a comment on the state of the marriage market.[31] By 1911 fifty-six per cent of Irishwomen aged between twenty-five and thirty-four were single, compared to thirty-six per cent in England and Wales, while in 1901, emigration attracted a hundred females to every eighty-two males. It has been suggested that missionary work (like entrance to a Catholic convent) offered middle-class females an alternative fulfilling lifestyle at a time when marriage opportunities for women in Ireland were receding. However, it is difficult to gather clear evidence for this tidy thesis. Certainly female missionaries were of marriageable age, and a large proportion did, often with a rapidity that disturbed their fellow-workers, find husbands on the mission field. Of the eighteen Irish Presbyterian missionary women in Manchuria between 1889 and 1913, seven were married within a short period, all to serving missionaries in the Presbyterian Church of Ireland or Scotland. Other women, however, approached their work with the single-minded conviction of a life-absorbing commitment. Emma Crook, writing from Manchuria in 1904, confided in a friend that though she regarded marriage as 'instituted by the greatest of all beings', she had parted from a dearly loved man because 'being a missionary I could not marry him . . . my conscience would not let me, as I felt it was my duty to be a missionary'.[32] Marriage may not have been a primary motivation in the choice of missionary work abroad, but it undoubtedly increased the likelihood of finding a partner from a similar background and with similar aspirations.

[30] Jordan, *Margaret Byers*, pp. 49–50.
[31] Daly, *Women and Work in Ireland*, p. 38.
[32] *Women's Work* (1904).

Back in Ireland, those seeking employment on finishing school could chose between an expanding service sector and teaching. While teaching in Ireland as elsewhere was an important outlet for educated middle-class and upper-working-class women, census statistics indicate that the proportion of female to male national school teachers was about ten per cent less than in the rest of Britain.[33] Moreover, while it was perhaps more culturally and socially appropriate for pupils of middle-class girls' colleges to return to their old schools as teachers, such positions lacked security in terms of pension rights, and were also poorly paid (arising from the misplaced assumption that middle-class teachers were less in need of grant-aided salaries). Alison Jordan demonstrates that such secondary-level schoolmistresses in England were paid a much higher salary than their Irish counterparts, and that 'as a result there was a steady exodus of highly-qualified Irishwomen across the Irish sea to take up better paid posts in England'.[34] Irishwomen taking up the option of obtaining a university degree also found few outlets for their talents or aspirations at home. To take medicine as an example, although the Royal College of Physicians (Ireland) opened their examinations to women in 1877 and the first women graduated from the Irish College of Surgeons in 1890, the attitudes of the male-dominated medical authorities were discouraging. The BMA considered that, while the perseverance of medical women deserved admiration, 'we cannot honestly congratulate the women in their victory. For the great majority of woman physicians, only disappointment and failure await them. This experiment is a palpable mistake that will end in wasted years and energy.'[35]

This certainly seems to have been the case in Ireland, particularly for the first three decades. The Royal Victoria Hospital in Belfast did not admit its first female medical student until 1889.[36] Ten years later, when Kathleen Lynn received her medical degree from the Royal University of Ireland, she was elected as resident doctor at Adelaide Hospital, but found that objections from other doctors meant she could not take up her position.[37] Women practising as physicians,

[33] Census of Ireland.

[34] Jordan, *Margaret Byers*, p. 43.

[35] *Medical Times and Gazette*, 1 (31 March 1877).

[36] R. S. Allison, *The Seeds of Time being a Short History of the Belfast General and Royal Hospital 1850–1903* (Belfast, 1972), p. 90.

[37] Myrtle Hill and Vivienne Pollock, *Image and Experience: Photographs of Irishwomen c1880–1920* (Belfast, 1993), p. 151.

surgeons, or general practitioners do not appear on the Irish census until 1901 (when there were five), and by 1911 numbered only thirty-three (in comparison to over two thousand males). While it was clearly difficult for women everywhere to break through prejudice, Ireland does appear to have been particularly resistant to change. While the sample is small, there were clear implications for the most highly-qualified women, particularly when it is noted that women in Ireland accounted for a higher percentage of university students.[38]

It is against this background, and in the light of Daly's contention that 'religion should be seen as the most rapidly expanding career for women in post-famine Ireland',[39] that female missionary work assumes a new significance as a full-time professional career, albeit for a small minority of women. Missionary bodies certainly expressed particular interest in the growing number of female university graduates whose academic training was regarded as a sound basis for the demands and trials of the mission field:

> not only because of the knowledge thus gained, but quite as much because her idea of life is widened and deepened. All sorts and conditions of people are met at college. One is taught self-control, self-reliance, humility, sympathy with the view of others, *esprit de corps*. Unselfishness and helpfulness are also encouraged. This moral part of university education is as important as a degree, when in the mission field one will have to live months and years perhaps, with fellow-workers of widely different temperaments.[40]

The upholding of moral, and specifically female, virtues over intellectual achievement is of course in keeping with contemporary religious discourse. In 1892 the founding of a Student Volunteer Missionary Union established a body of potential recruits, young women who pledged their 'purpose, if God permits, to become a foreign missionary'.[41] The weekly meetings for prayer and mutual support were also seen as an important example to less committed young academics.

There is no doubt that women working in the foreign mission field were able to take their professional skills and build on them in a way that was not possible at home. This presented an exciting challenge to

[38] Daly, *Women and Work in Ireland*, p. 38.
[39] Ibid., p. 39.
[40] *Women's Work* (1911).
[41] *Women's Work* (1894).

this first generation of women graduates – compare this job description to teaching at home, where women faced considerable restrictions on both their personal freedom and their professional advancement:

> the teaching lady has charge of the training of Biblewomen, usually managing one or more boarding or day schools in the central station, teaching in school academic as well as religious topics, to high standard. Probably also several smaller schools in out-stations under her charge, also the training of teachers, evangelising and other work.[42]

Before her journey to the mission field, such a woman would have benefited from training in the most progressive teaching methods – kindergarten teaching, regarded as an important experiment in the 1870s, is probably the best example.[43] They would also be much more likely to be able to move to the top of the ladder in their chosen profession than if they had remained at home in Ireland.

Female doctors too were offered a wide scope for their skills and expertise; following training in the treatment of tropical diseases,

> these medical ladies have charge of a women's hospital – operating, treating out-patients, training dispensers in medical and surgical work and in dispensing medicines, teaching and preaching to the in and out patients as well as the general control of all hospital management, including of course, all the finances.[44]

While, as we have noted, there were no Irish female doctors in Ireland in 1891, there was already one based in India with the Female Association. By 1901, when there were twenty female doctors working in Ireland (two of whom were returned missionaries), five more were in the employment of the same missionary association. By 1908 five out of the eight women this mission sent to Manchuria were doctors. While further research is necessary to ascertain the number of Irish women serving as missionary doctors overall, twenty, or just over twenty per cent of the 102 women sent to India and China by this one mission before 1930, were doctors; in the same period ten per cent of the male missionary body were doctors. This same trend was noted in

42 *Women's Work* (1894).
43 *Report of the Female Association* (1877).
44 *Women's Work* (1894), p. 314.

all major Protestant female missionary associations. A Methodist missionary pointed to the irony of the situation: 'How strange that the call to our women to advance in medical science and in the study of theology, and then to travel thousands of miles alone, and to live alone in a foreign land, should come from the intensely feminine women of the East.'[45]

Salaries for female missionary doctors and teachers also compared favourably with home-based career opportunities,[46] and of course, their work enabled, indeed encouraged, specialization. Dr Margaret McNeill, for example, used periods of furlough to take several higher degrees (L.R.C.P., M.B., B.Ch., B.A.O.) in the course of her work as medical missionary in Kuanchengtzu, China, where she served for 26 years. Her experience in the removal of large tumours was written up in the *British Medical Journal*.[47] On the down side, there were of course considerable hazards in this type of work. Annie Gillespie, the first female medical missionary to China, died of dysentery after only eight months.[48] Dr Mary McGeorge drowned when returning to China from her first furlough, and her body was never recovered.[49] In many cases, however, these personal tragedies, rather than acting as a deterrent, appear to have encouraged an influx of income and interest – as Kathleen Bliss put it, 'though this falls under no category of Christian service, martyrdom has profoundly to do with the health and vitality of the Church and its power to propagate its faith'.[50]

However, individual personality traits and social or economic circumstances combine with other factors to render it virtually impossible to disentangle the religious and secular motivations of these women. As already indicated, by the beginning of the First World War, missionary service in mainstream Protestant traditions was becoming more of a profession than a calling, with the divine origin of the missionary impulse coming to be seen as less important

[45] Quoted in N. W. Taggart, *The Irish in World Methodism* (London, 1986), p. 66.

[46] Salaries for female missionaries were on par with those well-experienced first-grade female National School teachers, considerably higher than the wages of a male skilled worker. See John Lynch, 'A tale of three cities: Belfast, Bristol and Bath' (Queen's University of Belfast Ph.D. thesis, 1996), appendix 2.

[47] *The Fisherwick Messenger* (1944).

[48] *Report of the Female Association* (1899).

[49] *Report of the Female Association* (1893).

[50] Kathleen Bliss, *The Service and Status of Women in the Churches* (London, 1952), p. 115; see also V. Hayward, *Christians and China* (Belfast, 1974), p. 17, who notes that within six years of the Boxer Rebellion the number of Protestant missionaries had risen dramatically.

than other, more easily identifiable, qualifications.[51] An article in the Presbyterian women's missionary magazine of October 1911 urged a straightforward approach to the question of suitability:

> What is this call? (1) Do you love the Lord Jesus and are you willing to obey him? (2) Have you good health? (3) Have you any duties at home that would prevent you (let us say) from marrying a suitable man? If you can answer all these questions (except the last) in the affirmative, then you have no need to wait for a call – you have the command 'Go.'[52]

As Stuart Piggin has pointed out, the traditional boundaries between spiritual and secular perhaps need to be redrawn, 'because frequently secular motives were spiritualised while spiritual motives were often emptied of altruism'.[53] In the case of these women, it is clear that respectability, education, teaching, healing, and, in particular, the progress of women were regarded as trademarks of civilization, arising from and reliant upon Christian faith. The 'language of rescue', already familiar to middle-class Irishwomen, from both temperance and proselytizing campaigns, gave divine force to not only religious, but secular activities: 'over a hundred and fifty-one millions of women and girls, not one of whom can read or write, fast bound in the prison-house of densest ignorance and superstition, with none to loose their chains, none to tell them of his freedom wherewith Christ makes his people free'.[54]

But if missionaries regarded educational and medical work primarily as weapons in a war against religious idolatry, the indigenous people they aimed to save were clearer about the distinctions and were usually anxious to maintain them. Reports frequently noted that parents, while acclaiming the academic curriculum of mission schools, generally retained their hostility to religious teaching. As Miss Staveley complained in 1889,

> This school would be very much more largely attended were it not for the prominent place given in it to religious instruction. So

[51] See, for example, Kathleen L. Lodwick, *Educating the Women of Hainan: The Career of Margaret Moninger in China, 1915–1942* (Lexington, 1995).

[52] *Women's Work* (October, 1911).

[53] Stuart Piggin, 'Assessing nineteenth-century missionary motivation: some considerations of theory and method', in Derek Baker, ed., *Religious Motivations*, SCH 15 (Oxford, 1978), pp. 327–37.

[54] *Women's Work* (January 1914).

> much in advance is it of all similar schools in Surat where only secular subjects are taught, that higher fees have been offered if only the Bible lesson would not be insisted on.[55]

Some years earlier, the baptism of a child of an important Parsee family caused local uproar and led to 'violent articles' in the press and the withdrawal of children from mission schools.[56] In the area of the Zenana, too, where it was hoped that missionary women would develop a special empathy with their Indian counterparts, differing expectations of their role frequently resulted in conflict. In 1888, for example, Miss McDowell was obliged to refrain from house-teaching until tempers cooled when a child informed her mother that the teacher 'was trying to make Christians of them'.[57]

Such clashes reflected the complexities and ambiguities of the wider relationship between Christian missions and imperial expansion which has dominated twentieth-century missionary historiography. Identification with 'the greatest Protestant Empire that has as yet existed in the world'[58] was of particular significance to Irish Protestants during this period when a burgeoning Home Rule movement threatened to sever the political connection which they believed to be the basis of their economic prosperity.[59] Moreover, the interpretation of that empire as 'a God-given trust' was believed to justify fully Western intervention in the cultures of the East.[60] As Belfast citizen Mr Thomas Sinclair told the 1879 Annual General Meeting of the Presbyterian Foreign Mission:

> I value the mission because it furnished an answer to the great question, why does England hold India? we govern India, not to enrich our merchants, or to find openings for our adventurous youth, or to win renown for our soldiery, or to add jewels to the crown of our beloved Queen, but to share with the peoples of that dark continent the light of life – through which our own favoured land has grown great.[61]

[55] *Report of the Female Association* (1889).
[56] *Report of the Female Association* (1881).
[57] *Report of the Female Association* (1888).
[58] The Reverend R. M. Edgar, *The Presbyterian Churchman* (1886).
[59] See Hempton and Hill, *Evangelical Protestantism in Ulster Society*, ch. 9.
[60] Brian Stanley, *The Bible and the Flag: Protestant Missions and British Imperialism in the Nineteenth and Twentieth Centuries* (1990), p. 69.
[61] *Report of the Female Association* (1879).

Margaret Byers also considered that it was 'invigorating to feel yourself part of a great nation',[62] and female missionary discourse reflects this sense of pride and superiority which served to further highlight the subservient, victim status of the women of the East:

> When the bills come in, there is a row, and the poor young wife takes a dose of opium. Sometimes the husband (who has power of life and death over a woman) orders her to do this, and she has to obey. It is a hard place for women.[63]

A patronizing tone is all too often evident in their descriptions of 'so many with no-one to look after them'.[64] That indigenous women were themselves effectively silenced in these discourses, reinforces the image of 'pathetic', grateful, victims.[65] The prison metaphor was frequently employed, as was the parallel with slavery – Eastern women, according to an article in *Women's Work*, were 'slaves of father, husbands, sons'. Emancipation was dependent upon salvation, and the privileged white woman, educated and independent, rose to the challenge of spreading the civilizing message of the gospel. Race was thus another component in the representation of the women of the East as 'Other', different and inferior, although in 1907, one British woman missionary reached across racial boundaries to appeal to a group of Indian women reformers on the basis of class. After outlining 'what Christian missions have done for the women of India', she strove to pass on the ideology of middle-class service:

> Your poets are fond of looking back to a golden age in some dim, far-away past; but the golden age for India is yet to come, and it will come only when ladies of family, and wealth, and education, like those assembled here today, realise their responsibilities to their poorer, less-favoured sisters, and are willing to step down from their high places to spend and be spent in the service.[66]

As the twentieth century progressed, a new emphasis on the importance of an indigenous Church would significantly alter both the methodologies and the content of the missionary message.

In this period, however, while female missionaries were in many

[62] Jordan, *Margaret Byers*, p. 64.
[63] *Women's Work* (July, 1910).
[64] The Revd F. W. S. O'Neill, *Dr. Isabel Mitchell of Manchuria* (London, 1918).
[65] R. H. Boyd, *Manchuria and our Mission There* (Belfast, 1908).
[66] *Women's Work* (October, 1907).

ways themselves a challenge to the Western, Victorian ideology of pious femininity which they simultaneously endorsed, there were clear limitations to their potential to alter radically the lives of indigenous women. Liberation would, it was believed, come through salvation and cultural change rather than political action. Their responses were not, of course, monolithic, and some individuals did mount more public challenges and attempt to influence legislation dealing with the treatment of women or children.[67] But, given a dominant ideology in which race, class, and gender were intricately interwoven, most, despite personal risks and hazards and a range of secular qualifications, interpreted their role in foreign missions in purely spiritual terms.

It is clear that for many young women in late nineteenth- and early twentieth-century Ireland, a combination of religious, cultural, and educational influences, strength of personality, and lack of challenges on the home front, made missionary work an attractive option. A professional female missionary body emerged which, in the context of limited career opportunities, enabled women to support themselves and to earn respect and authority as experts in mission affairs. While this topic requires more extensive research, it does seem that Janet Lee's conclusion is as fitting for Irish as for other women: 'In essence, missionary work allowed women to stay within the confines of socially sanctioned notions of femininity, yet stretch these boundaries and experience opportunities normally reserved for men.'[68]

Queen's University, Belfast

[67] Amy Carmichael (1867–1951) is a fine example. Born in County Down, she founded a settlement in Dohnavur, India, and persistently lobbied for parliamentary action to prohibit the dedication of young girls to temple service. The Carmichael papers are in the Northern Ireland Public Record Office D4061. See also F. L. Houghton, *Amy Carmichael of Dohnavur* (1992).

[68] Janet Lee, 'Between subordination and she-tiger: social constructions of white femininity in the lives of single, Protestant missionaries in China, 1905–1930', *Women's Studies International Forum*, 19, no. 6 (1996), pp. 621–32, esp. p. 624.

'THERE IS SO MUCH INVOLVED . . .' THE SISTERS OF CHARITY OF SAINT CHARLES BORROMEO IN INDONESIA IN THE PERIOD FROM THE SECOND WORLD WAR

by LIESBETH LABBEKE

> Palembang, 17 April 2603.[1] I am here together with sister Catherinia, sister Timothée, sister Paulie, sister Rumolda and sister Theresetta. The others live in the camp of Bengkoelen. We are all happy and healthy. There is plenty of work. We help the women and the children. Life is always beautiful and worthwhile, but especially the present time is praiseworthy. There are so many causes for gratitude, if one manages to keep considering things in a transcendental way. We have no information about the sisters on Java. Yours sincerely, Sister Laurentia, women's camp, Palembang.[2]

IN 1943, Sister Laurentia de Sain wrote this message to her congregation's mother house in Maastricht, in the Netherlands. At that moment, she was imprisoned in one of the concentration camps built by the Japanese troops in the Dutch East Indies after the invasion of March 1942. Sister Laurentia was a member of the Congregation of the Sisters of Charity of Saint Charles Borromeo, a Dutch congregation of Roman Catholic sisters which was founded in 1837. The sisters combined a life of prayer with charity work that consisted mainly of nursing and diverse activities in the field of education. In the course of the nineteenth century, the congregation spread over the Netherlands, opening many convents and accepting tasks in several schools, hospitals, homes, and orphanages.[3]

As a Ph.D. student, I am studying the developments within this congregation and its missionary work in Indonesia from 1940 until

[1] This telegram was sent in 1943, during the Japanese occupation of the Dutch East Indies. Therefore, the date is given in Japanese chronology.

[2] Maastricht, Mother House of the Congregation of the Sisters of Charity of Saint Charles Borromeo, Archief van het Algemeen Bestuur 1837–1967, inv. no. 46.

[3] The basic work on the history of the congregation from 1837 until 1940 is José Eijt, *Religieuze vrouwen: bruid, moeder, zuster. De geschiedenis van twee Nederlandse zustercongregaties, 1820–1940* (Hilversum, 1995).

1988. My purpose is to analyse the factors that effected important changes in the fields of legislation, organization, spirituality, and charity work. Special attention will be paid to the effects of decolonization in Indonesia and the renovation brought about by the Second Vatican Council.

The year 1940 was chosen as a starting point because it can be considered as the point of departure for some important changes in convent life. The outbreak of the Second World War created a split in the congregation's history. After the war, both Dutch and Indonesian society changed radically and the sisters had to adapt to these alterations. As a result, convent life was reformed thoroughly. The year 1988 can be regarded as the provisional end of a time of experiments and reforms in the congregation. In that year, new constitutions were ratified officially by the Vatican. A period of reflection on and adaptation to the ideas of the Second Vatican Council was tentatively wound up.

This paper discusses the positions of Dutch and native sisters in the congregation in Indonesia. Relations between both groups changed radically during the Second World War, which can be seen as a turning-point in this process. In my opinion, some events in Indonesia changed the position of native sisters within the congregation and prepared them for a kind of emancipation. A growing self-confidence, combined with social and political changes in the years after the war, led the native sisters to search for their own identity. They were members of a Dutch congregation in a former Dutch colony, yet they were striving for independence and their own cultural profile. Both Dutch and Indonesian sisters had to find a new balance in the convent. This process is still going on.

In order to draw as clear as possible a picture of this evolution, I will first discuss the sisters' missionary work in Indonesia before the Second World War. I will then focus on the relations between Dutch and native sisters and on the position of native sisters at the start of the Japanese occupation. The second part of this paper deals with the changing position of the native sisters during the war. The post-war tensions within the convents as well as between the sisters and the hierarchy will be focused upon in the third part of this article. I shall conclude with an epilogue in which a brief outline of the further evolution of mutual relations in the last decades will be given.

My research is not yet completed. The provisional conclusions presented here are the result of a study based on the archives of the congregation, which are kept in Maastricht, and on memorial books, edited by the congregation and written by its members. A valuable source with regard to the history of the congregation in Indonesia is a thesis written in 1976 by an Indonesian sister, named Louisie Satini, for her academic studies in history, and edited by the congregation in 1992. It discusses the history of the congregation in Indonesia between 1918 and 1960. Not only based on the archives, but also on interviews with sisters, it gives an interesting picture of the relations between Dutch and Indonesian sisters within the congregation in Indonesia after the Second World War.[4]

Comments on the present situation within the congregation are based on personal observation and consultation with sisters in the Netherlands as well as in Indonesia. From 21 June until 1 September 1997, I lived in some of the congregation's convents in Indonesia. Within this period, two months were spent in the Panti Rapih convent in Yogyakarta.

THE YEARS BEFORE THE WAR

Missionary work in the Dutch East Indies, 1918–42

In 1915, the congregation was asked to send sisters to Batavia, the colonial name of the capital of Indonesia, where they were needed as nurses to open a Catholic hospital for the European inhabitants of the city. The congregation responded positively to this demand, but stated explicitly that it deeply regretted the absence of any possibility of performing missionary work among the local population. In January 1919, ten sisters started working in the Catholic Hospital Saint Carolus.[5]

For the first eleven years of their stay on Java, the sisters only looked after Europeans in Catholic hospitals in Batavia, Bandung, and Yogyakarta. It was not until 1930 that the congregation was permitted to work for the local population. From that year on, it started a polyclinic and opened wards for Javanese patients in its hospitals. The rates were lower in these wards, so treatment became affordable for natives. In the same period, the congregation opened schools for local

[4] Sr Louisie Satini, C.B., *Kongregatie van de Liefdezusters van de Heilige Carolus Borromeus in Indonesia. Haar geschiedenis van 1918–1960* (Maastricht, 1992).

[5] Eijt, *Religieuze vrouwen*, p. 265.

inhabitants. According to the sisters, only at that moment did the 'real' missionary work start.[6]

The opening of a noviciate

In the early 1930s, the congregation decided to open a noviciate in the Dutch East Indies, since it regularly received requests from local girls who wished to be admitted to the convent life.[7] The clergy supported the admittance of natives, for the main purpose of the missionary work was *fundare ecclesiam*, which meant the lasting foundation of a local Church. In the long term, this local Church was meant to function without European help. The education of a native clergy, as well as men and women religious, was considered one of the prerequisites for the realization of this goal. These ideas were expressed for the first time in 1919 by Pope Benedict XV in his encyclical *Maximum Illud*. During the 1920s, they were adopted and developed by missiologists.[8] In 1926, Pope Pius XI repeated them in his encyclical *Rerum Ecclesiae*.[9]

The way in which candidates were educated and trained reveals something of the missionaries' view of their work and their task in the colony. Although in theory an attitude of respect for local cultures and adaptation to their customs was given as a precondition for the establishment of strong local churches, these ideas did not take shape in the sisters' actual practice.[10]

Education in the noviciate was aimed at entrance into all aspects of a Dutch congregation. The life of Javanese and Chinese novices in Yogyakarta hardly differed from the life of Dutch girls who received their training in Maastricht. The local girls did not only have to adjust to the Dutch-oriented special customs of the congregation, they also had to get used to speaking Dutch. Moreover, their whole life was a copy of the Dutch way of life at the time. They woke up, prayed, ate, and worked at the same hours as novices in the Netherlands did, they

[6] Satini, *Kongregatie*, pp. 21–45.

[7] Eijt, *Religieuze vrouwen*, p. 269.

[8] Carine Dujardin, *Missionering en moderniteit. De Belgische Minderbroeders in China 1872–1940* (Louvain, 1996), pp. 258–61 and 434–7.

[9] Edouard Loffeld, C.S.Sp., *De grondgedachte van missiewerk en missieactie* (Gemert, [1942]), pp. 12–18.

[10] Dujardin, *Missionering*, p. 435. As early as 1926, Pope Pius XI even pleaded for the foundation of special congregations for natives, adapted to the local culture, in his encyclical *Rerum Ecclesiae*. See Loffeld, *De grondgedachte*, p. 16. I have not yet found out why the congregation did not follow this recommendation.

ate the same food, and they even wore the same thick, heavy, black habits, although sisters who had taken their vows were allowed to dress in white habits which were more suitable for the tropical heat.[11] For many of the girls, adapting to these rules was a laborious process, as I was told by Indonesian sisters during my stay in the Panti Rapih convent of the congregation in Yogyakarta.

Convent life in the colony had to be an exact copy of that in the Netherlands. In order to stimulate this uniformity, until the beginning of the Second World War Dutch postulants and novices were sent to Yogyakarta in order to receive their training alongside local girls. In at least one congregation, native candidates were sent to the Netherlands in order to complete postulate and noviciate over there. The sisters of the Third Order of St Francis sent all candidates to the congregation's mother-house in Etten.[12] This would suggest that in other congregations too the training of postulants and novices was aimed at teaching natives the Dutch style of religious community life.

The position of native sisters in the congregation before the Second World War

As a result of this situation, the congregation was mainly a Dutch congregation performing missionary work in a Dutch colony. In 1935, the first native sisters took monastic vows. By 1940, there were about 155 sisters in the Dutch East Indies, of whom seventy per cent were Dutch.[13] All the native sisters were still very young, which means that none of them had ever occupied a responsible position within the congregation. They were used to following the guidance and example of the Dutch sisters who were much older and more experienced in convent life. Furthermore, the natives' education was restricted by regulations of the colonial government. In nursing for example, the highest diploma natives were allowed to obtain was the one of *mantri* or nursing assistant.[14] Consequently, native sisters were not used to taking decisions or bearing responsibility.

[11] Eijt, *Religieuze vrouwen*, pp. 269–70.

[12] Sr M. Annette, P.R. (m.m.v. Pater Gerlach, O.F.M. Cap.), *Geschiedenis der Penitenten-Recollectinen van Etten* (np, 1951), pp. 230, 240, and 242.

[13] Eijt, *Religieuze vrouwen*, p. 272.

[14] Satini, *Kongregatie*, p. 78.

THE SECOND WORLD WAR

This situation was altered suddenly by the outbreak of the Second World War. Japanese troops attacked the Dutch East Indies in March 1942. The capitulation of the colonial government soon followed.[15] After the invasion, the Japanese army started to confine the Dutch in camps. The Dutch sisters too were locked up behind the bamboo fences of the women's camps on Java and Sumatra. Only thirty-six members of the congregation remained free. They were natives, apart from a Slavic and a German sister: twenty-four Javanese, eight Eurasian, and two Menadonese sisters. Quite suddenly, they were left on their own. Precautions had been taken though, since the possibility of internment was known in advance: a missionary board of Eurasian sisters had been elected to replace the Dutch sisters in case of imprisonment. In addition, all native and Eurasian sisters had been gathered in Central Java, so that they could try to carry on their work together. During the war, they continued to work in the Panti Rapih hospital in Yogyakarta and in the orphanage, the school, and the hospital of Ganjuran, a village nearby.

All at once, the native sisters had to bear full responsibility for their convent life. They had to organize the convents by themselves, as well as the hospitals, the school, and the orphanage in which they went on working. They even managed to continue educating and professing novices. With help and support from the doctors in the hospitals, the sisters coped with the shortage of money, food, and medicine. Besides that, they also had to endure interference by Japanese commanders.[16]

15 August 1945 was a joyful day for both the native sisters in the hospitals and schools on Java and the Dutch sisters in the camps. Somehow or other, the news of the surrender of Japan reached them all. In the following months, little by little the sisters returned to their convents. Dutch and native sisters were reunited, while gradually the missionary work started again. Two days after the capitulation of Japan, Sukarno had proclaimed the independence of the Republic of Indonesia. The Netherlands did not recognize this independence, and the war was followed by a severe battle between the colonial

[15] M. C. Ricklefs, *A History of Modern Indonesia c. 1300 to the Present* (London and Basingstoke, 1981), p. 184.

[16] Satini, *Kongregatie*, pp. 58–60 and 75–84.

government and the new Republic. A period of struggle which would last until December 1949 began.[17]

THE YEARS AFTER THE WAR: A SEARCH FOR A NEW BALANCE IN THE CONGREGATION

Different perceptions

At the return of the Dutch sisters to the convents, some problems arose. The reunification of Dutch and native sisters did not go as smoothly as expected. Both Dutch and native sisters had looked forward to the reunion, but they could hardly have predicted each other's reactions to the dramatic events of the war, nor the effect of the proclamation of independence. As a result, expectations ran high on both sides and were difficult to reach. Native sisters hoped for some recognition for their work during the war, while the Dutch sisters who had been imprisoned only wanted to return to the safe prewar situation as quickly as possible.

Both Dutch and Indonesians sisters have written on these events within their congregation. The way in which the two groups of sisters look back on the years after the war is fascinating. The Dutch perspective can mainly be found in memorial books written by members of the congregation.[18] As in Sister Laurentia's letter quoted above, these memorial books are written in a very optimistic tone. They contain enthusiastic stories about the reconstruction of the missionary work, the arrival of more Dutch sisters in Indonesia, and the natives' gratitude and helpfulness.

Dutch sisters also highly commended the virtues of the native sisters. For instance, in the memorial book published in 1968 on the occasion of the fiftieth anniversary of the missionary work in Indonesia, Sister Laurentia gave the Indonesian sisters high praise in a chapter on the war: 'In that time, they proved they were full, mature religious women, who managed to maintain Panti Rapih in a

[17] Robert Cribb and Colin Brown, *Modern Indonesia. A History since 1945* (Singapore, 1995), pp. 17–31.

[18] Three memorial books have been published since the end of the war: *Lustrum in het zilver. 125 Jaar Liefdezusters van de H. Carolus Borromeus 'Onder de Bogen' Maastricht* (Nijmegen, 1962), 192 pp.; Sr Laurentia de Sain, C.B., *Een ster ging mee naar het Oosten . . . 50 jaar missiearbeid in Indonesia van de Liefdezusters van de H. Carolus Borromeus* (Nijmegen, 1968), 49 pp.; and Sr Timothée van Bemmel, C.B., *50 Jaar inzet voor Zuid-Sumatra 1930–1980* (Nijmegen, 1988), 79 pp.

heroic way and who made Ganjuran the centre of the aid to the people.'[19]

Texts which deal with the problems that arose in Indonesia after the war are very rare. Even visitation or meeting reports hardly mention the existence of smaller or larger problems in the congregation's convents in Indonesia. Not all the material has been studied yet, but a general overview of the material available only yielded a visitation report written in 1965 in which Mother Rosalinde Borst, superior of all the convents in Indonesia at the time, describes some problems between Dutch sisters and a Javanese mother superior in a convent. She remarks that 'the difference in character between the races is inevitable'.[20]

On the side of the Indonesian sisters, a different picture of the same period is presented. Only one of them was the author of a text about this period. The graduation paper by Sister Louisie Satini cited above informs us about the view of a young Indonesian sister on the matter in the mid-1970s.[21] Her study, however, is based on material which cannot be found in the convent's archives. She used letters which are kept in the archives of the archbishoprics of Jakarta and Semarang, written by sisters to members of the hierarchy. These letters, written shortly after the war, show how difficult life could be from time to time in an international congregation.

It is not yet clear to me why so little material is available on the matter. Did the Dutch sisters not notice the existence of serious problems in the convents, or did they refuse to pay attention to this issue? Another question is to what extent the Indonesian sisters experienced the situation as problematic at that time. The feelings of repression which appear in Sister Satini's graduation paper might date from later years. In any case, special research will be required to discover what was going on between Dutch and Indonesian sisters after the war, since the material available in the Netherlands mainly presents a positive image to the outside world. It is clear, however, that many problems arose when the Dutch sisters returned from the camps.

[19] De Sain, *Een ster*, p. 49.

[20] Maastricht, Mother House of the Congregation of the Sisters of Charity of Saint Charles Borromeo, Archief van het Algemeen Bestuur 1837–1967, inv. no. 733, p. 1.

[21] Satini, *Kongregatie.*

Tensions within the convents[22]

Moving into the convents again, Dutch sisters immediately replaced the missionary board of Eurasian sisters. All Indonesian sisters were brought back to the positions they held before the Japanese invasion. They barely had the chance to report on the past events. This was a bitter disappointment for the native sisters. During the war, they had discovered that they were capable of managing the congregation on their own. When the prewar situation was reinstated without any consideration, they felt their qualities were neglected by the Dutch sisters. As early as May 1946, the secretary of Mgr Soegyapranata, the Dutch Jesuit Father de Quay, raised the matter in a lecture entitled 'Our Javanese sisters'.[23] The lecture was given at a conference for mother superiors of different congregations in Indonesia. Father de Quay expressed his observations on the return of the Dutch sisters to the convents as follows: 'And now, they [the Dutch sisters] came back. And now they say the Javanese sisters did a good job. And now they take everything in their own hands again.'[24]

In the same lecture, Father de Quay mentioned another important issue in relation to the contact between Dutch and Indonesian sisters: 'The last few years, the Javanese sisters have become more Javanese, and now they have to adapt to the Dutch again.'[25] Japanese policy during the occupation aimed at erasing all Western influence from Indonesian society. For example, speaking Dutch was strictly forbidden, along with everything that had some connection with the West.[26] The years of separation from the Dutch therefore had given the native sisters the opportunity to adapt convent life slightly to their native culture. They had become used to speaking Javanese and cooking local dishes, for example.

The battle for independence also complicated living together. Although the congregation as an institution chose a policy which

[22] Unless it is explicitly indicated, the following paragraphs are based on Satini, *Kongregatie*, pp. 103–18.

[23] Heythuysen, Archive of the Dutch Province of the Franciscanessen van Heythuysen, Circulaires van de missie-oversten in Nederlands-Indië/Indonesië; Bijlage: voordracht van G. de Quay sj, 17-5-1946, p. 2. I thank Sr Antonius Gussenhoven and Gian Ackermans for making this text available to me.

[24] Circulaires van de missie-oversten in Nederlands-Indië/Indonesië; Bijlage: voordracht van G. de Quay sj, 17-5-1946, p. 2.

[25] Ibid.

[26] Henk Maier, Dan van Minde, and Harry Poeze, *Wisseling van de wacht. Indonesiërs over de Japanse bezetting 1942–1945* (Leiden, 1995), p. 8.

respected Indonesia's nationalist aspirations, this situation was difficult for some of the Dutch sisters to accept. They regarded striving for independence as a token of pride and ingratitude from the Indonesian people towards the Dutch, and they tried to convince the Indonesian sisters that it would be better to re-establish the colonial government. The Indonesian sisters felt split between their respect for the Dutch sisters and their feelings of loyalty towards their own people and country.

Moreover, some discriminatory measures by the colonial government, like the one which limited educational possibilities for natives, were still valid. Some of the sisters also often felt that a mistake was considered worse when it was made by a native than by a Dutch sister. Therefore, Indonesian sisters complained that they were not treated equally within the congregation.

Tensions between the sisters and some of the Church leaders in Indonesia

Problems were not limited to these internal tensions between sisters in the convents. Some of the Dutch sisters worried about the attitude of the Church leaders in Indonesia. As I mentioned above, ideas about missionary work had been changing since the 1920s. The activities of European missionaries had to be directed at making themselves redundant. A new cultural policy therefore had to be developed. A fundamental respect for indigenous cultures was necessary to further the development of strong, local churches. This new vision of missionary work had some practical consequences. For instance, in the nineteenth-century missionary model, native clergy only held a subordinate and secondary position. During the 1920s the training of a native clergy who could take over all responsible positions within the Church became an important issue.[27] As a result of this policy, the first Javanese was ordained bishop in 1940: Mgr Soegyapranata was to become apostolic vicar of Semarang.[28] This apostolic vicariate was created in 1940 by splitting off Middle Java from the apostolic vicariate of Batavia. It was in the vicariate of Semarang that important decisions concerning the future of Indonesia were made in the years after the war, since Yogyakarta became the centre of the struggle for independence.[29]

[27] Dujardin, *Missionering*, pp. 433–6.

[28] Jan Bank, *Katholieken en de Indonesische revolutie* (Dieren, 1984), pp. 38–9.

[29] M. P. M. Muskens, *Indonesië. Een strijd om nationale identiteit: nationalisten, islamieten, katholieken* (Bussum, 1969), p. 396, and Huub Boelaars, *Indonesianisasi. Het omvormingsproces van de katholieke kerk in Indonesië tot de Indonesische katholieke kerk* (Kampen, 1991), p. 82.

In the years after the war, Mgr Soegyapranata succeeded in starting all missionary work again in his diocese. European missionaries were allowed to return to their convents and resume their former tasks. This was possible because Mgr Soegyapranata openly supported the Indonesian claim for independence. Although the Vatican prescribed political neutrality, Mgr Soegyapranata recognized the new state and tried to contact its leaders. He took the role of intermediary between the Catholic Church and the Republic of Indonesia, in order to speak out in favour of the mission.[30] In his contact with the Republican authorities, he emphasised the supranational character of the Church. In order to safeguard the missionaries' work, he stated that Church and mission transcended national disputes and struggles. Being Catholic did not imply being Dutch. Dutch missionaries lived and worked in Indonesia as members of the Catholic Church, not as Dutch citizens. The altered political relations did not change the relations between Dutch and Indonesian Churches.

This attitude had some consequences for the daily life of the Dutch sisters. While in the years before the war their life in Indonesia was pretty much characterized by Dutch accents, after the war they had to adapt to an ongoing 'Indonesianization' of the country. The outcome of this adaptation was not easily accepted by all the sisters. Especially when alterations affected their daily life, they were hard to take; the small things which appear trivial at first sight, were of greater significance in the sisters' lives.

The fact that more and more Javanese was spoken particularly worried them. In 1943, Mgr Soegyapranata started translating the rules of the congregation into Javanese. It is not clear when he finished this work, but Mother Emmanuel Lemmens, who was the superior of the whole congregation at that time, wrote a letter about the matter to Father de Quay in 1947. In her letter, she quoted a letter she had received from a Dutch sister who lived in Indonesia. The name of this sister is not known, nor the exact date of her letter to the general mother superior. In relation to the translation of the congregation's rules, this sister wrote: 'His excellence is quite opposed to everything that is Dutch . . . we did not use this translation very much yet. . . .' In the same letter, she named other regulations by Mgr Soegyapranata which she considered hard to accept. Those regulations must have been enacted between the end of the war and 1947, the year in which

[30] Bank, *Katholieken*, p. 121.

this letter was written, but I have not yet been able to retrieve the exact date of promulgation. Singing Dutch songs, including religious songs, was forbidden, even within the convent walls. At Christmas, sisters who had already taken the vows could sing Dutch Christmas songs in the refectory, if a special permission was given. The feast of Saint Nicholas, very important within Dutch culture, could not be celebrated any more. The sister concluded her letter: 'All this seems only a small matter, but there is so much involved with this ban. It's quite difficult for me.'

The altered views of the Vatican on missionary work and the new political situation in Indonesia required considerable adaptability on the part of the sisters. They were to sacrifice a part of their identity as Dutch sisters in order to become more Indonesian. Many of them considered this as threatening, especially in a country whose future they were not sure about.

CONCLUSION

Two major evolutions in the first half of the twentieth century have effected an emancipation of Indonesian religious women within the congregation of the sisters of Charity of St Charles Borromeo. First of all, new ideas concerning missionary work, expressed in Vatican documents since the 1920s, made possible the enthronement of a Javanese bishop, who began the 'Indonesianization' of the Catholic Church in his country. Secondly, there was a growing self-confidence among Indonesian sisters. During the war, they had discovered that they were able to manage convent life on their own, and to run schools and hospitals in difficult circumstances while the Dutch sisters were imprisoned in camps.

Adaptation to this growing independence was rather difficult for at least some of the Dutch sisters. When they returned from the camps, they were longing to resume their prewar life. Isolated and cut off from the outside world, they had received little information on what was going on in the country and among the people. Therefore, they were not able to estimate correctly what had happened to the native sisters during the war. For a few years, both Dutch and Indonesian sisters had lived in different circumstances. This situation made them develop in different ways. When they had to start living together again, problems arose. Moreover, the world in which these sisters lived and worked appeared to have changed as well. Their leader, the apostolic vicar, supported and instigated innovation, which was even more threatening.

EPILOGUE: FURTHER DEVELOPMENTS AFTER THE SECOND WORLD WAR[31]

In the next decades, the congregation evolved from a Dutch congregation performing missionary work into an international congregation composed of two independent provinces, Dutch and Indonesian. Evolution in the education of novices, in the assignment of administrative functions, and in certain habits, for example, show a certain 'Indonesianization' within the Indonesian province. These developments run parallel to the decolonization of the country.

After the recognition of independence by the Dutch government, two separate noviciates were created in Indonesia. In the original noviciate in Yogyakarta, the everyday language became Javanese and later Indonesian. The novices learned Dutch as a second language. Girls who had no command of the Indonesian language were sent to a new noviciate, opened in Jakarta in 1953, where Dutch was spoken and Indonesian was taught. The 'Dutch' noviciate of Jakarta was closed again in 1964, because by then all applicants spoke Indonesian.

As far as leadership in the congregation is concerned, more and more leading positions were taken over by Indonesian sisters from the 1960s on. In 1967, Indonesia became an independent province within the congregation, with its own provincial board. Two years later, Indonesian sisters were sent to the Philippines in order to start missionary work there.

From the 1970s on, the Indonesian sisters tried to give their province a typical identity by adapting European traditions to Indonesian culture. Experiments with the postulants' entrance ceremony show how the sisters tried to combine Western and Indonesian cultures in a harmonious way. During those ceremonies, postulants used to be dressed as brides, since the symbol of the sister as a bride of Christ is a central theme in the spirituality of women religious in the West. When Dutch sisters in Indonesia started to train native candidates for convent life, not only did they give the postulants a Western education, they also installed the original entrance ceremonies, filled with Western symbolism and customs. The sisters of the

[31] This paragraph is the result of personal observation in several convents in Yogyakarta, Bandung, and Jakarta (Indonesia).

young Indonesian province dressed postulants as Javanese brides in order to give this typical European tradition an Indonesian touch. This idea was abandoned again, though only for practical reasons. During the ceremony, the brides have to change into the congregation's habit. Changing out of the Javanese *kain* and *baju* into the habit appeared to be much more difficult and time-consuming than replacing a Western wedding dress.

To this day, the congregation is a mixture of Dutch and Indonesian elements. Only three Dutch sisters are still living in Indonesia, but all sisters older than fifty-five are familiar with the Dutch background of the congregation. Daily life in an Indonesian and a Dutch convent differ thoroughly. In Indonesia life is adapted to the local rhythm and customs. Sisters in the Indonesian province make their own choices. For example, Indonesian sisters still dress in the congregation's habit when they go out officially as sisters. In the Netherlands, wearing the habit is no longer common practice. It should be noted that although spirituality is the same within the entire congregation, its practice differs. Praying the rosary, for instance, is much more important for Indonesian sisters than it is in the Dutch province.

At the same time, some Dutch elements still exist in the sisters' lives in Indonesia. The elder sisters know Dutch and some even pray in that language. Dutch songs are sung in Indonesian translation. At special occasions, a double feast is served: there is not only a local dish on the menu, but also Dutch food is part of the festivities. 'Hollands eten',[32] as the sisters describe it, is a luxury reserved for special occasions. At such moments, a remarkable division takes place in the congregation. Most of the sisters who are over fifty line up at the 'Dutch buffet', while younger sisters prefer Indonesian cuisine – a simple but striking illustration of a Dutch congregation's rapid and radical evolution in the course of the last decades.

Catholic Theological University of Utrecht

[32] Dutch food.

MISSIONARIES, MAU MAU AND THE CHRISTIAN FRONTIER

by JOHN CASSON

I

IN May 1955, the Archbishop of Canterbury, Geoffrey Fisher, visited Fort Hall in Kenya's Kikuyu native reserve. The colonial government had declared a state of emergency nearly three years before in response to a secret and violent Kikuyu anti-colonial movement which it knew as Mau Mau. In the ensuing guerrilla war several thousand were killed, almost all of them Africans, and some eighty thousand Kikuyu were held in detention camps. At Fort Hall, laying the foundation stone of a new 'Church of the Martyrs' to commemorate Kikuyu Christians killed by Mau Mau's violence, the archbishop addressed a vast open-air congregation of Kikuyu:

> Here we are at the very heart of the struggle of Jesus Christ to deliver men from evil. In the hearts of every one of you this struggle is being fought out. How I long to be able to meet face to face with those who have been led into the hateful ways of Mau Mau. Those who are of this evil belief are only destroying good things; . . . they are destroying life while Jesus Christ comes to give life abundantly.

At this, the official report recounts, '4,000 tribesmen' rose and sang 'The Lamb of God'.[1]

The polemics of Mau Mau deal in binaries. The emergency represented a crisis for all actors on Kenya's contested colonial stage, challenging their competing versions of Africa's past, present, and future and the accompanying moralizations of colonial relationships. The response on all sides was to harden the polemical frontier in order to legitimate violence and to negotiate unity. The pain and ambiguities of moral choices[2] were submerged beneath forceful dualisms of rhetoric and iconography.

[1] Cambridge University Library, Royal Commonwealth Society's Collection [hereafter RCS], Pamphlet -46p2: Government of Kenya Department of Information, *The Archbishop's Tour of Kenya*, p. 12.

[2] Cf. Frederick Cooper, 'Mau Mau and the discourses of decolonization', *Journal of African History*, 29 (1988), pp. 313–20.

> Both dissidents and rulers tried to justify action and attract allegiance by contrasting the most compelling symbols of upright conduct in their own culture with the barbarity of their opponents; to explain why their world deserved to be either bloodily defended or bloodily destroyed. But neither side was united on what they most had to preserve or fear, what methods of combat were legitimate and to what future purpose.[3]

The rhetoric of white churchmen and missionaries was no exception. Mau Mau was a crisis for theologies of history which variously interpreted the shared assumptions that Africa stood within a trajectory of progress, and that missionaries were agents of that African future. First, missionary responses to Mau Mau had to theologize failure. Written in 1952, Roland Oliver's classic *The Missionary Factor in East Africa* expressed complete confidence in the 'inevitable progress of Christianity over paganism'.[4] Mau Mau dispelled such confidence: the overwhelming majority of Kikuyu church members, when forced by the emergency to choose, had transferred their allegiance to Mau Mau. For most whites, 'Mau Mau was an ungrateful stab in the back, "a revolt of the domestic staff. It was as if Jeeves had taken to the jungle."'[5] Missionary relationships suggest a different idiom: the friendly, if exasperating, Kikuyu church members had stalked off leaving empty churches and redundant priests. Second, missionaries had to theologize evil: the violence of Mau Mau was both brutal and intimate. 'It was hard to believe', wrote one observer, 'that gangs were preparing to burn alive or hack to death their own neighbours, their wives and children.'[6] Among 'the green hills of Kikuyuland'[7] missionaries had hoped to cultivate an ordered future of Christian progress for the Kikuyu:[8] now something monstrous was growing in the garden. Mau Mau was, in the words of an early Church Missionary

[3] John Lonsdale, foreword to Greet Kershaw, *Mau Mau from Below* (Oxford, 1997), p. xxi.

[4] Roland Oliver, *The Missionary Factor in East Africa* (London, 1952), p. 291.

[5] John Lonsdale, 'Mau Maus of the mind', *Journal of African History*, 31 (1990), p. 407, citing Graham Greene, *Ways of Escape* (London, 1980).

[6] Margery Perham, letter to *The Times*, 22 April 1953, cited by Peter Bostock in his unpublished 'Reminiscences' (1993).

[7] This phrase from the souvenir account of the Archbishop's tour of Kenya echoes the language of many missionary descriptions, e.g. T. F. C. Bewes, *Kikuyu Conflict: Mau Mau and Christian Witness* (London, 1953); and Syliva Bewes's foreword to Mary Rickman, *Seven Whole Days* (London, 1950).

[8] Cf. John Casson, '"To plant a garden city in the slums of paganism": Handley Hooper, the Kikuyu and the future of Africa', *Journal of Religion in Africa*, 28 (1998), pp. 387–410.

Society report, 'a sudden eruption of violence and subversive activity', interwoven with 'mystery and secrecy'.[9] Missionaries sought clear and stable categories to make sense of something that was baffling and unexpected in a world they had presumed to know.

In order to explain and defeat Mau Mau, whites constructed it as united[10] and uniquely evil. The movement was demonized as a reactionary antithesis to the various ideals of civilization, progress, modernity, or Christianity. Mau Mau was, in its violent particularity, a regression into the irrational, the tribal, its ritualistic oathing stirring memories of an all too recent past: 'the Mau Mau oaths are very reminiscent of travellers' tales from the "Darkest Africa" of fifty years ago.'[11] In the various constructions, Mau Mau can be seen as a mirror reflecting the overlapping understandings of self and society of each writer. Mau Mau appears as untamed savagery, 'a perverted and atavistic cult',[12] as disease,[13] as a coherent political organization modelled on the structures of the colonial administration,[14] and as mass psychological breakdown.[15] The London-educated evil genius, Jomo Kenyatta, is likened to the witch-doctor,[16] to Hitler the demagogue,[17] to Marx the dangerous theorist,[18] and to a maverick anthropologist conducting a vast sociological experiment.[19]

But in the missionary mirror, Mau Mau was demonized above all as

[9] RCS, Pamphlet -46p2, Church Missionary Society Bulletin Special Issue, *Mau Mau: What Is It?*, p. 3.

[10] A recent shift in the historiography of Mau Mau moves away from 'lumping' analyses to explain Mau Mau as a fractured movement whose competing wings came together in competition, not under central control. Cf. Kershaw, *Mau Mau from Below*, and John Lonsdale, 'The moral economy of Mau Mau', in Bruce Berman and John Lonsdale, *Unhappy Valley: Conflict in Kenya and Africa* (London, 1992).

[11] CMS, *Mau Mau: What Is It?*, p. 4.

[12] J. F. Lipscomb, *White Africans* (London, 1954), p. 143.

[13] CMS, *Mau Mau: What Is It?*, p. 6.

[14] C. J. M. Alport, 'Kenya's answer to the Mau Mau challenge', *African Affairs*, 53 (1954), pp. 241–8, at p. 241.

[15] See Michael Kerby, 'The unhappiness of the Kikuyu', *East Africa Medical Journal*, 34 (1957), and J. C. Carothers, *The Psychology of Mau Mau* (Nairobi, 1955).

[16] Bishop Walter Carey, *Crisis in Kenya: Christian Common Sense on Mau Mau and the Colour-Bar* (London, 1953), p. 37: 'the power of Jomo Kenyatta to sway crowds by his words, and, above all by his eyes, is overwhelming. . . . He has the witch-doctor's eyes: shrouded, menacing, compelling – and all for evil.'

[17] Ibid., p 27.

[18] L. J. Beecher, 'Christian counter-revolution to Mau Mau', in F. S. Joelson, ed., *Rhodesia and East Africa* (London, 1958), pp. 82–92, at p. 82.

[19] Idem, 'After Mau Mau – what?', *International Review of Missions*, 44 (April 1955), pp. 205–11, at p. 206.

a grotesque anti-Christian religion. To Cecil Bewes, CMS Africa Secretary returning in 1953 to his former missionary home in Kikuyuland, Mau Mau was 'a fusion of social and political grievance and pagan witchcraft',[20] with 'its roots deep in the past', characterized by a 'nostalgia for barbarism'.[21] The old Kikuyu religion of witchcraft and hypnotising magic was staging a last desperate bid for control in the face of Christian advance, asserting the tribal in the face of Christianity's multiracial universalism. But to many missionaries Mau Mau represented something very different from the now familiar adversary of traditional religion. They observed that the only vigorous resistance to Mau Mau outside the Church could be found among Kikuyu traditionalists. Mau Mau's diabolical depravity was a new menace. It drew on the pagan past, but was dressed in Christian clothes, propagated in Kikuyu independent versions of the mission schools and captivated the popular imagination with blasphemous versions of creeds and hymns that replaced the name *Jesu Kristo* with that of Jomo Kenyatta. To Leonard Beecher, Kenya's Anglican bishop and a former CMS missionary, Mau Mau was more than a parody of Christian methods, it was a self-conscious challenge to his vision of the Christian re-fashioning of the social economic and political patterning of African life, a counter-revolution to the missionary project.[22] Mau Mau's unexpected resilience and brutality could best be explained by the extraordinary power of the spiritual. As the CMS reported, 'Mau Mau is the expression of something that is deeply entrenched in many of the Kikuyu people . . . it is a spiritual movement, albeit of the devil . . . Africa is in the grip of forces which do not submit to control.' The missionary demonization of Mau Mau was literal: it represented, in Bishop Beecher's words, 'the black mass of Kikuyuism'.[23]

[20] Bewes, *Kikuyu Conflict*, p. 43.

[21] T. F. C. Bewes, 'Behind the Mau Mau headlines', *East and West Review*, 19 (Jan. 1953), pp. 3–8.

[22] Beecher, 'Christian counter-revolution', p. 82.

[23] Beecher, 'After Mau Mau', p. 206. The view of Mau Mau as religious conflict was shared by Philip Mitchell, Governor of Kenya until 1952: 'The black and blood stained forces of sorcery and magic, stirring in the vicious hearts and minds of wicked men, and as the churches, and the schools speak over the land, whispering to them "Kill, kill, kill, for your last chance in Africa is at hand".... The light is spreading and these dark and dreadful distortions of the human spirit cannot bear it' (*Afterthoughts* [London, 1954], cited in R. Buijtenhuijs, *Mau Mau Twenty Years After* [The Hague, 1973], p. 45). Louis Leakey likewise argued that Mau Mau must be understood as religion: *Defeating Mau Mau* (London, 1954).

'The Christian frontier', wrote Bishop Beecher, 'extends right into the heart of Kenya.'[24] Missionary accounts invested Mau Mau and the Kenyan political landscape with great theological and teleological significance. Economic and social factors were recognized, but purely secular explanations were avoided. The struggle in Kenya was a clash of the gods, a religious battle between dark and light, 'between good and evil'.[25] This was the rhetoric of the colonial religion steeling its soldiers to fight, but was also an assertion of the vital importance of the Church and the missions in a continuing colonial argument. Missionaries constructed Mau Mau in a way which mapped the Christian frontier on to Kenya's emergency and placed the Church in the front-line of the struggle. 'When the history of these times comes to be written', Bishop Beecher told the 1953 Kenya Church Synod, 'it will be seen that a diabolical movement which had its origins in the midst of the irreligion of detribalized African society . . . pitted itself against all those things which have constituted the way of freedom in good society. . . . Nothing short of the extermination of Christian life and witness was among its aims.'[26]

II

At first sight the boundaries seem clear: the evils of Mau Mau on one side, its opponents on the other. But on closer examination, the Christian frontier, like any frontier, reveals itself to be disputed territory. How far could the Christian frontier be equated to the two sides of an untidy colonial struggle? How would Christian advance relate to colonial victory? Missionary theologies revealed the divisions and ambiguities in the broader white community over the effects of colonial rule on native peoples, and the natives' supposed potential for progress. They differed over eschatology and ecclesiology: how did the Kingdom of God relate to human history and contemporary progress, and in what way was the Church to extend that kingdom? Mau Mau was an episode in the much larger story of how missionaries theologized their relationship to the political projects of colonialism and nationalism.

[24] Beecher, 'After Mau Mau', p. 210.

[25] See CMS, *Mau Mau: What Is It?*, prayer on p. 13, and the Council of Churches of Kenya statement on p. 16.

[26] Henry Martyn Library, Cambridge [HML], Kenya Church Year Book 1954, p. 7.

In the early months of the emergency Walter Carey, formerly Anglo-Catholic Bishop of Bloemfontein, now living in Kenya, produced a pamphlet entitled *Crisis in Kenya*.[27] In Carey's hands the Christian frontier coincides closely with a paradigm of slow cultural evolution from primitivism to civilization. Mau Mau represents a reversion to the deeply entrenched savagery of African life. In ways in which the citizens of Cambridge, London, and Bournemouth cannot imagine, Africa is a place where evil is a dynamic force, personal and awful, kept at bay only by the presence of those of a more advanced culture which has been shaped over centuries by conformity to Christianity. 'If we departed there would be savagery again in 10 years time. . . . They have no equivalent terms for gratitude, love, honour, integrity, virtue: such words don't exist in their language.'[28] The Christian boundary between good and evil is mapped on to that between primitive and civilized cultures, and even on to the contrast between the geographical space of England and Africa.

> Out here it's full grown, and if you don't feel in its presence the onset of something personal, vile, rejoicing in iniquity, hating God, loathing Christ, a deadly enemy to all goodness and innocence and beauty, then you are just blind, blind, blind. If you don't trust me, try St Paul or even Kipling.[29]

The spiritual forces of good and evil co-exist in a Manichaean balance of power, but in Carey's imagination the redemptive possibilities of Christ lack the potency of the darkness. The solution to Mau Mau, the redemption from evil, can only be found in the distant prospect of a two-hundred-year evolution of African life under the slow civilizational influence of education according to the principles of Christ and Moses, disseminated through a colonial order idealized in the terms of a genteel Victorian master-servant relationship.[30] With regard to the present, the Bishop's pessimism is profound: there is no prospect of personal emancipation for the individual born in primitivism, and even European societies must beware of complacent superiority, continuing to cleave to Christ lest the darkness overwhelm them.[31]

[27] Carey, *Crisis*, pp. 13–37.
[28] Ibid., p. 17.
[29] Ibid., pp. 38–9.
[30] Ibid., pp. 17 and 35.
[31] Ibid., p. 29.

But Carey's views, voicing a politically conservative theology with the embittered and embattled tone of voice of the settler community, were the exception. The majority of Protestant missionaries broadly shared the liberal view on the basis of which the administration fought the war.[32] They argued that 'Mau Mau terror is a kind of tribal psycho-neurosis rather than primitive savagery', the result of 'the delayed consequences of the impact of Western secularism on the ordered life of an African tribe'.[33] Mau Mau reflected the trauma of transition as tribal life encountered bewildering social change in the inevitable impact of 'western civilization, like a typhoon, sweeping everything before it'.[34] The mainstream missionary view did not demonize an essentialized Africa, rather it took a de-sacralized view of Western, modernizing civilization, whose inevitable progress was 'not exactly anyone's fault',[35] but whose impact was ambivalent. For colonial administrators, modernization threatened to undermine itself, dissolving the boundaries between rural and urban, African and European, on which the colonial project relied;[36] for missionaries, many of whom saw Western secularism as antithetical to their own purposes, the ambivalence was even more pronounced.[37] Where Carey saw Mau Mau as characteristically African, the mainstream missionary position explained it in terms of the advanced degree of Westernization of the Kikuyu,[38] and took pains to deny all suggestions that the struggle between light and darkness was in any sense a racial conflict.[39] The missionary mainstream offered a less potent account of evil, following the broader liberal consensus in rendering it largely in the language of

[32] Cf. Lonsdale, 'Mau Maus of the mind', which delineates liberal and conservative positions in the white community. The liberal view is articulated by L. S. B. Leakey in *Defeating Mau Mau* and *Mau Mau and the Kikuyu* (London, 1952), and in its psychologized form by Carothers, *Psychology*.

[33] L. J. Beecher, 'Education in Kenya today', *East and West Review*, 20 (October 1954), pp. 110–17, at p. 111.

[34] Bewes, *Kikuyu Conflict*, p. 36.

[35] T. F. C. Bewes, 'The work of the Christian Church among the Kikuyu', *International Affairs*, 29 (1953), pp. 316–25, at p. 320.

[36] Cf. Luise White, 'Separating the men from the boys', *International Journal of African Affairs*, 23 (1990), pp. 1–25, and Lonsdale, 'Mau Maus of the mind'. The blurring of categories is what makes the independent schools and churches troublesome for Beecher: they are neither one thing nor the other.

[37] Cf. Casson, '"Garden city"'.

[38] CMS General Secretary Max Warren called Mau Mau 'profoundly unAfrican' in his *CMS Newsletter* (February 1954).

[39] For example, J. W. C. Dougall, *Building Kenya's Future* (Edinburgh, 1955), p. 17, and Carey Francis described in L. B. Greaves, *Carey Francis of Kenya* (London, 1969).

psychological trauma and manipulation.[40] The Christian frontier was internalized. The struggle between good and evil lay not on the boundaries of the slow march of civilization, but, democratic and immediate, in the inner conflict within every human soul.

III

The conclusion to which Bishop Carey's logic points is that of Kenya's settler community: the Kikuyu as an entity were guilty of the evils of Mau Mau.[41] Missionary mainstream views, by contrast, reflect a very different experience of Kikuyuland as their home, and their descriptions frequently juxtaposed the anti-Mau Mau idiom of Kikuyu country as dark and brooding, against the established missionary tradition of casting the reserve as a rural idyll. As with the landscape, so with the people. Relating good and evil to the inner frontier of moral choice, missionary writings disaggregated Kikuyu society, and emphasised the significant numbers of Kikuyu who opposed Mau Mau. Above all, they focused on the extraordinary perseverance of the small Christian remnant, who, fired by the intense spirituality and fellowship of the East African Revival, resisted the Mau Mau oath, even to the point of death.

The heroism and faithfulness of the Kikuyu remnant gripped missionary imaginations and theologies. Many could not conceal their exhilaration at the humbling witness and martyrdom of the Kikuyu remnant. This was New Testament faith recovered,[42] 'a return to the simple gospel of Jesus Christ'.[43] 'I have never seen anything like it', wrote Cecil Bewes, 'their witness cannot but tell.'[44] Missionaries recounted revivalist testimonies which contrasted initiation by the

[40] Cf. Carothers, *Psychology*, pp. 12–15: '[Mau Mau] arose from the development of an anxious conflictual situation in people who, from contact with an alien culture had lost the supportive and constraining influences of their own culture, yet had not lost their "magic" modes of thinking. It arose from the exploitation of this situation by relatively sophisticated egoists.'

[41] 'I don't say that all Kikuyus are actual murderers, but they all . . . screen, protect and justify these murderers.' But Carey denied that he was 'a negrophobe': 'I myself mix with Africans most freely, having meals with them (generally tea, but sometimes chicken and so on at lunch), but then I'm a professional and it's part of my work, they know it, and I know it' (*Crisis*, pp. 31–3).

[42] N. Langford Smith, 'Revival in East Africa', *International Review of Missions*, 43 (1954), pp. 77–81, at p. 81.

[43] Bewes, *Kikuyu Conflict*, pp. 48–9.

[44] Bewes, 'Mau Mau headlines', p. 8.

blood of Jesus with initiation by the blood of Mau Mau oaths.[45] In contrast to the uncertainties of Christian faith in a secularizing world, Mau Mau provided a dramatic stage on which the ambiguities of the internalized Christian frontier within each heart, could be resolved into simple binaries of external allegiance around a single point of decision. The conversionist emphasis on a once-and-for-all moment of decision for Christ or Mau Mau re-drew the frontier once again. This was a time for undivided hearts; the Kikuyu were either lapsed or loyal. As a Kikuyu rural dean told them, 'When they drag you out of your hut at night to make you take the oath, that is the time for you to prove whether Jesus Christ means everything to you, or whether he means nothing at all.'[46]

The missionaries situated Mau Mau within a local Christian teleology. The tension for the Kikuyu Church had always been how far the Christian frontier should be left to hidden moral and spiritual ambiguity, and how far it should be attached to external marks of allegiance. During Mau Mau, missionaries told a history of the Kikuyu Church in which numerical growth and the accompanying nominalism of a 'mixed Church' were confronted by periodic moments of frontier definition and enforcement which cut away the nominal dead wood to reveal shoots of spiritual re-birth. As with the female circumcision crisis, and the independent schools crisis, so now with Mau Mau.[47] 'Perhaps this was the purge the church had been needing', Bewes told the Institute of International Affairs in 1954.[48] Making theological sense of the crisis swung the balance back towards the ecclesiology of the 'gathered Church'. 'In any nation,' the Archdeacon of Nairobi reflected later, 'it has not been the multitude that have come deeply under the control of Christ . . . the sickness of the world is due to the fact that only a tiny minority place themselves under the control of Christ.'[49] Nominalism blurred the boundaries. It was the missionary equivalent of the liberal anxiety over the transitional African, neither one thing nor the other. In Cecil Bewes's description

[45] Phillips, *From Mau Mau to Christ*, pp. 19–20; Bewes, *Kikuyu Conflict*, p. 51; E. M. Wiseman, *Kikuyu Martyrs* (London, 1958), pp. 12, 20; and more recently Dorothy Smoker, *Ambushed By Love* (Fort Washington, PA, 1994), demonstrate the perception of an all-or-nothing moment of decision.

[46] RCS, pamphlet -46p2, E. M. Wiseman, 'The story of the CMS in Kenya', (nd), p. 12.

[47] For a missionary construction of Kikuyu church history, see CMS, *Mau Mau: What Is It?*

[48] Bewes, 'Work of the Christian Church', p. 324.

[49] Bostock, 'Reminiscences', pp. 171–2.

it raised the prospect that church members might be elusive to missionary categorization, comprehension, and control: 'At the foot of the hill there is a flat open space where dances are held night after night when the moon shines. Members of your own congregation may be there, their eyes glazed in a sort of ecstasy; they appear self-hypnotised, they do not even see you.'[50]

Nominalism made it hard to tell which side people were on in the missionary project to advance the Christian frontier. Mau Mau made clear who were the 'real Christians',[51] *individuals* whose *personal* experience of Christ was evidenced in joyful hospitality, rather than the sullen faces which the 'accumulating mass'[52] of the Kikuyu under occupation turned towards white visitors.[53]

In his foreword to the early CMS report on Mau Mau, Geoffrey Fisher offered a theological perspective on confusing events: 'God is in this world working out His good purposes. In the midst of man's disorder we may with the eye of faith discern God's design and our part in it.'[54] To the missionaries the only discernible signs of God's activity, and the only hopes of the future of the Church in Kenya, lay in the powerful witness of the Christian revivalists. Surveying the African scene they articulated a remnant theology informed by biblical and revivalist models. Mau Mau was a time of testing, which would produce a purified and faithful remnant, a gathered Church, who would advance God's kingdom not by worldly power or numerical strength, but by the cruciform redemptive power of suffering.[55]

To invest events with a theological trajectory of divine agency was to lay claim to specific human strategies and agency. It was, the missionaries believed, the revival that had saved the Church.[56] Kikuyu Christians inspired by an African-initiated spiritual movement had been the primary agency of God's purposes, and missionaries were prepared to admit the lesson that theirs had been a secondary role.[57] The frontier lay within Kikuyu hearts and minds: 'such direction as

[50] Bewes, *Kikuyu Conflict*, p. 26.

[51] Bewes, 'Mau Mau headlines', p. 8.

[52] Bewes, *Kikuyu Conflict*, p. 47.

[53] CMS, *Mau Mau: What Is It?*, p. 10.

[54] Ibid.

[55] Dougall, *Building Kenya's Future*, p. 29: 'out of travail and tragedy a new inter-racial Christian community is being born.'

[56] M. A. C. Warren cited in C. P. Groves, *The Planting of Christianity in Africa*, 4 vols (London, 1958), 4, p. 312.

[57] Beecher, 'Christian counter-revolution', p. 83.

may have effect must come from within, and herein lies the immense significance of the African church.'[58]

But facing in the direction of colonial arguments, the missionaries found in the resilience of the Christian remnant new grounds to assert the essential part which Christian faith, and specifically missionary enterprise, must play in the African future. The Church, in their construction, had proved to be Mau Mau's natural and most intimate enemy, singled out in violence as the central obstacle to Mau Mau's designs on the African soul. Only Christian faith, personal and powerful, had proved itself capable of the fundamental remaking of people for the demands of modernity.

Missionaries thus envisaged a central role for themselves in the government project of rehabilitation. This was the outworking of the liberal analysis of Mau Mau as psychological regression, which sought to counter Mau Mau's madness by attention to both environment and moral responsibility. Its screening procedures, at once punitive and therapeutic, sought to restore colonial order by delineating the colonial frontier in clear categories of guilt and innocence embodied in different detention camps graded from black to white. Both the missionaries' conversionist theology and the administration's psychological idiom placed great weight on the transformative power of confession in this process, and both sides welcomed the co-operation of the other in the project of re-making the Kikuyu.[59] White missionaries and Kikuyu revivalists were active evangelists in the camps, and for the first time in Kenya a significant para-church structure of community development emerged through the Kenya Council of Churches.[60]

For the missionary mainstream rehabilitation represented a theology of redemption that corresponded to the individualized, internalized account of evil. It was a theology confident of the 'power of the Christian message to cleanse from the chains of oath-taking',[61] in the face of some secular doubts about the redeemability of the most 'hard-core' Mau Mau cases. Christ, in the revivalist paradigm, offered transformative power which secular psychology could not. The loyal

[58] CMS, *Mau Mau: What Is It?*, p. 12.

[59] Government officials explicitly welcomed missionary involvement: 'Rehabilitation is an undoubted opportunity for the churches to re-establish Christian values' (J. Nottingham and C. Rosberg, *The Myth of Mau Mau*, pp. 337–40). Missionary Keith Cole made explicit the parallel between rehabilitation and Christian confession (*Hanging in the Middle Way* [London, 1959], p. 45).

[60] Cf. Bostock, 'Reminiscences', and Beecher, 'Christian counter-revolution', p. 84.

[61] Bostock, 'Reminiscences', p. 163.

Christian remnant represented the firstfruits of what God can do to transform Africa. As the Mau Mau oath produced immediate slavery to fear, so conversion offered individual transformation that was immediate and universal.

But the theology of Christian rehabilitation did not exclude broader views of Christian transformation as offering some kind of social amelioration with a horizon of progress beyond the spiritual health of the individual soul. In fact in its emphasis on social transformation through individual conversion, the idiom of rehabilitation offered a very precise account of the Christian impact on society. The living power of Christ within individuals would produce the Christian character which alone could cope with the bewildering moral demands of modernity. In Bishop Beecher's account, conversion would replace the 'sordid mass of agglomerated humanity', by creating morally responsible citizens for the modern world.[62] Christian faith would produce the 'politically respectable, guilt-conscious middle class'[63] which the administrators desired, replacing Nairobi's dark primitive overcrowding with decent homes in whose domesticity a man could live with one house, one wife, and one job.[64]

The missionary theology of rehabilitation envisaged the remaking of men and women by conversion of character and reform of society. Uniting around the need for action in a time of crisis, the very specific content of the rehabilitation project forged a theological consensus which knit together the varied Christian frontiers of conversionist and socially progressive theologies. By the faithfulness of the Christian remnant would the prosperity of the land be restored.[65] Christ engages with both society and individual, but without individual conversion, rehabilitation and reform will prove ineffectual. 'Rehabilitation workers and others whose own lives are shrouded in spiritual defeat are by the very nature of the case not likely to achieve much success.'[66] It was a new articulation of an older missionary case, around which conversionists and social progressives could agree: only in so far as

[62] Beecher, 'Christian counter-revolution'. Cf. J. C. Dougall's emphasis on Christianity's role in creating personal responsibility, *Kenya's Future*, p. 13.

[63] Lonsdale, 'Mau Maus of the mind', p. 416.

[64] Cf. White, 'Separating the men'. Note too Cecil Bewes's comment that in Nairobi, 'no home life is possible' (*Kikuyu Conflict*, p. 37), and Mary Rickman's belief that 'hope for the church of the future lies . . . with the promise of Christian homes, where the wife is the husband's helpmate, and they bring up the children together' (*Seven Whole Days*, p. 52).

[65] Wiseman, *Story of the CMS in Kenya*, p. 11.

[66] Beecher, 'After Mau Mau', p. 210.

Western civilization is Christian will Africa advance under its impact. Only with a specifically Christian account of rehabilitation could missionaries reconcile themselves to modernization, which had caused all the trouble in the first place.

IV

John Lonsdale has characterized the landscape of missionary theology in Kenya's last decade of colonial rule as polarized between a conservative theology of Christian withdrawal from the world, and a liberal theology of active social and political involvement.[67] I have argued, however, that the exigencies of the Mau Mau emergency forged a moment of mainstream missionary consensus around the practical project of making Christian citizens in the power of Christ, centred on individual conversion. Contained within such a consensus were theological ambiguities and tensions, competing answers to long-running missionary problems about the nature of the missionary enterprise and its relationship to political and cultural exchange in a colonial situation. But I want to suggest, in conclusion, that this constellation of inconsistent theologies is best explored not by reducing it to the categories of conservative withdrawal and liberal engagement, but by reference to the more slippery concept of the Christian frontier, borrowed from Bishop Beecher. For the ambiguity of that terminology hints at the way in which questions about the relationship of the kingdom of God to the complexities of secular history (eschatology), and questions about the relationship of Church and mission to the state, to society, and to the purposes of God (ecclesiology), overlap in missionaries' accounts of their world and work. Missionaries worked to advance an elusive Christian frontier that could never be clearly mapped.

Missionaries were clear about the enemy. Mau Mau was demonized; its defeat was in some sense a Christian victory. But there was rarely a corresponding sacralization of the forces ranged against Mau Mau. Western society was secularized of direct correspondence to divine purpose, and was viewed by all missionaries with some ambivalence, whether they were conversionists, social progressives,

[67] John Lonsdale with Stanley Booth-Clibborn and Andrew Hake, 'The emerging pattern of church and state co-operation in Kenya', in Richard Gray *et al.*, eds, *Christianity in Independent Africa*, pp. 267–9.

or even politically conservative advocates of Christian civilization such as Bishop Carey. But also, conversely, even the most world-denying of missionaries reveal traces of a lingering paradigm of civilizational progress, which links certain superiorities of Western society to its historic allegiance to Christ.

The liberal-conservative dichotomy does not do justice to these contradictions. Bishop Carey's conservative politics and establishmentarian theology, for example, although profoundly pessimistic about the power of good to effect a transformation in the immediate present, opens up a horizon of broad Christian advance within African civilization over a period of two centuries. By contrast, the comparative optimism of missionary mainstream liberals and evangelicals who, placing their hope in Christ's advance in the immediacy of individual conversion, refused to abandon Kikuyuland to evil, implicitly collapses the trajectory of Christian advance into spiritualized moments of individual transformation. The arch-conservative Carey reveals a liberal's trust in the gradual effects of civilization to erode African primitivism, while liberal hopes of social advance in the face of Mau Mau's barbarity look to a more confrontational conversionist paradigm.

Missionary ecclesiology proves similarly ambiguous. The witness of the Kikuyu remnant under Mau Mau led missionaries to articulate a vision of a purified Kikuyu Church called out from the world into the fellowship of radical Christian allegiance as the locus of God's advance. But within their own white context missionaries operated with a parallel, alternative ecclesiology. For much of Kenya's colonial history the Church Missionary Society and the Church of Scotland Mission had functioned as a quasi-established church,[68] receiving government educational funding, welcoming successive Governors to address the Synod, and relations with government strengthened during Mau Mau. While it was not uncommon for missionary rhetoric to close accounts of Kikuyu conversions with a call to whites to be sure of their Christian allegiance, the over-riding impression is of the Church envisaged as a public institution, leavening society by restrained influence.

The development of accounts of world-denying and revivalist Kikuyu Christianity did not prompt missionaries to radical denial of their own world. With decolonization only a decade away, missionaries

[68] Ibid., p. 268.

were unanimous in accepting the colonial state as a benevolent framework for the struggle for the African future.

> It was a rare Christian voice black or white which affirmed that this was a situation in which all were guilty; and it took a significant amount of moral courage for Christian leaders to denounce state terror against Mau Mau, whether casually employed or institutionalised by the gallows. For a great many Christians the defeat of Mau Mau was a Christian victory.[69]

Neither establishment nor revivalist ecclesiologies provided the Kenyan Church with a tradition of prophetic engagement with the state, but missionaries were aware from their attention to the persecuted Kikuyu remnant that the Kikuyu revivalists suffered from both sides in the conflict, and no more identified with the government cause than with Mau Mau.[70] But it was an establishment, and not a revivalist, strand of thought with which certain missionaries defended their decision to confront government abuses of power.[71] They appealed to the Christian character of Western civilization as the basis for colonial responsibility in Africa. 'If we cannot fight as Christian men,' said Carey Francis, 'we had better not fight at all.'[72]

Finally, if the Christian frontier was at times uncertainly drawn, so too was the role of the missionary as pioneer of the frontier. The conversionist, revivalist impulse was ultimately a democratic one in which the agents of Christian advance were not the missionaries, but the African Christians, and God.[73] But missionaries justified their existence at the court of white opinion where a different ecclesiology held sway. For a while, amid the flattery of the Department for Community Development and Rehabilitation, their place seemed secure as the established religion of the colonial enterprise. A theology to justify the missionary endeavour in a post-colonial world had yet to be articulated.

The Mau Mau emergency offered missionaries a brief, seductive glimpse of a Kikuyuland in which the sides drawn up on each side of

[69] Lonsdale, 'The emerging pattern', p. 270.

[70] Bewes, *Kikuyu Conflict*, p. 67; Dougall, *Kenya's Future*, p. 18; CMS, *Mau Mau: What Is It?*, p. 10.

[71] See for example, Beecher, 'After Mau Mau', p. 208.

[72] Cited in Greaves, *Carey Francis*, p. 122.

[73] As Bewes was happy to admit ('Mau Mau headlines', p. 5): 'Our European kindly paternalism is now out of date. Europeans do consistently insult Kikuyu by treating them as inferior.'

the Christian frontier could be clearly identified. But beneath the rhetorical simplicities lay unresolved and unresolvable tensions of the missionary enterprise. The Christian frontier was fragmented and contested territory.

University of Cambridge

INDEX